MENTAL HEALTH CARE IN THE EUROPEAN COMMUNITY

MENTAL HEALTH CARE IN THE EUROPEAN COMMUNITY

Edited by Steen P. Mangen

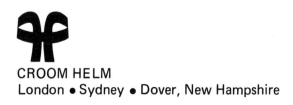

CROOM HELM
London • Sydney • Dover, New Hampshire

©1985 Steen P. Mangen
Croom Helm Ltd, Provident House, Burrell Row,
Beckenham, Kent BR3 1AT

Croom Helm Australia Pty Ltd, First Floor,
139 King Street, Sydney, NSW 2001, Australia

British Library Cataloguing in Publication Data

Mental health care in European Community.
   1. Mentally ill—Care and treatment—European
   Economic Community countries
   I. Mangen, Stephen P.
   362.2'0425'094   RC450.E9

   ISBN 0-7099-1755-4

Croom Helm, 51 Washington Street, Dover,
New Hampshire 03820, USA

Library of Congress Cataloging in Publication Data
Main entry under title:

Mental Health Care in the European Community.

   Includes Bibliographical References.
   1. Mental Health Policy — Europe. 2. Mental Health
Services — Europe. I. Mangen, Stephen P. (DNLM:
1. Health Policy — Trends — Europe. 2. Mental Health
Services — Trends — Europe. WM 30 M5457)
RA790.7.E9M45   1985   362.2'094   85-6661
ISBN 0-7099-1755-4

Printed and bound in Great Britain
by Billing & Sons Limited, Worcester.

CONTENTS

Preface
Acknowledgements

PART ONE: INTRODUCTION

PART TWO: COUNTRY REVIEWS

PREFACE

The idea for this book originated just before I left Britain to become a research fellow at the Universitäts-Nervenklinik, University of Kiel in West Germany. Coming to work in a system so different to that from which I was accustomed was indeed a challenge but, at the beginning, it was frustrating too. At every level there were so many things to learn, so many new ways of approaching what, for me, had previously been routine. Therefore, as part of my research I began to plan a project comparing the mental health systems of Britain and West Germany. Gradually the project grew. After several years in Germany I went to Paris to extend my research to France in collaboration with the late Françoise Castel. Whilst there, I was based at the Psychiatric Epidemiology Department of INSERM and at the Department of Social Medicine at St. Antoine Hospital. At the same time I set about extending the project to include all full member states of the European Community. Over time I was able to build up a network of people working on the same sorts of problems as myself and together we planned the topics we should cover for this book. In the intervening period manuscripts have been going to and fro all over Europe. The end result of my editing is, I hope, worthy of their original contributions.

ACKNOWLEDGEMENTS

The planning of the project was made possible by
the award of a British Council Travelling
Scholarship to the Federal Republic of Germany.
The initial stages of the research were financed by
the Social Science Research Council, London.
Funding of the programme of research visits to
many clinical and administrative centres in France
and Germany, as well as to institutions in other
Community countries, was made available by the
Deutscher Akademischer Austausch Dienst and the
Präsidium of the Christian-Albrechts-Universität,
Kiel, Federal Republic of Germany.

The people who have helped in this project are
too numerous to name. Grateful thanks go to the
researchers, clinicians, planners and
administrators in Germany and France and to staff
at the World Health Organisation in Copenhagen and
the European Commission Headquarters in Brussels,
without whose assistance my research would not have
been possible. I should also like to acknowledge
the help given to me by my former colleagues in
Kiel and Paris and by my present colleagues at the
Institute of Psychiatry in London.

Finally, especial thanks go to Yvonne Waters
and Maureen Marks who helped to type the several
drafts of this manuscript.

Chapter One

PSYCHIATRIC POLICIES: DEVELOPMENTS AND CONSTRAINTS

Steen Mangen

This book is a study of developments and constraints in the mental health policies of the full-member states of the European Community (1). Discussion is largely devoted to issues in the sixties, seventies and early eighties, although the contributors have attempted to set each nation's policies in the wider historical context. Each case study links the expansion of psychiatric services 'in the community' to changes occurring in the health and welfare services generally. In so doing the authors describe and assess the scale of political, financial and planning constraints - some peculiar to the country, others common to all the countries in this era of recession - and endeavour to outline the prospects for mental health care for the rest of this decade. The subjects primarily addressed in each chapter are national mental health policies and the services they have promoted in the field of general adult psychiatry. It must be emphasized that in all countries there have been serious and long-term regional inequalities in the distribution of mental health services. 'National' profiles are therefore, at best, tentative affairs. The book contains less in the way of treatment of dominant clinical orientations of psychiatry and other mental health disciplines. In this respect the Italian chapter is an interesting exception, since the attempt at reform of services there is inseparable from the challenge it poses to clinical and professional ideologies.

The ultimate selection of contributors was made on several grounds. Apart from trying where possible to choose collaborators whose work I already knew, an important consideration was that the authorship should reflect a multi-disciplinary approach to mental health. Among the contributors are psychiatrists engaged in clinical work, research, or planning and administration; an economist who researches issues related to the financing and planning of services; a lecturer and researcher in social work; social science advisers to health ministries; and a psychologist and a sociologist (myself) who are involved in research on services evaluation. I was aware that both alternatives of a native or foreign author had advantages and limitations. Of course, there are other permutations, but in the event there is a mixture of the two, selection being determined by the overriding principle that each contributor, of whatever national origin, should have a thorough grasp of the problems in the country under review.

The choice of the working language for projects of this kind can prove a major headache. Having fallen prey to some prime examples of the professional translator's art, almost as an occupational hazard, I was anxious that the authors of this book should be able to communicate with me - and to write - in a language in which they felt comfortable. In most cases this was English, but the inclusion of French and German as working languages proved to be of great benefit.

THE SCOPE OF THE ANALYSIS

As editor I wanted to avoid the outcome of some 'comparative' studies in which a collection of disparate case reports is produced, the content of each being determined by the academic predilections of distant contributors, some of whom might have poor facility in English. Equally unsatisfactory would have been the extended questionnaire approach, forcing contributors into an analytical straitjacket, which may be productive of 'facts' but is barren of meanings. The authors were therefore asked to discuss a set of central pre-determined issues and to draw on additional themes where these would highlight particular problems in each country.

Our analysis focuses on policies formulated in the course of the past twenty-five years, primarily designed to create psychiatric services outside - and sometimes independent of - the network of old mental hospitals. Some of these services were

2

intended as complementary to existing inpatient services, others as alternatives. To varying degrees - and increasingly so in certain EC countries - in combination they are an attempt at a gradual dismantling of the hospital base, the ultimate goal being its replacement by a 'community-based' service. The pace of these developments varies considerably among the sample of countries. In order to understand why, contributors were asked to identify and assess the major constraints inhibiting change in each country. For this purpose the list of policy problems compiled by a World Health Organisation working group appeared to me to be highly relevant. Among the key constraints they cite: the lack of a comprehensive policy with clear goals; the quality of psychiatric legislation; maldistribution and poor coordination of services; lack of relevant research; and internal resistance to change (WHO, 1977). Also in their list are the still prevailing negative attitudes to mental illness which frustrate attempts at normalisation and integration of ex-patients. Here, there is a surprising paucity of relevant comparative European research and, unfortunately, our limited resources did not allow us to elaborate on this important subject (for a partial review of the field see Townsend (1978)).

The approach adopted in this book has been influenced by the work of Leichter (1979). His comparative model incorporates situational factors (e.g. political events), structural factors (e.g. socio-demographic structure, political constraints), cultural factors (e.g. historical legacy, political norms and ideology), and environmental factors (e.g. diffusion of policies from one country to another). Equally, we have drawn on the research of Hall and her colleagues (1975) on change-promoting and change-inhibiting factors in a system they describe as 'bounded pluralism'. Although they are essentially writing about British social policy their analytical approach comfortably crosses the Channel.

We can make no great claim that our analysis is in the strictest sense evaluative. We have attempted to examine the connexion between formal policies, resource plans and actual resource flows. However, we have been handicapped by having to rely on global input and process variables, since differentiated outcome data are in extremely scarce supply. It may be that the current interest in

3

cost-effectiveness studies in several Community countries will go some way towards rectifying this deficiency.

We must be equally cautious about making too confident a claim of an exhaustive comparative analysis. The need to rely on routine official statistics and the problems caused by the lack of functional equivalence of such concepts as 'community', 'care', 'treatment', or even conventional labels like 'outpatient', 'day care' or 'psychiatrist' can daunt even the most zealous of empirical scientists. It has therefore not been possible to compile a comprehensive catalogue of descriptive statistics of the type attempted by May (1976). What we have tried to achieve is a comparative analysis of trends and patterns of relationships among countries at a similar stage of development, which form an economic union with the longer-term goal of closer political integration.

Judged in terms of its contribution to theory comparative research of social policy has been less than impressive (Higgins, 1981; Madison, 1980). So far, the majority of studies have provided useful, albeit episodic descriptions of particular policies, but the approach has been atheoretical and the sample of countries frequently haphazard. Certainly, methodological problems can be immense and the generated data of too poor a quality to permit vigourous hypothesis testing. Even in closely similar countries concomitant variation, as Przeworski and Teune (1970) term it, may defy parsimonious explanation, with a great number of system-specific variables accounting for the large 'residua' of the unexplained. However, one of the strengths of comparative research of this kind lies in its utility to the planner and administrator. It can add an extra dimension to the perception of policy problems and it may also provide cues for new approaches to their resolution. Nevertheless, it would be naive to entertain too great an expectation that cross-national research will offer tailor-made solutions to pressing domestic problems.

THE SAMPLE

The EC countries share a long history of state involvement in the problems of the containment of the mentally ill, although direct responsibilities

4

typically have been undertaken by provincial and
local authorities. And, whilst long-term political
stability has not been a common feature among the
sample, what is shared - and in the present context
is critical - is a marked degree of administrative
continuity ensured by powerful bureaucratic
organisation (Altenstetter, 1980).

(a) Historical Trends

The origins of present policies on community care
are closely interwoven with the history of the
mental hospital which has dominated psychiatric
history in EC countries in the past century and a
half. The history of the network of asylums must
therefore be our departure point, since it is a
shared history. The history of policy in the
twentieth-century has been more varied, a critical
determinant being the speed at which the need for
change was recognised and then implemented. Until
recent years, some countries made few moves to
provide alternatives to the hospital and, instead,
devoted their capital budgets to constructing new
hospital beds (see Table 1.2). Other countries
were more active in the promotion of alternatives
and achieved a decline in bed numbers earlier.

In what can only be a superficial historical
review some of the more significant developments in
the past hundred years or so are discussed. And in
the case of the early extra-mural services outlined
here, their historical significance lay in their
role as models for the future, rather than in the
speed of their implementation or the original
extent of their diffusion.

Several points arise immediately from even the
most perfunctory reading of psychiatric history: to
perceive events in terms of discrete eras can be
greatly misleading; many ideas and attempts at
innovation are merely recycled (Allderidge, 1979);
the presence of insanity alone is insufficient to
account for the mass construction of asylums: it
was the synergic interaction of madness and
pauperism that is crucial, since the need to
accommodate the insane poor, no longer accorded a
place in an urbanising society, was the paramount
consideration; the conceptual boundary between the
curable and the incurable was continually
withdrawn and it has shaped the kind of services
created, with the present divisions between the
acute and chronic sector owing much to nineteenth-
century ideas of eligibility and less eligibility;

the connexion between innovation and the possibility of cure has been critical; finally, the failings of nineteenth-century psychiatry must be assessed in relation to the comparative lack of success of medicine as a whole before 1900.

The years following the end of the Napoleonic Wars were a time during which the problems of lunacy became a favourite cause of social reform in several European countries (Dörner, 1975). Around 1820 parliamentary enquiries and plans for reform were in progress in France, Britain and Denmark; and in the period after the Prussian reform the first of the large public asylums in the German states was opened. Within thirty years many of the countries had passed psychiatric legislation that was to remain on the statute books into the next century, in some cases remaining in force to this day: France (1838), Netherlands (1841), England (1845) and Belgium (1850).

Thus, by the middle of the nineteenth-century most pauper lunatics throughout Europe were no longer 'at large' (Scull, 1979). Almost synchronously the European states had solved the problem of containment: the seclusion of the mad in institutions of their own became the treatment of first choice. Insanity became 'administered' (Blasius, 1980); the alienist entered into an enduring relationship with the law and the state.

Some of the early asylums were places of intense activity and therapeutic optimism. They were the institutions most influenced by the principles of non-restraint and moral therapy. These ideas spread rapidly, for it was a period in which the grand psychiatric tour first became popular among influential alienists (Pirella & Casagrande, 1981). But, although ideas spread, they were put into practice in few institutions. Doubts about the effectiveness of the asylum system soon arose, as did the reluctance of local administrations to commit themselves to enormous expenditure on what appeared to be a Sisyphean task. Overcrowding and insanitary conditions became features of even the newest asylums.

Thus, by the 1860s criticisms of the role of the asylums were being openly expressed by an enlightened minority of alienists and liberal politicians. Castel (1976) traces the enduring crisis of faith in psychiatry to this period, when all elements of the asylum system were under attack. Nevertheless, the demands on asylums to accommodate ever-increasing numbers grew everywhere, though it had little to do with therapeutic effect. Some of the disillusioned turned to old alternatives for solutions. The colony at Geel became a favourite destination for those seeking 'new' ideas and, despite the opposition of alienists against dispersal, there was a growing number of local projects to establish colonies and boarding-out schemes. One of the cottages for lunatic patients in the village scheme at Bicknill in England was even put on show at the Paris Exhibition of 1867 (Parry-Jones, 1981).

In fact one of the earliest colonies was the farm-hospital of Sainte-Anne, then on the outskirts of Paris, established by alienists at Bicetre asylum in the 1830s. Other French colonies were to follow in 1884 and 1892. Colonies were established elswhere: for example, at Schleswig, then under Danish administration, Einum and Berlin. In Scotland, too, there were celebrated boarding - out schemes. At the same time after-care associations were founded to help asylum inmates resettle after discharge. One of the earliest was formed in Germany in 1829, but most were founded in the period after 1860.

By the end of the century the network of asylums was more or less complete, with relatively few of the insane escaping incarceration. But there were also signs of change. Local 'open door' experiments occurred in France as early as the 1890s (Panse, 1964). From the turn of the century neuropsychiatrists were beginning to set up practices outside the hospitals, creating a division between inpatient services and outpatient office psychiatry that remains in force in most EC countries today. At the same time there was a growing number of university psychiatric clinics, luring the best qualified psychiatrists away from the asylums and creating another institutional division. Freudian theories began to open up new possibilities, attracting a new and more affluent clientele. However, psychoanalytic practice remained a rare provision in Europe in the years before the Second World War and was proscribed in Germany from 1933. Interest grew after the War, but it has never posed a serious challenge to the dominant neuropsychiatric model.

In England, at least, the First World War conferred new functions on psychiatry in the treatment of the shellshocked, although the possibility of a 'war neurosis' was officially denied in defeated Germany (Fischer-Homberger,

1975; Pichot, 1983). It was a period, too, of growing interest in prevention, eugenics and mental hygiene. Actually, ideas on prevention became fashionable in the 1890s, the argument being that it was better to try to prevent what one could not cure. However, it was not until the 1920s that the mental hygiene movement gained a foothold throughout Europe: with associations, for example, in France (1920), the Netherlands (1920), Italy (1924) and Germany (1924). The Twenties and Thirties saw the beginnings in certain towns of new outpatient services, some designed for a new clientele which became models for developments elsewhere (e.g. in Gelsenkirchen, Erlangen, Paris and Amsterdam). These services offered screening, early treatment and domiciliary care and the field was gradually extended, as child guidance, family guidance and marital counselling services were introduced. However, developments were geographically restricted, with perhaps the greatest expansion occurring in Britain, the Netherlands and Denmark. For the majority of patients in Europe the mental hospital, and in places office psychiatric practices, were the only services available.

Some of the asylums, too, adopted new practices during this period. Increasingly ward doors were being opened and in Germany, for example, there were experiments with wards administered by the patients themselves (Panse, 1964). Industrial therapy achieved swifter diffusion. Originally introduced by Simons at Gutersloh mental hospital as a way of coping with serious understaffing, its therapeutic benefits were widely extolled, even if in the process many patients were doing essential maintenance work. It was only later, with the employment of occupational therapists and industrial supervisors, that industrial therapy has taken on explicit rehabilitative functions.

The grim events in the Third Reich are outlined in the chapter on the Federal Republic of Germany. The United Kingdom and French chapters illustrate how, again, the war years provided fresh opportunities for psychiatry, with the development of group therapy by the British Army psychiatric service and the beginnings of institutional psychotherapy at St Alban. New physical treatments were introduced in the Thirties and Forties which, for a time, brought hopes of cure. It was during this period that sickness insurance liabilities

8

were gradually extended. A common trend in post-war reconstruction was the substantial increase in state involvement in social and economic planning, with each of the countries pursuing its own interpretation of the welfare state.

Insurance coverage was extended to larger proportions of the population and governments assumed a greater role in supervising the schemes. Only Britain opted for a state-operated health service. Though few countries would yet claim a large degree of success in the achievement of a locally-based comprehensive psychiatric service, some countries were particularly handicapped in the expansion of extra-mural care by the lack of an agreed means of ensuring long-term funding, either by the insurance funds or by public authorities. There is ample evidence in the case studies that several countries have still to resolve these problems. It is partly for this reason that the introduction of the phenothiazines, which in anglo-saxon countries was to prove a catalyst in the moves already underway to discharge patients to other forms of care, did not have such clear-cut effects in many of the continental countries. Thus, whilst the mid-Fifties marks the start of the period in which many of the components of what is now accepted as conventional 'community care' were either initiated or developed further - psychiatric units in general hospitals, day hospitals, night clinics, new outpatient services, sheltered workshops, half-way houses and other hostels - and some elements were present in all countries, at least as specially-funded experimental services in one or two centres, the point at which they were formally integrated into an official policy varies considerably. These issues and subsequent events are taken up in the case studies.

(b) Health Systems

State intervention in the field of health and social insurance occurred at a comparatively early stage in most countries in the sample. The outcome is that health systems differ in organisation and financing, although most countries have retained an insurance-based system. In terms of a broad financial categorisation, Denmark, the United Kingdom and Italy form one group, in which individual sickness funds have been replaced by unified schemes and/or general taxation funding. In these countries most treatments are free to the

9

individual and do not attract specific reimbursement. The other group is formed by Belgium, France, the Netherlands, Luxembourg and West Germany, and most forms of care there attract a specific fee directly or indirectly reimbursed by the various insurance schemes. On its own is Ireland whose system has features of both groups.

Whatever the specific system, by international standards member states are among the highest spenders both on health care and the social budget as a whole. However, as Table 1.1 demonstrates, there is substantial variation in percentage terms. Although the two statistics refer to different years they do give some broad indications of trends: Germany and the Netherlands, for example, have high expenditure on both counts, whilst the United Kingdom is at the bottom of the league. Beyond that, the association between the two statistics is more complex. Of course, these sort of data are notoriously difficult to interpret, as Hezel (1978) in his comparative analysis of health expenditures has shown. Certainly, low GDP percentage expenditure on health care cannot be taken to mean poorer services. It may be the product of a variety of factors which collectively represent 'value for money', whilst the high expenditure of other countries might reflect high administrative and salary costs.

Table 1.1: Social Expenditures (Percentage of Total GDP)

	Health Care 1981	Social Budget (1) 1982
Belgium	6.4	30.2
Denmark	6.9	29.3
France	9.3	27.2
F.R. Germany	8.2	29.5
Ireland	8.2	22.0(2)
Italy	7.0	24.7
Luxembourg	9.5(2)	27.1
Netherlands	9.1	31.7
United Kingdom	5.9	23.5

Notes: (1)   The social budget comprises all forms of public services in the field of health, welfare, housing, education etc, as well as social insurance and social assistance expenditure and tax concessions.

(2)   Data are for 1980

Sources

(a)   Estimated health care expenditure: to be
       published by OECD with the provisional title
       of 'Health OECD: Facts and Trends, 1960-1983'.
(b)   Social Budget expenditure: Donnees Sociales:
       1984. INSEE, Paris, 1984.

Equally, GDP expenditure on health care as a
whole gives no indication of the amount spent on
the psychiatric sector, nor of the relative quality
of the services it contains. Unfortunately, as
Alan Maynard complains in the next chapter, cross-
national expenditure data for the mental health
services are extremely hard to come by. But the
data that are available for the United Kingdom,
France, Ireland and the Netherlands, and which are
cited in the case studies, confirm that psychiatric
services receive a relatively small share of the
health budget, with at least eighty per cent of
what is allocated continuing to be spent on
inpatient services, despite official policies on
community care.

The traditional separation of physical illness
and mental illness services has contributed to the
impoverishment of the psychiatric sector in all
countries under review. It is partly for this
reason that differences in the general health
systems of the sample become less acute when
analysis is restricted to mental health: psychiatry
everywhere was a 'cinderella' service. The reasons
for this are clear. For a long time mental health
care meant asylum care, which was almost
exclusively financed by local welfare authorities.
It was relatively late in the day before insurance
funds accepted some liability. Even now large
numbers of chronic psychiatric inpatients are
dependent on some form of social assistance, either
for treatment or subsistence costs, which partly
explains why in all countries the average costs of
a psychiatric bed are much lower than a general
bed.

The special system of financing psychiatric
care has limited the scope for the creation of
services outside the mental hospitals. In the
early days these services were almost entirely
dependent on public or charitable funding. Only
when insurance liability was extended could extra-
mural services develop nationally. Even now, as

11

some of the case studies show, the means of reimbursing the costs of extra-mural care are far from settled to the satisfaction of all parties. Apart from office neuropsychiatrists, non-hospital services in many countries are therefore comparatively thin on the ground and most countries are still heavily reliant on the old mental hospitals.

The insurance-based system administered by a variety of separate schemes seems set to be retained in the majority of EC countries. Indeed, insurance is being extended to new areas: in two countries (Luxembourg and the Netherlands) compulsory 'heavy risk' insurance has been introduced as a means of paying for the costs of long-term care and, thereby, relieving the burden on social assistance budgets. Currently, West Germany is also considering introducing a similar supplementary insurance scheme. However, there has been growing recognition that some of the forms of reimbursement by insurance are inappropriate in psychiatric care. The fee for each item-of-service and the hospital daily fee are being replaced in several countries by forms of global reimbursement, whilst other countries are still considering reform.

A major impetus for change has been the desire of governments to instigate more effective cost-containment and cost-monitoring procedures. Initially attention was concentrated on the hospital sector and by the late 1970s all the countries had established stricter hospital planning machinery (Abel-Smith & Maynard, 1978). More recently governments in several countries have been anxious to extend these controls to other sectors, including outpatient and community psychiatric services. Pressures for cost-containment have come at a time when calls are being made for expansion of these services; but sometimes official policies in favour of priority services are forgotten in the bid to effect expenditure cuts where it is easiest to do so. Thus, as Zöllner (1981) argues, where cost containment measures have been most successful it is not unusual to discover that community-based services have suffered most.

(c) Mental Health Policies

Among EC countries the period during which major new policies or administrative reforms were

12

formally instituted stretches from the late-1950s to the early-1980s, with two peaks: the period around 1960 (e.g. France and the United Kingdom) and the mid to late-Seventies (e.g. West Germany, Belgium, the Netherlands, Italy, Denmark). Innovations at the local level had been in progress for several years beforehand and in several countries they became 'model' services on which the proposals for reform were based.

The problems facing mental health policy-makers were remarkably similar, for Community countries are inheritors of a common legacy: a network of overlarge and decaying mental hospitals remote from the populations they serve, their major task being to accommodate long-stay patients, even though late in their life they increasingly turned to an acute clientele. Beyond these mental hospitals the boundaries of the psychiatric system are less distinct and vary among the countries. In some countries there is a comparatively long tradition of providing locally-based outpatient, residential and day care facilities, either by religious and charitable organisations or as municipal undertakings. Each of these countries approached the task in its own way, with the result that services in the same category take on diverse forms. Other countries relied almost exclusively on the mental hospital and the office psychiatrist and the development of alternative facilities occurred much later.

Nevertheless, in more recent times, one can identify a significant degree of convergence of mental health policies among the Nine: the adoption of some form of sectorisation of psychiatric services, including internal sectorisation of hospitals; drives to improve physical conditions which remain poor inside many of the old hospitals; the move to resolve the problem of overcapacity in the inpatient sector, either by closure of hospitals or their reduction in size, with large numbers of patients being transferred to accommodation elsewhere; preference for psychiatric units in general hospitals, even though current building programmes in all countries ensure that these units will continue to provide a small proportion of total beds in the planable future; the desire to extend the range of provisions by the creation of small locally-based services; the growing reliance on services in the private sector, in some cases a policy being actively pursued, in others relied on as a default option; emphasis placed on the multi-disciplinary specialist team with, however, the recognition that the bulk of psychiatric treatment will continue to be administered by family practitioners or office psychiatrists; a renewal of interest in lay and self-help, sometimes generated by the interests of the public purse; and new psychiatric legislation which places emphasis on care as well as control and, to varying degrees, affords the patient greater legal safeguards. There is no claim that the list is exhaustive and other issues of shared concern are introduced later in this chapter.

Some readers will surely be arguing that the Italian experience must be an exception. Although conforming to many of the trends outlined above there is no doubt that Italy is the outlier in our cluster of countries. Its formal national policy is drastically to restrict admissions to psychiatric hospitals, with an energetic strategy being pursued in certain regions to secure their closure. It is as yet early days to assess the full impact of these policies which, as Shula Ramon stresses in her chapter, have still to be rigorously applied in all areas of Italy.

Criticism of the Italian reform has been growing within and beyond Italy in recent years. Wambach (1980) believes that a fundamental mistake has been to regard the reform as something rather more definitive than it really was. He maintains that in practice it is a conglomeration of what for him are ambivalent liberalisation measures influenced by alternative psychiatry and anti-psychiatry. Jones and Poletti (1984) during their tour of Italian services found the situation confused and contradictory. There are now regular newspaper articles in Italy highlighting the lack of day care and residential facilities. They report scandals about destitute patients whose only places of shelter are the large railway termini and the appalling conditions endured by patients in some hospitals starved of adequate funds. Benaim (1983) asserts that some of the most vociferous opponents of the reform were formerly among its staunchest supporters. Centre and right-wing parties now favour an amendment of the legislation with proposals for the re-establishment of long-stay institutions. Left-wing parties are opposing these plans.

At the present stage of the reform services in several of the largest cities and in the south leave a lot to be desired. Certainly, in some

14

regions new mental health services have hardly been
implemented. Yet the strengths of the reform
should not be under-estimated. There is a genuine
attempt at demystifying the role of the 'expert'
professional. Mental health workers in many areas
are engaged in genuine negotiation, not only with
clients but also with the wider community. The
reform demonstrates how crucial it is to generate
and maintain political and trades union support.
On present (inadequate) evidence it would appear
that the proscription of new admissions to mental
hospitals (though not, of course, to psychiatric
units) is being strictly adhered to. Furthermore,
the reform was promoted precisely because
conditions in the mental hospitals were so
appalling. Supporters of the reform argue that
where this situation persists it is largely due to
the inertia and lack of commitment of local
politicians and mental health staff. It should
also be conceded that appalling conditions and
destitution also occur in countries whose attempts
at reform have been far less radical.

None the less, complaints about services and
opposition to the reform must be taken seriously.
As Shula Ramon acknowledges in her chapter, only
when evaluative studies of different parts of the
country have been completed can the <u>Italian</u>
experience be more fully assessed.

(d) Problems in Policy-Making

Heidenheimer and his colleagues (1983) remind us
that power and the perception of the possible are
engaged in a dynamic relationship. The case
studies provide supporting evidence of the
interaction of politics and mental health policy:
there are situations which become issues for
resolution, those which are politically too
sensitive to disturb, and those that are regarded
as non-issues. Each strategy is limited by the
prevailing system; to have any chance of success it
needs political opportunity. In this respect there
seems to be no clear distinction between federal or
centralised political systems. In any case, in an
era when all countries are moving towards major
decentralisation of health and welfare services,
the dichotomy becomes increasingly blurred.

But there may be something in the argument
that some federal systems have responded sluggishly
to reforms. In Germany, for example, proposals for
reform of mental health services can fall victim to

influential interest groups, which may have been able to marshal their power more effectively at the federal state level than perhaps might be the case at the central level in a distant capital city. This issue deserves further investigation and a closer comparative analysis of the situation in West Germany with that in, say, the Netherlands might be instructive. The Netherlands ventured on social and community psychiatry at an early stage, whilst West Germany was relatively late on the scene. Yet both countries have similar insurance-based health systems and share a long tradition of office neuropsychiatric practice. One major difference is that, until recently, the Dutch government retained considerable responsibility for health affairs and might therefore have been able to impose its will more effectively than state-level governments.

Of necessity one of our central concerns is the devolution of powers of policy-making and relations between the various tiers of government. A common theme throughout is the decentralisation of responsibilities for the administration of high spending health and social services, although in most cases these moves have been accompanied by increased efforts at cost-containment at the central level, with the closer monitoring of budgetary allocations. At the same time there has been an increasing tendency to contract out responsibility for direct management of services to the private sector. This is especially so in the case of nursing homes and long-stay residential accommodation. Too often the outcome has been an unhappy liaison between central, regional and local-level public and voluntary agencies with a highly-damaging organisational division of the health and personal social services. Each country in its own way has attempted to devise appropriate means of coordination, but none can claim unqualified success.

Most EC countries have actively encouraged voluntary provisions, especially at the local level. Indeed, in certain countries non-profit making organisations have pride of place in the management of welfare services. It is also true that many of the innovative psychiatric services in Europe owe their existence to local voluntary bodies and there are many examples of local organisations being set up specifically for this purpose. But local experiments can be difficult to reproduce on a national level. And, although most governments have eagerly advocated an extension of this pluralist system, the introduction of an increasing number of policy-making and management agencies in mental health care exacerbates the problems incurred in negotiating a comprehensive policy. Each level of government may have competing policy priorities; and these in turn may be difficult to reconcile with the goals of voluntary and private services, not all of which may be described as 'progressive'. Problems are made worse by the fact that, on all but rare occasions, mental health reform does not enjoy a high political profile and can rarely count on sustained political support at the highest level.

Incremental reform may therefore be extremely difficult to negotiate and policy implementation can often be a tediously slow affair: in some cases so slow as to be almost imperceptible. But the few countries that have attempted radical reform are exposed to other risks, especially in the initial stages when it is easiest for critics to point to the deficiencies of an inchoate development of services and when a large measure of faith in the future is demanded. The current situation in Italy presents us with an interesting example, where opposition to the psychiatric reform is gaining ground.

(e) Planning and Community Care

Mental health plans have a common failing in being impressive in scale but limited in vision. Many countries have adopted a highly technocratic approach to planning, in which 'community care' and some form of sectorisation are essential ingredients. Yet, they frequently appear as mere catchwords, poorly conceived and capable of conflicting meanings. In most plans 'community care' is watered down to mean an emphasis on non-hospital, locally-based services (e.g. the French term 'extra-hospitalier'). It has become an administrative term for a diffuse range of outpatient, day and residential provisions 'in' not 'of' the community (it is interesting that the Germans use the term 'Gemeindenahe'). Earlier local experiments and present efforts in parts of Italy may have wider political dimensions. But, for the large part, 'community care' was the brainchild of a select few: influential psychiatrists and receptive officials. Other mental health professionals and members of the

17

public were brought in - if at all - only after plans had reached an advanced stage. Despite this 'community care' became a popular slogan, leapt on by those disillusioned with the existing state of affairs but with no real notion of the full implications of what they were espousing.

Therapeutic optimism, combined with an almost total loss of faith in the future of the mental hospitals and a desire among politicians to test potentially cheaper alternatives were key change promoting factors. Incrementally, developments in the name of community care have reorganised and, indeed, extended the psychiatric field. The rapid growth in the mental health professions occurred simultaneously with the appearance of new and 'alternative' therapies. Castel (1981) questions whether collectively these events represent the aggiornomento of psychiatry - and not simply to the benefit of psychiatrists - with new territories, new specialisms, new competences.

The planning process has proved no match for the tasks demanded of it by this new system. All EC countries report they are a long way off from achieving planning goals. Hospital planning is precarious enough, but when planning remits are extended to the wider field, to incorporate a broad range of services managed by separate and independent bodies, strategic planning becomes illusory and, in the absence of effective means of coordination, planning remains a fragmentary, ad hoc affair.

Many of the new plans got off to a relatively bad start: apart from funding for special 'model' schemes, there has been a common assumption that additional finances, if forthcoming at all, would build up slowly. Budgetary redistribution was therefore to be the solution, but it was rarely specified how funds would be reallocated or what the long-terms effects on the whole service network were likely to be. Reliance on this approach has been all the more problematic because several countries started to formulate new plans in the early 1970s, in the years of comparative plenty, only to discover that the years of implementation of the plans had become decidedly leaner. In such an unfavourable economic climate some governments have increasingly turned to the private sector, the desire being to cut public budgets by withdrawing from direct service provision. This has served to complicate the planner's task still further. Castel (1981) argues that it has also given rise to a curious paradox in which many governments are extolling the virtues of strategic planning at the same time as promoting a gradual withdrawal from the provision of services for which they wish to formulate effective plans.

(f) Services

Many of the proposals for new services in Community countries in the post-war period were, of themselves, not particularly innovatory. What was innovatory was the concept of the service network into which these individual elements were to be integrated. It is the degree of coordination at the local level that is the acid test of all the catchment area/sector models in operation in the EC. Most services developed incrementally, sometimes into a patchy national provision. Formal planning and legislative reform came much later. In some countries those services continue to rely on ad hoc or short-term funding and every country has yet to resolve the problems of how to finance a comprehensive locally-based psychiatric service, though some have recently instigated funding reforms. The present service network is therefore patchy and may give rise to serious misplacement of patients. In countries which retain an item-of-service and hospital daily fee system this problem is exacerbated by the illogicality of the means of reimbursement of treatment costs: where individual institutions do not receive an integrated budget for the inpatient and outpatient services they provide moves to reduce inpatient numbers by extending outpatient services can lead to overall budgetary reductions if bed occupancy rates fall.

Some of the newer, innovative services are the first victims of unstable funding. Frequently, they are too small-scale, under-staffed and over-reliant on unqualified personnel. Sometimes the development of new services has been made possible by extra-ordinary time-limited budgetary allocations; here emphasis has been on 'model' services or 'demonstration' projects. In some cases there have been complaints that unrealistic standards have been set which, in normal circumstances, cannot be maintained. Enthusiasm generated in the short-term is all too easily dissipated when key personnel leave or reservations about the quality of care start to be expressed, a process Dellman (1980) has topically termed the 'Basaglia effect'.

19

Statistics on the full range of psychiatric services are remarkably difficult to obtain in most EC countries. Routine official statistics are generally restricted to the psychiatric hospitals and, even then, merely to an enumeration of inpatient beds. With such limited data available to mental health planners in many EC states it is difficult to see how any claim of even the most rudimentary attempt at monitoring can be justified. For the purposes of comparative research there is the added problem of a lack of functional equivalence of the terms used: for example, a psychiatric bed can mean any number of things and psychiatrists appear to come in a wide range of assortments. The failure to provide adequate definitions in official national statistics precludes the possibility of presenting anything approaching a rigourous comparative analysis of the data. Rather than reproduce the inpatient statistics published separately by each country, I have referred to statistics supplied by health or information ministries of the Nine to the World Health Organisation. This does not overcome the problem but at least it does provide some overall impression of trends. Of course, the data provide no indication of the wider range of psychiatric services. Furthermore, increases or decreases in bed numbers tell us nothing about the quality of inpatient services: capacity might be increased to make good past deficiencies, especially in countries with historically low bed ratios, and reductions in capacity may be made without adequate alternative services being available.

The WHO statistics in Table 1.2 show the trend in psychiatric hospital bed capacities since the early Fifties, roughly the period during which ideas about community care gained currency. Once again it should be emphasized that the statistics are not strictly comparable, since some countries have reported the total number of mental hospital beds available and this may include provisions for neurological patients and/or the mentally retarded. The immediate impression is that over the entire period there is no one salient trend. Taking the whole sample into account crude economic factors appear to have little explanatory power. There is little overall relationship between increases or decreases in bed capacity and periods of boom or recession. Some countries substantially added to their bed stock precisely at the time when others were reducing capacity. However, if we restrict ourselves to the Seventies a clearer trend emerges, with all countries reporting a decline, although in several cases it is of quite a small order. This latter trend gives some indication of the effect of active community care policies, although, as some case studies show, the large-scale transfer of chronic patients to ostensibly cheaper forms of institutional provision has been a major contributory factor.

Table 1.2: Beds in Psychiatric Hospitals: Trends since the Early Fifties

Belgium	1951	19841			
	1960	27450			
	1970	26553			
	1979	24567	Ratios	(a)	2.5
				(b)	2.6
Denmark	1951	10907			
	1962	10640			
	1969	10708			
	1979	9547	Ratios	(a)	1.9
				(b)	2.1
France	1952	93000			
	1962	85864			
	1970	121200			
	1977	105500	Ratios	(a)	2.0
				(b)	2.6
F.R. Germany	1953	86640			
	1962	95306			
	1970	115496			
	1979	107965	Ratios	(a)	1.8
				(b)	1.9
Ireland	1951	19568			
	1962	19357			
	1970	16629			
	1979	13838	Ratios	(a)	4.1
				(b)	4.1
Italy	1954	88241			
	1961	113040			
	1970	113556			
	1979	80480	Ratios	(a)	1.4
				(b)	1.5

Luxembourg (All beds)	1952	776			
	1962	1242(1)			
	1970	1348			
	1979	1292	Ratio	(b)	3.6
Netherlands (All beds)	1950	25000(2)			
	1962	26000(2)			
	1970	26782			
	1979	26734	Ratio	(b)	1.9
United Kingdom (All Beds) England & Wales	1952	156493			
	1962	148520			
	1970	128161			
	1979	88425(3)	Ratio	(b)	1.9
Scotland	1952	21120			
	1962	21556			
	1970	18858			
	1979	17063	Ratio	(b)	3.3
N.Ireland	1952	5530			
	1962	7460			
	1970	7219			
	1979	6632	Ratio	(b)	4.3

<u>Source</u>

World Health Organisation Statistics Annual: 1962 (issued Geneva, 1965); 1970 (issued Geneva, 1974); 1983 (issued Geneva, 1983 & 1984).

<u>Notes</u>

(1) Luxembourg figure includes beds in facilities for the mentally deficient

(2) Dutch figures are estimates

(3) 1979 figure for England is not reported in the WHO Publication. The cited figure is that of the 1979 Mental Health Enquiry for England (London, DHSS, HMSO, 1984).

(a) Ratio of beds in psychiatric hospital per thousand population at last cited date.

(b) Ratio of all psychiatric beds per thousand population at last cited date.

The marked variation in bed ratios among the EC countries has therefore continued. From the latest figures shown in Table 1.2 ratios are highest in Ireland, Scotland, Northern Ireland and Luxembourg. In the case of the first three bed ratios have traditionally been high. Most of the other ratios at present hover around two per thousand with, pointedly, Italy having the lowest ratio. To these figures should be added the psychiatric beds located elsewhere. The Seventies in particular were a period when most countries increased priority for psychiatric units in general hospitals. Some indication of how active these policies have been pursued is given by the difference between ratios (a) and (b) in Table 1.2, although some of the statistics from which the ratios are derived also include beds located in other specialist hospitals. Most countries appear to have made only modest progress. Unfortunately, the official statistics of most EC states do not provide additional information on the percentage of beds in psychiatric units. However, on the basis of the available data, which do not include Italy, only in Britain, France, Denmark and the Netherlands do percentages reach double figures. In all cases, however, the proportion of admissions to these units is much higher, an indication of their focus on acute inpatient treatment. In most countries units continue to be built far too small to undertake full catchment area responsibilties.

Several of the EC states are now confronted with the problem of serious overcapacity in the mental hospitals. This is a more complex issue than it may initially appear. Overcapacity tends to be concentrated in the acute sector, but its eradication there will still leave hospitals with large numbers of patients on long-stay wards. Hospital closures are therefore not a simple procedure, as several countries are now discovering. EC countries differ in their long-term policies for the network of old mental hospitals. Italy has an explicit policy of mass closure, although it is a long way from being fulfilled. In Britain the process was intended to be far more gradual, although in recent years the pace has quickened, with the announcement that about one-third of hospitals are destined for closure in the medium-term. In France and Germany large numbers of patients are being transferred to nursing homes and other long-stay accommodation, but the overall strategy is far from clear. On the other hand, in the Netherlands a major hospital construction programme was announced some years ago which despite mounting criticism appears to be going ahead.

(g) Staff

Among mental health staff only the qualifications of psychiatrists are mutually recognised in the EC countries. In most countries the training of psychiatrists has continued to be along strong neuropsychiatric lines. In several member states it was not until the late 1960s that neurology and psychiatry were formally separated. Most countries retain the system of office neuropsychiatric practice. Moreover, many office specialists continue to practice in isolation from other psychiatric provisions, despite official policies for integrated and comprehensive services at the local level. However, office psychiatrists in some countries also have sessional contracts for hospital work.

The statistics in Table 1.3 can provide only the broadest of indications of the number of psychiatrists in practice in Community countries, since each national source reports the data in a different way. Excluding the figure for Belgium, which includes neurologists, and Italy, which is confined to psychiatrists working in publically-owned hospitals, the broad range is between five and eight psychiatrists per 100,000 population.

Table 1.3   Ratios of psychiatrists

Ratio per 100,000 population

Belgium	(1984)	12.7
Denmark	(1982)	8.3
France	(1980)	5.1
F.R. Germany	(1982)	8.3
Ireland	(1981)	5.3
Italy	(1981)	2.1
Luxembourg	(1977)	6.6
Netherlands	(1982)	6.1
UK (England)	(1981)	7.6

Sources

Belgium: Information et Statistiques, Institut National de la Securité Sociale, Brussels, 1984. Data include all registered doctors in neuropsychiatric practice, including neurologists.

Denmark: Sygehusstatistik 1983: Personale og Økonomistatistik for Sygehusvaesenet. Sundhedsstyrelsen, Copenhagen, 1983. Data include all doctors employed by the psychiatric services.

France: Données Sociales: 1984. INSEE, Paris, 1984.

F.R.Germany: Berufe des Gesundheitswesen: 1982. Statiotisches Bundesamt, Wiesbaden, 1984. Data also include psychiatrists with additional neurological caseloads.

Ireland: Data supplied by Dermot Walsh from information obtained from the Irish Division, Royal College of Psychiatrists.

Italy: Annuario Statistico Italiani: 1983. Instituto Centrale di Statistica, Rome, 1983. Data refer only to psychiatrists employed in public hospitals.

Luxembourg: Annuaire Statistique. STATEC, Luxembourg, 1977.

Netherlands: Data supplied by Nederlands centrum geestelijke Volksgezondheid, Utrecht. Data exclude neuropsychiatrists primarily engaged in neurological work.

UK(England): Facilities and Services in Mental Illness and Mental Handicap Hospitals in England, 1980-1981. DHSS, HMSO, London. Data include all doctors working in mental illness hospitals or units with more than 200 beds.

Statistics available for other psychiatric personnel defy interpretation and I judged it wisest to omit them. The categories of qualified and unqualified nurses and nursing assistants, for example, are often subsumed under one statistic. Furthermore, even where statistics for qualified nurses are given they do not necessarily indicate that staff have specific qualifications in psychiatric nursing. In Germany, Italy and Denmark psychiatric nursing is not offered as a basic qualification (EEC, 1983) and many of those enumerated as trained are general nurses. Similarly, in the remainder of the sample (where three-year courses in psychiatric nursing are available) statistics on qualified staff sometimes include those with general nursing qualifications.

(h) Psychiatric Legislation

In some countries basic psychiatric legislation in force today is over one hundred years old; in France legislation has been on the statute book for almost 150 years. However, in those EC states that have not introduced major revisions of legislation in the past fifteen years, parliamentary bills are at various stages of redrafting or official enquiries are in progress. The operation of mental health legislation varies considerably within the Community. Some countries have retained the role of the magistracy in authorising certification (e.g. the German federal states); in others the mayor or a government official is charged with these duties (e.g. France and Italy); whilst in others authorisation is vested in psychiatrists and other medical practitioners (e.g. Republic of Ireland and England and Wales).

Information in Table 1.4 demonstrates that certain countries have encountered considerable delay in passing new legislation. In the case of Belgium, for example, several revisions of a reform bill have been debated in both parliamentary chambers in the last fifteen years without an ultimate resolution of contentious clauses. A similar process has occurred over a briefer period in the Netherlands. Some Irish psychiatrists maintain that new legislation in the Republic was hastily passed without adequate prior consultation with the mental health professions. In the event the 1981 Irish Act has not been implemented and is currently being reviewed. Successive French governments have considered plans for the reform of

the 1838 Act but none has won widespread
parliamentary and professional support. In recent
years there have been several official reports on
the working of the Act and fresh proposals are now
being discussed.

Table 1.4 Psychiatric Legislation in Force since the Early Fifties

Belgium	(a)	1850/1873
	(b)	1969 Bill and subsequent revisions not yet passed
Denmark	(a)	1938
	(b)	Parliamentary Enquiry in progress
France	(a)	1838
	(b)	1968 Amendment. Review under discussion
FR Germany (1)	(a)	From Early 1950s
	(b)	New Legislation from mid-1970s
Ireland	(a)	1945
	(b)	1981 Act not implemented and now to be revised
Italy	(a)	1904
	(b)	1968 Amendment. New Act 1978
Luxembourg	(a)	1880
	(b)	1982 Bill not yet passed
Netherlands	(a)	1884
	(b)	1979 Bill and subsequent amendments not yet passed
England & Wales	(a)	1930
	(b)	New Acts 1959, 1983

Notes

(a) Laws in force at the start of the period

(b) Subsequent amendments

(1) Psychiatric legislation in the Federal
     Republic is a responsibility of the federal
     states. Each of the states began to implement
     its own legislation from the early Fifties and
     this has been revised in new laws introduced
     from the mid Seventies.

     The more recent legislation has been framed in
the light of the priority attached to community
care policies. Measures designed to prevent the
need for compulsory admission - prevention, early
treatment and crisis intervention - feature
prominently. The right to treatment has
supplemented the former dominant considerations of
protection and control. In general, the newer laws
have attempted to enforce a stricter specification
of the categories of patients who may be
compulsorily detained. There is also an increased
emphasis on confidentiality and the safeguarding of
patients' rights. Appeals and review procedures
have been extended (Curran & Harding, 1977).
Legislation in Italy and in England and Wales has
formalised the patient's right to consent to
certain treatments.
     Statistics on compulsory admission are an
extremely imperfect indicator of the number of
patients who have entered hospital involuntarily.
In the face of heavy pressure exerted by relatives
and doctors some patients may feel that they have
little choice but to accept admission. Others, who
are informal patients, may be certified if they
attempt to discharge themselves. Finally, some
patients may be the subject of guardianship orders
as an alternative to certification. Few countries
routinely publish data on the number of patients
subject to formal detention orders. I have based
my tentative estimate of the annual percentage rate
of formal admissions on an extrapolation of the
available statistics. Denmark appears to have the
lowest rate at three per cent; the rate in the
United Kingdom is ten per cent; in Ireland, the
Netherlands and France it is fifteen per cent;
whilst the rate varies enormously among the German
federal states, with some areas reporting rates as
low as five per cent and others as high as forty
per cent. The rate of compulsory admissions has
been coming down dramatically in Italy but,
nationally, it was still as high as twenty per cent
in 1979, the latest year for which data are
available. This figure needs to be interpreted
against the background of a tremedous fall in the

number of total admissions: between 1977-1979, for example, there was a fifty per cent reduction in the admission rate.

(i) Mounting Problems for the Future

In addition to our outline of general policies EC countries are experiencing problems in providing adequate specialist services for particular client groups. First among them are the elderly mentally infirm. Population projections for all Community countries suggest that the numbers of those aged over 85 years, the age-group most 'at risk', will rise sharply, in some cases doubling by the end of the century. Psychogeriatric services in their present form would be unable to cope with any major increased call on their resources and most countries are now attempting the hazardous task of developing plans for a differentiated and community-oriented service for the future.

European countries are also experiencing a tidal wave of alcoholism and alcohol-related disorders. Consumption of alcohol has increased everywhere, partly as a result of the failure of prices of alcohol to be maintained in real terms. Many countries now report that alcoholism and related disorders are the major diagnoses among (male) first admissions. Readmissions have also risen sharply. With some exceptions, treatment has largely been restricted to an inpatient basis, but some countries are now investigating whether an increase in specialist services on a day or outpatient basis would offer a more appropriate treatment model.

Although the concept of psychiatric disability has become widely accepted models of social and occupational rehabilitation remain poorly specified. Additional research in these areas is urgently required, since large numbers of long stay patients are being transferred to alternative day care and residential provisions. Rehabilitation services are nowhere adequate, despite some expansion in the past twenty years, notably in Britain, Denmark and the Netherlands. The new Italian psychiatric service has tended to opt for a more informal rehabilitation model, with emphasis on self-help and patient cooperatives. In France, however, there has been general criticism of the retrograde nature of the 1975 Handicapped Persons Act, which it is claimed was influenced by a perception of psychiatric disability as a static condition.

Industrial rehabilitation policies have so far tended to be formulated without due regard to their relevance to the local employment market. Many patients are engaged in work activities which are primarily intended to break the monotony of life on a long-stay ward. Much of the available contract work is of an unskilled packing and assembly type that is in rapidly diminishing supply in outside employment. Some patients who might otherwise have reasonable chances of obtaining open employment are therefore receiving inadequate preparation. For the rest there is a desperate shortage of long-term sheltered workshops.

NOTES

(1) Greece has been excluded from our analysis since its history and current provision of psychiatric services differ substantially from the other EC states. Regional inequalities in services are even greater than elsewhere in the Community. Half of all psychiatric beds are located in the two largest cities. Three large hospitals account for sixty per cent of available beds (total ratio: 1.5/1000). Sixty per cent of psychiatrists practise in Athens (total ratio 6.8/100,000) (Stefanis & Madianos, 1979). Outpatient and community services are of very recent origin. The first day hospital was established as late as 1977. Services are now supplemented by two community mental health centres (Madianos, 1982). Currently approximately nine per cent of the total health budget is allocated to the psychiatric services.
Since 1982 the Greek government has been attempting to establish a national health service. Individual sickness funds, which collectively cover 95 per cent of the population, will be integrated into a unified scheme and private hospitals are being brought into public ownership.

REFERENCES

Abel-Smith, B. & Maynard, A. (1978) The Organisation, Financing and Cost of Health Care in the European Community. Commission of the European Communities, Social Policy Series No. 36.

Allderidge, P. (1979) Hospitals, Madhouses and Asylums: Cycles in the Care of the Insane. British Journal of Psychiatry, 134, 321-334.

Altenstetter, C. (1980) Hospital Planning in France and the Federal Republic of Germany. Journal of Health Politics, Policy and Law, 5, 309-332.

Benaim, S. (1983) The Italian Experiment. Bulletin of the Royal College of Psychiatrists, 7, 7-10.

Blaslus, D. (1980) Der verwaltete Wahnsin: Eine Sozialgeschichte des Irrenhauses. Fischer Verlag, Frankfurt.

Castel, R. (1976) L'Ordre Psychiatrique: L'Âge d'Or de l'Aliénisme. Éditions de Minuit, Paris (Also available in German).

Castel, R. (1981) La Gestion des Risques: de l'Anti-psychiatrie a l'Après Psychiatrie. Éditions de Minuit, Paris.

Curran, W.J. & Harding, T.W. (1977) The Law and Mental Health: Harmonising Objectives. International Digest of Health Legislation, 28, 725-885.

Dellman (1980) Die Psychiatrie Reform in der Phase der Konsolidierung aus der Sicht des psychiatrischen Krankenpflegedienstes. In: K. Dörner (ed) Gütersloher Fortbildungswoche: 1980. Landschaftsverband Westfalen-Lippe, Gütersloh.

Dörner, K. (1975) Bürger und Irre. Fischer Verlag, Frankfurt (Also available in English).

EEC (1983) Psychiatric Nursing: Report of the Advisory Committee on Training in Nursing. Ref: III/D/258/6/80. Commission of the European Communities, Brussels.

Fischer-Homberger, E. (1975) Germany and Austria. In: J.G. Howells (ed) World History of Psychiatry. Balliere-Tindall, London.

Hall, P., Land, H., Parker, R.A. & Webb, A. (1975) Change, Choice and Conflict in Social Policy. Heinemann Educational, London.

Heidenheimer, A.J., Heclo, H. & Adams, C.T. (1983) Comparative Public Policy: The Politics of Social Choice in Europe and America. Macmillan, 2nd Edtn, London.

Hezel, F. (1978) Entwicklung einiger zentraler Hypothesen für einen internationalen Vergleich von Gesundheitssystemen. In: F. Hezel & W. Thiele (eds) Gesundheitssysteme im Internationalen Vergleich. BASIG, T.U. Berlin.

Higgins, J. (1981) States of Welfare: Comparative Analysis in Social Policy. Basil Blackwell/Martin Robertson, Oxford.

Jones, K. & Poletti, A. (1984) The Mirage of A Reform. New Society, 69, 10-12.

Leichter, H. (1979) A Comparative Approach to Policy Analysis: Health Care Policy in Four Nations. Cambridge University Press, Cambridge.

Madianos, M.G. (1982) Mental Illness and Mental Health Care in Greece. Public Health Review, 11, 73-93.

Madison, B.Q. (1980) The Meaning of Social Policy: The Comparative Dimension in Social Welfare. Croom Helm, London / Westview Press, Colorado.

May, A.R. (1976) Mental Health Services in Europe: A Review of Data Collected in Response to a Questionnaire. World Health Organisation, Geneva.

Panse, F. (1964) Das psychiatrische Krankenhauswesen, Thieme, Stuttgart.

Parry Jones, W. (1981) The Geel Lunatic Colony and its Influence on the Nineteenth-Century Asylum System. In: A Scull (ed) Madhouses, Mad-Doctors and Madmen. Athlone Press, London, 201-217.

Pichot, P. (1983) A Century of Psychiatry. Roche, London (Also available in the original French).

Pirella, A. & Casagrande, D. (1981) John Connolly-von der Philanthropie zur Sozialpsychiatrie. In: F. Basaglia (ed) Was ist Psychiatrie? Suhrkamp, Frankfurt, 141-157 (Also available in the original Italian).

Przeworski, A. & Teune, H. (1970) Logic of Comparative Social Inquiry. Wiley, New York.

Scull, A.T. (1979) Museums of Madness: The Social Organisation of Insanity in Nineteenth-Century England. Allen Lane, London.

Stefanis, C.N. & Madianos, M.G. (1979) Mental Health Care Delivery Systems in Greece: A Critical Overview. In: G.N. Christodolou (ed) Aspects of Preventive Psychiatry. Karger Verlag, Basel.

Townsend, J.M. (1978) Cultural Conceptions and Mental Illness: A Comparison of Germany and America. University of Chicago Press, London.

Wambach, M.M. (1980) Nachbemerkungen als Nachruf auf eine alternative Zukunft. In: M.M. Wambach (ed) Die Museen des Wahnsinns und die Zukunft der Psychiatrie. Suhrkamp, Frankfurt, 379-403.

WHO (1977) Constraints in Mental Health Services Development: Report of a Working Group. WHO, Regional Office for Europe, Copenhagen.

Zöllner, H.F.K (1981) European Health Strategies in the Absence of Economic Growth. Scandinavian Journal of Social Medicine, 28, 73-81.

Chapter Two

THE ECONOMIC EVALUATION OF MENTAL HEALTH POLICIES

Alan Maynard

Policy-makers in the psychiatric services of all the countries in the European Community are confronted with a common set of problems arising from the recognition of what generally have been poor standards of care in the old mental hospitals, with the belief that socio-clinical outcomes might be improved through the development of a variety of alternatives loosely, and often vaguely, termed 'community care'. Thus, despite differences in the time of initiation and speed of implementation, one can trace a general move among the member states to deinstitutionalise psychiatric patients, even though evaluative evidence to sustain this radical change of policy is less than complete. The expansion of community care has sometimes been accompanied by substantial augmentations of resource allocations outside the hospital sector, but whether the new treatment modes provide the most efficient forms of care has yet to be demonstrated.

The aim in this chapter is not to advocate re-institutionalisation, but rather to analyse recent policy trends from an economic perspective. In the first section an outline of the health economist's approach to health care is presented. This is followed by an examination of the reasons why community care programmes have not been subject to economic evaluation. Finally, the nature of economic appraisal of mental health care is discussed.

A psychiatrist or hospital administrator might define efficiency in terms of, say, a shorter length of stay or the cheapest form of care for each patient group. Careful appraisal of these responses reveals their weaknesses. A shorter length of stay may minimise costs to the hospital service but provides no information about treatment outcomes or, alternatively, the costs and benefits of care outside the hospital. On the other hand, the cheapest form of care for some patient groups may well be in institutions. Thus, for efficient decision-making one needs to take account of alternative ways of achieving the same socio-clinical goals in order that the full social costs and benefit for any one mode of care can be assessed.

Superficial definitions of efficiency fail to take account of the differences between and within patient groups and they ignore the distinction between 'inputs', 'processes' and 'outcomes'. Yet the distinction between these three terms is essential. Health care inputs such as expenditure on staff, drugs, beds and other facilities are combined in differing quantities to produce health care processes. These are activities or measures of throughput such as the number of outpatient attendances, the number of inpatient days, the length of stay and so on. Outcomes are measures of the impact of inputs and processes on the patient's health: the extent to which they improve or avoid reductions in the length and quality of life (i.e. produce quality adjusted life years - QALYs)..

This input-outcome relationship is an essential part of the economic approach to the evaluation of health care and the creation of improvements in health status. On the inputs side the ubiquitous characteristic of all individuals, institutions and societies is that they face limited budgets (means) and infinite ways (ends) of allocating them. Because of scarcity, choice and rationing are unavoidable. The consequence of scarcity is that each choice involves a foregone alternative. For example, if the increase in the budget is spent on hiring a new psychiatrist, the value of alternative actions such as the employment of a nurse or the purchase of equipment is foregone. The value of these foregone alternatives is the 'opportunity cost' of the decision to hire another psychiatrist.

All decisions involve opportunity costs; there is always an alternative way of spending society's scarce resources. Because of the scarcity of resources inputs and the presence of opportunity costs, it is logical to seek to use the limited inputs efficiently to maximise the production of desired outcomes. Economic efficiency can be defined as the minimisation of costs <u>and</u> the maximisation of benefits. A failure to achieve economic efficiency incurs opportunity costs which could have been avoided without reducing the production of QALYs. Conversely, reallocation of inputs and the achievement of economic efficiency minimises the opportunity costs of achieving the given output.

THE FAILURE TO EVALUATE POLICY OPTIONS

The failure to evaluate community care policies now being adopted in many European countries may lead to long-term inefficiency in the use of scarce resources. This situation is not helped by the tendency for most health care systems to have incentive structures which themselves induce inefficiency. Individuals are typically insured by private or social agencies or the state providing third party reimbursement of the costs of treatment. Thus, there is no incentive for patients to economise on their use of health care facilities; equally there is no incentive for the treating agent to economise: the third party pays again.

To these factors militating against economy amongst providers and consumers, must be added the asymmetry of knowledge between the two groups. Psychiatric patients, for example, have a limited ability to determine their appropriate diagnosis and treatment, let alone predict outcome. As a consequence, the 'expert' provider determines the nature of the treatment. In this way the provider (supplier) may play a crucial role in determining demand in the health care market and, unlike in some markets, the consumer's ability to identify over-supply or inappropriate treatment is minimal. This situation is unlikely to be the product of a conscious strategy on the part of the medical practitioner, for he is generally unaware of the true costs of various treatments and is not trained to evaluate the costs and benefits of alternative patterns of care. Indeed, some doctors, particularly in the acute sector, tend to argue that there are no alternatives to a particular treatment, whereas an economist will always argue that there is at least one alternative: doing nothing. The orientation of medical school training means that doctors may tend to be 'benefit maximisers', concerned with outcomes for the individual patient, although they are often relatively ignorant of the benefits of the treatments they offer. Moreover, it has to be said that this approach will meet with patients' approval since they are not concerned about or are ignorant of the financial costs of treatment.

One decision maker in the health care system concerned directly with the minimisation of costs is the treasurer. However, in allocating resources he tends to minimise the costs of his particular service, for instance a hospital, rather than taking a wider view of the system as a whole. This failure to take account of the full opportunity costs of care - costs to each agency in the public and voluntary sector, to private profit-making services, to families and individuals - results in inefficient decision-making. Yet, in the British system for example, those whose job it is to minimise costs to the hospital in times of cash limited national health service budgets may have every incentive to move chronic psychiatric patients to accommodation elsewhere, because this reduces hospital expenditure by transferring responsibilities to other service budgets and/or to the family. Conversely, in a system as in West Germany, where a hospital earns a daily fee for each occupied bed, the hospital administrator may have a vested interested in maintaining a high occupancy rate and may have less incentive to discharge patients who might benefit from forms of extra-mural care since such action would eventually reduce the hospital budget.

All health systems manifest this kind of budgetary and intellectual compartmentalism which results in a critical failure to share knowledge and concern of the true costs and benefits of health care programmes. Indeed, one group of decision-makers may be concerned to maximise benefits regardless of costs and another to minimise costs regardless of benefits. To take an example: a clinical evaluation of care for alcohol abusers may indicate that therapy 'A' meets a defined set of criteria of cure within eighteen months, whilst therapy 'B' leads to a cure within three years. Using this information the benefit (cure) maximiser may opt for package 'A'. However, this choice is based on a consideration of individual benefits (outcomes) alone. Let us say that the cost of each successful therapy in 'A' is £15,000 and in 'B' £5,000. If the alcohol treatment unit has a total budget of £150,000 - ten patients can be successfully treated by therapy 'A' but thirty patients can be cured by therapy 'B' before the unit's budget is exhausted. Thus, maximisation of individual benefits does not lead to efficiency in resource use and, moreover, in the above example it is unethical, since it would mean depriving twenty patients access to treatment from which they could have benefitted.

The lack of evaluation of the community care option in psychiatry is caused by factors which are endemic to all health care systems. Incentive structures are such that they induce inefficiency. They are protected by intellectual specialisms and separate trainings which compartmentalise knowledge and decision-making. The inadequate measurement and lack of integration of considerations of costs and benefits in the decision-making process results in a poor specification of policy issues and the failure to develop a systematic and comprehensive strategy.

ECONOMIC EVALUATION OF PSYCHIATRIC SERVICES: AN AGENDA FOR EUROPE

Economic evaluation is an aid to the decision-making process, rather than a definitive approach to policy options that produces unambiguous answers to difficult problems. What economic analysis can do - and this is vital at the current stage in Europe of planning new modes of care - is to generate data that inform policy-making, help establish appropriate norms of practice and assist in the evaluation of actual service performance.

At the present time mental health services in many Community countries are in the process of change, in several cases profound change. Yet these new policies are being enacted largely in ignorance of long-term or even short term effects, not only on patients but also on mental health budgets. Resources are being transferred from hospital to 'community' services; from health to welfare agencies. Powers of resource allocation and responsibility for service provision are being delegated by central ministries to regional and local authorities. The number and range of services and service providers are growing incrementally, making the health economist's task increasingly hard. In many countries reliable economic data on the mental health sector even at the national level are extremely difficult, and sometimes impossible, to obtain, since the required data collection would have to rely on the sustained cooperation of a large number of public and private agencies. Thus, routinely collected official statistics frequently provide too inadequate a basis for detailed economic analysis.

At this stage, therefore, what is required urgently in each country is a series of reasonably small-scale but comprehensive cost-effectiveness studies which compare outcomes of services currently being proposed as alternatives to be afforded priority in resource allocation. It is perhaps premature to advocate that such studies should be cross-national, since economic outcomes at least are closely linked to the organisational and financial systems of delivering health services which vary considerably among EC countries. The studies should help to identify the strengths and weaknesses of policies which are now shaping the long-term planning of services, frequently until the end of the century.

These cost-effectiveness analyses will be concerned with quantifying the real opportunity costs of alternative means of achieving therapeutic goals in terms of the impact on patients, their families and a wide range of health and social services, as well as the broader effect on the economy (Williams and Anderson, 1975; Drummond, 1980). To be of any great use to planners the problem for analysis should be well-defined, the alternative provisions clearly specified and the outcomes for each party (for example, the patient, the health authority, or society) identified and evaluated. It will be important to describe carefully the alternative modes of care in terms of the client groups served to avoid confusion about the validity and applicabilily of the results.

Since it is impossible to evaluate all costs and benefits accruing to alternative modes of care, the range of effects included becomes a vital issue. The costs of some services are difficult to measure because they are financed centrally and are distributed among many users (e.g. heating, lighting and water). Difficulties also arise in costing the services provided by voluntary workers; yet because these inputs involve opportunity costs - leisure time is foregone - their inclusion is appropriate. The efficiency with which benefits are identified will depend on the outcome measure used. Such measures may relate to morbidity, indicators of health status that assess physical, social and psychological well being (Wright, 1978; Culyer, 1983) or years of life gained.

The valuation of benefits raises some further problems. For instance, if a schizophrenic patient is returned to the labour force the benefit, as measured by his remuneration, is an increase in output. However, if the patient is a housewife or an old age pensioner, no return to the labour force will take place and output will not increase. This is because of the way in which Gross National Product (GNP) is calculated: it ignores, among other things, the value of household production by children, housewives and the elderly, thus helping to generate unequal benefit streams. Although adjustments can be made this remains a controversial issue.

Another area of controversy concerns transfer payments: that is, welfare benefits paid in money. Some people erroneously argue that, if health status is improved and transfer payments reduced, a benefit (or negative cost) accrues. However, such payments are merely redistributions of existing GNP; they do not affect its magnitude. Welfare payments therefore are not opportunity costs; they merely affect property rights in opportioning the existing national wealth.

Both benefits and costs may have time profiles over many years and these may differ between treatment programmes. Thus, the benefits of one programme may accrue in the short-term whilst those of another may only accrue over many years. To take account of the differential timing of costs and benefits, a procedure called discounting is required. Future cost and benefit streams are accordingly reduced (or discounted) to reflect the fact that money spent or saved in the future does not count as heavily with decision-makers as money spent or saved now. The application of an appropriate discount rate reflects these differential time preferences.

Finally, every evaluation of the costs and benefits of alternative therapeutic strategies contains varying degrees of uncertainty: for example, what is the effect of using different discount rates: two, five or seven per cent?; what is the effect of differential patient compliance rates on the costs and benefits of the treatment package? All cost-effectiveness studies will therefore need to include an analysis of the impact of alternative assumptions about factors such as these on the estimates of differential costs and benefits. And, most important, the investigators will need to ascertain that resources 'released' by the adoption of alternative care modes can be usefully exploited elsewhere.

CONCLUSION

At present in health care as a whole the kind of analysis advocated here is an exception rather than the rule. Yet only if such evaluate research is expanded rapidly can there be any hope of scarce psychiatric resources being allocated efficiently and ethically, rather than on the basis of current crude 'guestimates'. Furthermore, without the evidence produced by economic analysis innovations and extensions in the service network may merely exacerbate existing inefficiencies in resource use and deprive potential patients of care or existing patients of better care. The opportunity costs arising from such inefficiency are unethical and unacceptable.

REFERENCES

Culyer A. (1983) Health Indicators. Martin Robertson, Oxford and London.
Drummond M.D. (1980) Principles of Economic Appraisal in Health Care. Oxford University Press, London.
Williams A. and Anderson R. (1975) Efficiency in Social Services. Basic Blackwells, Oxford.
Wright K.G. (1978) 'Output measurement in practice'. In: A.J.Culyer and K.G.Wright (Eds). Economic Aspects of Health Services. Martin Robertson, Oxford and London.

Chapter Three

BELGIUM: PSYCHIATRIC CARE IN A PLURALIST SYSTEM

Franz Baro, André Prims and Pierre de Schouwer

In common with its northern and southern neighbours
a salient feature of Belgium health policy in the
last decade has been the decentralisation of powers
to regional authorities. Although the Brussels
health ministry retains certain policy-making
functions and undertakes a general supervisory
role, major executive powers have been entrusted
since 1979 to the two language Communities: Flemish
and French, each of which has its own regional
government. In addition other powers in the field
of environmental health have been delegated to the
three regions: Flanders, Wallonia and Brussels.
Any review of 'national' policy must therefore take
account of the cultural and linguistic
heterogeneity of Belgium which, in health care, has
found expression in a diffuse range of actors both
in policy-making and service provision. It is in
terms of the coordination of this system that
ultimately the success of national policy must be
evaluated.

POLICY-MAKING IN MENTAL HEALTH CARE

The Ministry of Public Health and Family Affairs
exercises central government functions in respect
of mental health policy and welfare assistance.
This ministry is responsible for health legislation
relevant to the whole country, for the basic
regulations concerning the financing of services
and national standards of accreditation of medical
establishments. Major planning functions have also
been retained through the 1963 Hospitals Act, which
came into force in psychiatry in 1972. The Act
enables the central ministry to set planning norms

and to authorise the permitted number of hospital beds in each area eligible for government aid. Sixty per cent of building and equipment costs comes from the state and forty per cent is guaranteed by the Hospital and Medico-social Institutions Building Fund. Hospital bed planning is thus one of the strongest controls central government has on the Communities in the field of health care. The Ministry shares with the Ministry of National Education and Culture the regulation of training in the paramedical professions, whilst this latter ministry oversees the training of doctors.

The Ministry of Social Security is responsible for legislation in the field of sickness and disability insurance. There are six groupings of sickness funds which now provide cover for the whole population. Some funds are occupation-based. The insurance system has traditionally been somewhat competitive; coordination has been attempted through the creation of the National Institute of Sickness and Invalidity Insurance (INAMI) which has the task of supervising the insurance system and distributing revenues among the various funds. Over one quarter of its budget comes from state subsidies.

Other ministries exercise special functions in the field of psychiatric care. The Ministry of Justice is responsible for legislation authorising compulsory detentions in psychiatric hospitals and also has control over services for the psychiatric offender. The Ministry of Employment and Labour supervises the special fund for the social rehabilitation of the disabled, which, in part, finances a range of services, including vocational retraining centres and sheltered workshops.

The formulation of policies for inpatient services and a variety of forms of extra-mural care now largely rests with the Communities. Unfortunately, in the present discussion, this devolution has made it impossible for us to collect and review data for the whole of Belgium, and in assessing policies introduced since 1974 we have concerned ourselves mainly with data provided by the ministry for the Flemish Community.

It is perhaps misleading at present to refer specifically to 'psychiatric' services, since Belgium is only now establishing separate provisions for the mentally retarded, many of whom remain in psychiatric hospitals solely because of the lack of alternative facilities.

Family doctors and specialists in office practice, who form the majority of neuropsychiatrists, receive payment for each item-of-service performed. Most doctors have signed agreements (conventions) with the insurance funds whereby persons who consult them are reimbursed most of the treatment fee, with the remainder - the ticket moderateur - being paid by the patients. Patients have direct access to medical specialists in office practice.

During the past ten years several general hospitals have established psychiatric units, the average size being thirty beds. However, the majority of inpatient services are provided by psychiatric hospitals, most of which were built in the last century. One important legacy is that 90 per cent of these institutions are adminsitered by religious orders; the Communities and certain provincial authorities administer most of the rest. Another legacy, but from much further back in history, is the former psychiatric colony at Geel. Care of the mentally ill has been provided for almost ten centuries, when Geel became a place of pilgrimage to the shrine of the Irish martyred Saint Dymphna. At present some one thousand mentally retarded and chronic psychiatric patients are accommodated at Geel, the majority being boarded out with local families, although the number of families willing to accept placements is now decreasing rapidly. A similar initiative was founded in the nineteenth-century at Lierneux.

Hospital inpatient services now receive an annual global budget instead of the former daily fee for each occupied bed, Outpatient services, however, continue to be financed on an item-of-service basis. Sickness insurance funds indemnify 75 per cent and the state 25 per cent of the general costs of inpatient care. Patients are expected to contribute a fixed sum towards 'hotel costs' and also pay a ticket moderateur for the hospital doctor's services they receive. Where patients cannot pay these supplements they may be eligible for a means-tested award of social assistance. In the current climate of spiralling costs, it is expected that patients' own contributions to the costs of treatment will increase sharply.

Relations between the psychiatric hospitals and the insurance funds are regulated by national agreements (conventions) which, among other things, specify that the funds must pay a supplement for the costs of medication.

Mental health service units - called 'dispensaires' - have been established in the wake of the 1975 legislation discussed later and provide counselling and preventive treatment. In fact, their origin goes back to the 1930s when a voluntary organisation, the 'League of Mental Hygiene' set up ten clinics, run on similar lines to those for tuberculosis. An impetus for further development was provided by a health ministry order in 1953 which sanctioned their work in the preventive field, but restricted the number of consultations permitted for each patient. Many dispensaires continue to be administered by the League, although local authorities and other voluntary organisations are also active in this field.

Patients using the services of the dispensaires are expected to contribute a certain proportion towards treatment costs or to apply for social assistance. The health ministry provides a 95 per cent subsidy for the operational and salary costs and Communities subsidise building costs.

Residential services, rehabilitation centres and a variety of nursing and long-stay homes are also provided. Medical and nursing components of care are covered by sickness insurance, but liability for the 'hotel costs' falls on the individual who may apply for means-tested welfare benefit. In these services the various forms of financing - global budget, item-of-service and daily fee - are often combined in a complex fashion.

Belgium currently spends about five per cent of GNP on health care. 37 per cent of total costs are administered by INAMI for distribution to the insurance funds; 25 per cent comes from the state, Communities and local authorities; and 38 per cent is met by the individual. Though reliable data specific to psychiatric care is not available, one is safe in assuming that individual liabilities are lower than the above figure and expenditure by public authorities considerably higher.

Current policies for mental health services date from the mid-Seventies, although psychiatric legislation from the mid-nineteenth century is still in force, and responsibilities for services were also amended by the creation of the Communities in 1979.

The major reform of inpatient services came in 1974 with the official endorsement of the principles of active treatment, in an establishment located as close as possible to the patient's own environment. Prevention, early detection and rehabilitation were essential by-words in the new policy. Organisationally the aim was to achieve what had been critically lacking in Belgium services: a coordinated and integrated service based on the sector principle.

Initial endeavours were directed at improving the quality inpatient services. Belgium at that time enjoyed the dubious privilege of having one of the highest bed ratios in north-west Europe. Hospitals were large and frequently in a poor state of repair. Inpatient numbers in the early 1970s decreased from 28,000 to 25,000 (1975), but the impact of this decline on improving standards was minimal; 25 per cent of hospitals still had over one thousand beds and two-thirds of patients were located in what in Belgium are called 'closed services'.

In the longer term the goverment wished to see a substantial reduction in the number of beds. The development of alternative outpatient and community services was expected to contribute to a decline in demand for inpatient care, as was the transfer of the mentally retarded to special institutions. These assumptions were built into the 1976 plan which specified the planning norms for future accredited services. The complex categorisation of inpatient facilities was amended, being replaced in adult general psychiatry by two classifications: service 'A' offering acute treatment and observation, either in psychiatric hospitals or DGH units, for urgent or crisis cases; and service 'T' in psychiatric hospitals only and offering a more long-term treatment programme focussed on rehabilitation. Both service are available for inpatients and day patients.

To meet the new standards of accreditation demanded by the 1974 policy the number of beds per ward was to be reduced and qualified staff ratios increased to allow for the creation of truly multi-disciplinary teams. There was also to be a closer collaboration with specialist services in physical medicine, primary care and other outpatient services to permit speedy and effective intervention in crisis situations.

The norms adopted in the 1976 plan allow for 0.65 beds per thousand population in the 'A' services, of which 0.15 would be in DGH units. For day care and night clinic patients the norms specify 0.15 places in psychiatric hospitals and 0.075 places in general hospitals. In the more long-term 'T' services, available only in psychiatric hospitals, the bed ratio is 0.9, supplemented by 0.4 day/night care places. Thus, the plan envisaged that the existing psychiatric hospitals would continue to provide the majority of inpatient services. Although the 1976 norms allow for a doubling of the 745 beds then located in DGH units, these services would provide acute treatment only and would still account for less than ten per cent of the planned total of some 15,000 inpatient places. In all, day/night care places would increase this capacity by forty per cent but, again, the majority of places would be attached to the psychiatric hospitals. Further norms were provided for child psychiatry and services for the elderly mentally ill.

Taking all inpatient services into consideration, it would appear that implementation of the plan is not proceeding as envisaged. Projections for the total bed/day place capacity in the Flemish Community, for example, indicated that by 1982 there would be 11,715 places, whereas, in fact, this figure was exceeded by some 3,400 or almost 30%. Moreover, despite the plan that the old inpatient service categories ('O' and 'P') would be phased out in the short-term, and would therefore not require inclusion in the longer-term plans for modernisation, by 1982 services in these categories were still supplying nearly a quarter of all accredited beds. The need to offer treatment and rehabilitative services as close as possible to the patient's home environment was taken into account in devising the 'T' service and in the establishment of day hospitals which, though the first was opened as early as 1960, were still in their infancy in the mid-1970s. Unfortunately, the plans for day/night care provisions have only been partly implemented: in the Flemish Community it was projected that by 1982, there would be 2700 day places in 'A' and 'T' services, yet only half of these places were in fact available by this date. Moreover, the insurance funds stipulations for day care have been rather inflexible: a minimum number of hours and frequency of attendance are specified in order to qualify for reimbursement of costs.

The Fund for the Social Rehabilitation of the Disabled, set up 1963 and administered by the employment ministry, has invested considerable sums in the establishment of rehabilitation centres and leisure facilities within psychiatric hospitals. The Fund has also helped local authorities and voluntary organisations to build rehabilitation and vocational retraining centres and sheltered workshops outside hospitals. Construction and operational costs of these units are met by the Fund. The costs of a patient's rehabilitation programme are reimbursed by the insurance funds, although the Fund contributes to any costs not falling within their liabilities.

Psychiatric rehabilitation services remain inadequate and the danger is that long-term patients will be transferred to residential and nursing homes, many of which are very large, without being offered an appropriate form of rehabilitation.

A royal decree in 1975 laid the foundations for a new system of preventive services in the community centred on the dispensaire, each of which was to serve a population of between 40,000 and 50,000. 196 dispensaires were planned for the whole of Belgium, approximately two-thirds of which are now in operation, treating an annual average of 25,000 patients.

One of the unfortunate features of the Belgium health care system is exemplified in the operation of these dispensaires. Their establishment was largely left to private or local authority initiative; those in charge of administering the psychiatric hospitals - the majority being members of monastic orders - were not party to these developments. Indeed, under the daily fee system prevailing at the time, the dominating interest was a high bed occupancy rate and hospital budget suffered if alternative services reduced the demand for inpatient care. A lack of real coordination with the hospital sector has continued to handicap the work of these clinics.

The staff of the dispensaire are now involved in a range of interventions which extend beyond their original narrow 'preventive' role. With the permission of the Health Ministry they may collaborate with other services, such as primary care teams, educational authorities, and Alcoholics Anonymous, to provide counselling and crisis intervention. Ministerial approval is required in order to facilitate the monitoring of the innovative role of these clinics and also to control their expenditure.

Each dispensaire consists of one or more multi-disciplinary teams directed by a psychiatrist. One of the prime focuses in the past has been work with children and parents. There have been some complaints of an inadequate service for adults, particularly in follow-up care for discharged patients. Services have proliferated, although staffing complements and the desired multi-disciplinary team membership have not always been achieved. However, although dispensaire staff are functionally independent of clinical teams in the inpatient sector, a cross-over of staff on a part-time basis is being officially encouraged.

One of the emphases of the 1977 policy statement concerned the effective coordination of what was a diffuse complex of services, in order to provide a continuity of care. Nevertheless, the health policies of the mid-Seventies represent something of a compromise, a political expedient attempting to accommodate fragmented budgetary systems and conflicting economic and professional interests. Real coordination has proved to be pious hope: agreements exist only on paper, their success depending on the cooperation of a large number of agencies with interests to protect, whose mode of operation could be seriously challenged by future moves to creat a community-based service. The identification of an appropriate means of coordinating services continues to elude policy-makers.

The formulation of the 1976 plan, which was based on policies adopted in the preceding two years, appears in hindsight to have been based on very questionable principles. The potential contribution of alternative services on reducing needs for inpatient beds was not fully assessed, with the result that developments outside the hospital have been inadequate, a situation which helps support a large inpatient sector. On the other hand, the number of mentally retarded patients who could be transferred in the short-run was seriously over-estimated. Some of the plan's

49

deficiencies have been officially acknowledged, but suggestions to appoint a working part to re-examine the whole basis of hospital bed planning have come to nothing. In the meantime, the health minister is considering fresh proposals to create additional sheltered accommodation for long-stay patients and to accelerate the programme of converting hospital accommodation into hostels or nursing homes. Proponents argue that these plans would lead to an improvement in the quality of psychiatric care at the same time as bringing about a financial saving to the state, by levying higher personal contributions to the costs of care.

PSYCHIATRY AND THE LAW

The status of psychiatric patients in Belgium is still governed by legislation passed between 1850 and 1873. The laws were primarily designed to control persons presenting a threat to public order, but there are also safeguards against illegal confinement. The legislation provides for the licensing and inspection of mental hospitals and stipulates the necessary conditions for certification; it does not refer to the forms of treatment and care patients should be given once they are admitted.

Patients may be admitted: on petition of their guardians or relatives; at the request of the local mayoral court in cases where there is a threat to public order; by a decision of the judiciary or, in urgent cases, the provincial governor; or at the request of other persons authorised by the mayor. Except in the case of a relative's petition, each request for admission must be accompanied by a medical certificate completed no more than fifteen days prior by a doctor independent of the admitting hospital. In urgent cases the certificate may be produced up to twenty-four hours after admission.

Within a day of admission a psychiatric report must be sent to the mayor, the provincial governor and certain public officials. The law requires that in the first five days the patient should be visited daily by a psychiatrist and a record maintained in a medical register. Thereafter, a written report must be filed at least once a month.

Since 1930 it has been possible to authorise a trial discharge of detained patients, given the written consent of the original petitioner of admission. A psychiatric patient may also be confined at home, subject to approval by a justice of the peace whose decision is based on two medical certificates: one completed by a doctor designated by the patient's family, the other, a doctor appointed by the justice of the peace.

With its emphasis on restraint, the existing law has long been held to be anachronistic. The current focus of Belgian psychiatry, as elsewhere, is voluntary treatment in 'open' institutions. Indeed, open units have been in existence in some Belgian hospitals for a considerable time, and a ministerial circular on the subject was issued as long ago as 1946. Yet the fact is that these open units, as, too, the new inpatient categories introduced in 1974, are technically operating against the law, since there is no provision for them in the nineteenth-century legislation.

A mental health reform bill was introduced in parliament in 1969. Its provisions are founded on the principle of patients' right to appropriate treatment in institutions close to their home environments. The bill stipulates that, first and foremost, treatment should be voluntary and made available as quickly and as freely as possible. Only as a last resort, where patients present a great danger to themselves or others, should compulsory admission to a psychiatric hospital be contemplated. The bill clearly specifies the conditions for admissions: emergency orders are limited to 72 hours; orders for 'a period of observation' may not exceed forty days; detention beyond this period is subject to two-yearly orders. In suitable cases certified patients could be boarded out or placed back with their own families.

Unlike later legislation in some other countries, the bill does not place emphasis on the patient's right to consent to treatment or restrict authorisation of certain treatments. However, there is an appeals procedure against detention, for which the patient may retain a lawyer or, alternatively, have one appointed by a justice of the peace.

One of the principle features of the bill is the abolition of closed psychiatric units (units containing locked wards only). In fact, the move away from closed units has been going on for some time. In 1955 there were some 20,000 psychiatric inpatients, 95 per cent of whom were in closed units; by 1981, of the 16,000 inpatients, 27 per cent were accommodated in these units. In terms of admissions the decline is even more dramatic: only 2.7 per cent of admissions in 1980 were to closed units.

The bill has been before both houses several times, on each occasions being amended. In subsequent revisions the proposals to extend boarding-out schemes have been less prominent, emphasis returning to hospital care, in spite of continued lip-service being paid to the importance of community-based psychiatry. Remaining contentious issues surround the relative status of the doctor and the judiciary in authorising compulsory admissions. The lower house holds that, since certification constitutes a deprivation of freedom, the exercise of such a power should be restricted to the magistracy. On the other hand, the general opinion in the upper house is that the psychiatrist is the appropriate person to decide on compulsory admissions; it is held that this would more closely align the status of the psychiatric patient with that of other patients since, by excluding juridical authorities from the process, it would emphasise the medical nature of the problem.

In the bill as it now stands the emphasis is firmly on the maintenance of juridical control, even though this entails the cumbersome process of the law. A final vote on the bill has yet to be taken. Meanwhile, in 1982, a working group formed by the Belgium League of Human Rights presented its proposals for new legislation to the Senate Committee of Justice. No official response has been forthcoming.

MENTAL HEALTH POLICY: OUTSTANDING PROBLEMS AND PROSPECTS

The coordination of the fragmented system of psychiatric services remains a major outstanding task. With a few notable exceptions, clinical teams in hospitals and dispensaires are separate, collaboration being achieved on an informal basis by individual team members. The coordinating committees envisaged in the 1975 policy have hardly been created and, where they do exist, are largely ineffective in the face of the very real divisions of economic and professional interests.

The laws governing compulsory admission are archaic and progress towards their replacement has been tediously slow. The outcome is that, in Belgium, there are serious legislative gaps in the protection of detained patients who, ipso facto, are deprived of control over their private means and certain other civil rights.

Despite some progress there remain considerable regional inequalities in services, with the south having more favourable provision than the north. These inequalities are superimposed on what are serious deficiencies in mental health services generally: most notably in the numbers of qualified psychiatric nurses; truly multidisciplinary teams in the dispensaires; and an adequate range of rehabilitative services and residential and nursing home provisions.

One of the most important challenges facing policy-makers is the significant increase in the numbers of the over 75 year olds: the 'old old'. This country has one of the most ageing populations in the world and pressure on residential, geriatric and psychogeriatric services is coming at a time when the economic recession is at its worst and where, for Belgium, the prospects of a strong recovery are not rated high. For the time being, policy options are limited and are generally aiming at reallocating funds away from other health service areas. There will be an increase in the financial liabilities of local authorities and families, and greater reliance on informal voluntary services.

These sorts of options are also being considered for general psychiatric services. In particular, state subsidies for day care and the dispensaires are at risk. Indeed, it is not an exaggeration to say that the whole social welfare system is endangered, with collective responsibility being increasingly replaced by private liability.

The present government has yet to issue its policy on the future of the mental health services, and general statements on health affairs made so far have hardly mentioned psychiatry. One clear policy, however, is the aim at reducing the permitted total number of psychiatric inpatient days. Hospitals which reduce the number of inpatient days below the permitted number will receive a 60 per cent subsidy for the cost of the bed whilst it is unoccupied. On the other hand there will be no reimbursement of the costs of hospitalisation for days beyond this number. Alternative provisions are permitted providing they produce a financial saving comparable to that saved by the reduction in inpatient days.

BIBLIOGRAPHY

Appelmans M. and Ternest J. (1982). Fondation 'Travail et Santé Mentale', Information Psychiatrique, 58, 1067-1075.

Coens D. (1980). Alternatives to psychiatric care in Belgium. World Hospitals, XVI, 21-22.

Dick D. (1980). Shaping new models in the European workshop. Health and Social Services Journal, LXXXX, 538-540.

Integrale Psychiatrische Gezondheidszorg: Studien van het Verbond der Verplegingsinstellingen van Caritas Catholica. XX, 1975, 1-88.

Ohrenbusch J. and Bastyns C. (1978) Fins et moyens de la nouvelle politique psychiatrique belge. Revue de I'Institut de Sociologie III, 209-227.

Ohrenbusch J., Bastyns C., Domb I.W., Toledo M. (1979). Traduction en terme de personnel de la nouvelle politique psychiatrique:
Vols 1 & 2: La Psychiatrie hospitaliere et non hospitaliere belge.
Vol 3 (1980). Annexes Statistiques. Institut de Sociologie, Brussels.

Ohrenbusch J. (1980). How to weld heterogeneous institutions into a homogeneous system of psychiatric care. In: E.A. Sand and F. Baro (Eds). Evaluation and mental health care. Centre interuniversitaire belge: Santé et facteurs psychosociaux. Brussels.

Prims A. (1981). (State of affairs in mental health care). In Psychiatrie en Verpleging. July 1981, 101-110.

Prims A. (1982). (Liberty and restraint in psychiatric care). In Vlaams Tijdschrift van Gezondheidswezen, July 1982, 223-235.

Prims A. (1984). (Services for psychogeriatric patients: wishes and realities). Welzijnsgids, February 1984, 1-19.

Chapter Four

DEVOLUTION AND REFORM OF PSYCHIATRIC SERVICES IN DENMARK

Erik Strömgren

THE ORGANISATION OF HEALTH SERVICES IN DENMARK

Health insurance was already common in Denmark in the last decades of the nineteenth century, initially on a private and voluntary basis. In 1933, at a time when more than ninety per cent of the population was already covered, compulsory insurance was instituted. The various sickness funds were abolished in 1973, when the county and lower-tier authorities assumed responsibility for financing and administering health services. Health care since then has been financed through taxation, each county deciding the rate of proportional income tax to be levied. The counties also receive financial assistance from central government through equalisation and supplementary subsidies in the form of block grants for the whole range of local services. These grants cover approximately forty per cent of total local authority expenditure.

The Ministry of Interior is the principal central government agency concerned with health care, though as this chapter outlines major functions have increasingly been devolved to the fourteen counties and the lower-tier authorities. The Ministry supervises certain preventive and domiciliary services which have not yet been or are not to be devolved. The enforcement of legislation controlling the training of health personnel is also one of its functions. County authorities are required to submit for ministerial approval their strategic plans for hospitals and nursing homes. Within the Ministry a directorate, the 'National Health Service', supervises and advises on hospital and other health services operated by central and local authorities. This directorate is also responsible for the collection of official health statistics.

The Ministry of Social Affairs supervises the health care reimbursement scheme, discussed below, including the approval of fees negotiated with the medical professional bodies. Welfare and rehabilitation services for the elderly and disabled are also its responsibility, as is the supervision of provisions for the mentally retarded which, for more than a century, have been completely separate from psychiatric services.

Since the last reform in 1976 two variations of the compulsory health scheme have been offered: one, to which over ninety per cent of the population have elected to subscribe, entitles the patient to free general practitioner treatment and to free treatment by a medical specialist in office practice on referral by a GP; the other gives partial reimbursement of the costs of primary care but allows the patient direct access to office specialists. For each patient the health scheme limits the number of office specialist consultations that are covered. Hospital treatment is free of charge in both categories of the scheme.

For long-stay patients there are special - and complex - regulations which have recently been revised. Most of the patients concerned are pensioners. Generally, when patients have been admitted for more than six months and when there is no likelihood that they will be able to manage without institutional provision, their pension is withdrawn as partial payment of care with a residual sum being left for personal expenditure. If patients have additional financial means up to sixty per cent of this income can be demanded as a further contribution to treatment costs. Similar rules apply to patients in nursing homes. Since patient contributions do not cover the operating costs of the institution the deficit is met equally by local authorities and the state. Under the present system it is financially more advantageous to local authorities for patients to be in hospitals rather than in nursing homes, a point discussed later. Among Danish politicans there has been an increasing recognition of the need for change in the complex and sometimes conflicting regulations governing long-term care and a revision of policy is possible in the future.

56

THE HISTORY OF PSYCHIATRIC SERVICES UNTIL 1950

The first psychiatric hospital in Denmark was established in 1816 by the municipality of Copenhagen in a rural area twenty miles from the city. Until then the mentally ill had been housed in meagre conditions in the poor house. In 1820 the first state hospital was built in Schleswig, which at that time belonged to the Danish kingdom. Since no borough other than Copenhagen was judged to offer reasonable care for the mentally ill, the state assumed this responsibility. With intervals of ten to twenty years new hospitals were built throughout the country, usually providing reasonable accommodation when new, but gradually suffering the common fate of ad hoc expansions which failed to solve the problem of overcrowding. The sharp contrast with the municipal and county general hospitals became increasingly apparent, especially during the first half of the 20th century when local authorities took pride in developing their own hospitals, advised and encouraged by the National Health Service, and with state reimbursement of the majority of running costs.

The state mental hospitals had a centralised administration which since 1921 has been in the Ministry of Interior Affairs, in the form of a special directorate completely independent of the National Health Service, although both directorates belonged to the same ministry. The obligations of the two directorates were different: whereas the National Health Service, staffed by doctors and jurists, had (and still has) only advisory and monitoring functions, the directorate for the state mental hospitals was also responsible for the financing and administration of these hospitals, thus having full power over them. The directorate, which had no doctors on the staff, was in administrative respects very efficient, not least with regard to keeping budgets low.

REPORTS, PLANS AND IMPLEMENTATION IN THE FIFTIES AND SIXTIES

During the 1930s and 1940s there was a growing public feeling, shared by many politicians, that the state mental hospitals were backward and needed

57

complete reorganisation and modernisation. In 1952 Louis le Maire, Professor of Criminal Law at the University of Aarhus, became director of the state mental hospitals and a new era began. A government commission was formed comprising politicians, administrators, psychiatrists and representatives of other medical specialisms. After several years of intensive work this heterogeneous membership managed to agree unanimously on a general plan for the modernisation and expansion of the mental health services. The report was published in 1956 and contains many of the general principles still directing policy.

The guiding principle was that psychiatry should be integrated with the rest of medicine. Until then most psychiatric hospitals had been built far away from the cities and the general hospitals. Most of them were too old, too large, and overcrowded. It was agreed that all new psychiatric hospitals should be built adjacent to, or as part of, general hospitals, and that they should be much smaller than existing hospitals, some of which had more than 1,000 beds. The optimal size was to be between 300 and 400 beds, giving them the capacity to serve a similar size catchment area as an ordinary county general hospital and to offer specialist psychiatric services. They were to be able to take care of all psychiatric patients at all stages of treatment, the distinction between acute and chronic hospitals being rejected.

Equally important in the commission's view was that psychiatric hospitals should have extended outpatient services. In fact, by the 1930s all psychiatric hospitals operated outpatient clinics, albeit relatively limited in scope mainly because of the hostility of the medical associations who feared the clinics would encroach on the territory of general practitioners and private specialists. This fear was quite unjustified since very few private specialists were in practice and general practitioners were usually happy to be relieved of some of their psychiatric caseload. Thus, although Danish psychiatrists very early on suggested that community psychiatric services should be created, the resistance of the medical associations delayed their introduction for several decades.

In 1956, when the report was published, the Danish economy was improving and it seemed quite realistic to plan for a rapid development of psychiatric services. In addition, geographical conditions were favourable: in twelve cities there was space enough to build psychiatric hospitals adjacent to general hospitals. One such innovation was already in progress when the commission was still working: the county of Copenhagen was in the process of building a 600-bed general hospital in Glostrup; a special law now provided possibilities for building a neighbouring psychiatric hospital. The opening of this hospital in 1960 became an historical event for Danish psychiatry, and the united general and psychiatric hospital has served as a model in later plans.

Although the combination of a general hospital and a medium-size psychiatric hospital was regarded as the ideal solution, it was obvious that it could not be realized in all locations. In areas where there was a need for psychiatric services, but where there was no possibility of building a full-scale psychiatric hospital on a site adjacent to the local general hospital, a smaller psychiatric unit had to be established. These small units could not cater for all psychiatric patients and therefore have had to rely on a psychiatric hospital elsewhere, especially for the provision of chronic care.

In 1956 there was much optimism about the future of Danish psychiatry and initially the new policy was implemented smoothly. In those places where new psychiatric hospitals were planned, local authorities were usually enthusiastic and cooperative and the financial basis for planning the hospitals was secured. But gradually obstacles arose. Although National Health Service members of the government commission had signed the report, it transpired that the head of the Service had viewpoints which differed from those of the commission. He argued that small psychiatric units in general hospitals should be promoted first and felt that the establishment of medium size psychiatric hospitals was not an urgent need. When politicians discovered this divergence of opinion among their professional advisers it was natural that they should be hesitant to act on the plans of the commission. Consequently, the whole planning process decelerated and long-delayed plans were overtaken by the beginnings of economic recession. At the expiry of the fifteen year planning period only four of the envisaged hospitals were in operation. On the other hand, some of the existing mental hospitals had been radically modernised, and a number of new nursing homes had been established which helped to reduce overcrowding in hospitals, especially among the many chronic patients who did not need active psychiatric treatment.

Another contribution to the improvement of the situation of the mentally ill was the 1957 law which provided for a substantial increase in welfare benefits and pensions. One of the consequences was that many old and mildly incapacitated persons, who had been unable to manage on their very small pensions and had been financially better off in institutions, could now be discharged with a reasonable chance of managing on their own.

During the late 1950s and 1960s a considerable number of small psychiatric units were established in general hospitals, a policy espoused by the National Health Service. For understandable reasons the building of these units was popular: there was a general feeling that they would be less stigmatising for their patients. Some also believed that if patients received adequate intensive treatment in such a unit the need for a longer admission to a psychiatric hospital could be avoided. It was also obvious to all concerned that cooperation between psychiatry and other medical specialisms was desirable. However, one cannot ignore the fact that the positive attitude of the somatic specialists towards the psychiatric units was sometimes influenced by their wish to erect new buildings for their own purposes and leave the old dilapidated buildings to psychiatry. It is also understandable that the establishment of psychiatric units was popular among younger psychiatrists, since they offered the possibility of a great number of permanent positions.

The psychiatric wards in general hospitals were soon treating a considerable number of patients. However, as the number of admissions to psychiatric hospitals did not decline it seemed that, on the whole, these small units catered for categories of patients who otherwise would never have received psychiatric inpatient treatment. The new units therefore did not reduce the workload of the psychiatric hospitals, most of which remained in an unsatisfactory condition.

The strong but uneven trend towards establishing small psychiatric units did not make the planning of mental health services at a national level any easier. Although the state had full responsibility for development of psychiatric provisions in the whole country (with the exception

of the city of Copenhagen), it could not prevent
counties from initiating similar services on their
own, often in conflict with ministerial plans
derived from the 1956 report. The 1952 commission
had, of course, discussed whether responsibility
for psychiatric services should be transferred to
the counties, which were responsible for general
hospitals, since it seemed logical that all
hospitals should be under the same administration.
There were, however, obstacles to bringing such
decentralisation about, at least in the short-run.
At that time the counties were relatively small and
the state hospitals were quite unevenly
distributed, most of them serving several counties.
No county was likely to be eager to take over a
large old psychiatric hospital which was far too
big for its own needs. Moreover, the counties felt
that the state had a duty to improve the
psychiatric hospital system before the transfer of
authority to them. Also during this period a re-
organisation of local government was planned with
the aim of radically reducing the number of
counties and communes (lowest-tier authorities).
It was thought that the new larger counties would
be in a much better position to assume
responsibility for psychiatric services.

During the 1960s plans for decentralisation
gained increasing currency in political circles.
The state was anxious to divest itself of some of
its responsibilities and the counties were eager to
take over. It was argued that local authorities
would be more interested in providing adequate
services for their own population than the
centralised administration in the ministry could
ever be. The superior state of general hospitals
under county control compared to state psychiatric
hospitals was believed to be proof of the greater
competence of local administration. In 1968 the
government assessed that the time might be ripe for
change, since the communal reform had now taken
place. A commission was appointed to consider
whether decentralisation would be advisable, but
soon afterwards with the change of government its
remit was altered to consider ways of how to
implement decentralisation, a policy to which the
new cabinet was deeply committed. Yet, after this
decision had been taken nothing more happened and
mental health services were left in a vacuum: the
state was, of course, not inclined to improve a
hospital system which was going to be transferred
to the counties, but the counties had no authority

61

to do anything for the psychiatric hospitals which were still under state management. No action, nor even planning was possible.

THE DANISH PSYCHIATRIC ASSOCIATION REPORT OF 1970

In this deplorable situation the Danish Psychiatric Association felt itself bound to take the initiative. A commission was formed which worked intensively for two years, publishing a huge report in 1970 giving details of what Danish psychiatrists wanted for the future. It was fortunate that this report was unanimously accepted by psychiatrists, despite the fact that there had been so much disagreement about organisational structures. The old controversy between those who were in favour of small units in general hospitals and those who felt that the whole of psychiatry should be moved to the general hospitals had in the meantime been resolved. Agreement was reached on a plan for minimum 60-bed psychiatric units with day patient facilities and extensive outpatient services. In addition, it was recommended that, where possible, up to four units should be attached to one hospital to improve efficiency and economy in operation. It was stressed that this combination of a few 60-bed 'atoms' with a larger 'molecule' was not to imply a deviation from the basic principle of sectorisation. Each of the 'atoms' was to serve its own population; on the other hand, it was desirable and practical that small units should share resources such as occupational therapy and clinical laboratories. It was supposed that a 60-bed unit could serve a population of about 30,000.

The principles of community psychiatry naturally included extended outpatient work and possibilities for home visits by hospital staff. The importance of appointing psychiatric nurses for domiciliary work was emphasised as was the establishment of close cooperation between various social agencies allied to mental health care.

This trend towards community psychiatry was apparent in other countries. In Denmark, however, pilot services had already been in operation for some time. In 1957 a community mental health project commenced on the island of Samsø, which is part of the catchment area of the Aarhus psychiatric hospital. Cooperation was established between the island's general practitioners and members of the hospital staff who visit Samso regularly to provide psychiatric treatment. The population of Samso at 6000 was supposed to be representative of the Danish rural population, and experiences occurring during the project were hopefully to have implications for other rural areas. The experiences during the first years indicated that the specialist psychiatric manpower required was not unrealistic. The project's results have been used as guidelines for much of the planning of Danish community mental health services.

THE DECENTRALISATION LAW OF 1975

The 1970 report of the Danish Psychiatric Association, though not in any way authoritative, had a great impact on mental health services planning during the 1970s. In 1975, the Minister of Interior Affairs finally proposed a law transferring the management of psychiatric hospitals from the state to the counties. He also appointed a new commission which was to formulate guidelines for the counties when taking over their new duties, a vital need since several counties had no experience at all of administering mental health services.

In accordance with the 1975 law the counties took over their new responsibilities in 1976. Since the guidelines were not yet published, it was inevitable that there would no immediate action. The intention was that, as soon as the counties had had time to study the guidelines, they should formulate their local plans which would then be sent to the ministry for comment.

The goal was that all counties should become self-sufficient in psychiatric resources, other than very specialised services, as soon as possible. As mentioned earlier, the baselines for the counties differed: in some there were new psychiatric hospitals, in others an old large institution, and in others, nothing at all. Those counties without psychiatric provisions of their own would be obliged to send patients to hospitals in other counties and to pay the relevant authority there. It was supposed that, gradually, these counties would build their own hospitals and thus provide their population with services in their own area. For the counties that already had hospitals

this plan could present problems: even if
modernisation of old institutions reduced bed
capacity, these hospitals might still be too large
and operating costs expensive. In some cases it
would therefore be necessary to use parts of these
hospitals for other purposes.

The first question counties asked was how many
psychiatric beds were needed. It was of course
easy for the ministry to reply that the prevailing
Danish average was 2.3 per 1,000 inhabitants, but
this was not a very useful answer because of
considerable regional variations in provision: for
example, whereas Ringkøbing in western Jutland had
1.3 beds per thousand population, the corresponding
figure for Copenhagen was 7 per thousand. These
huge differences within a small and relatively
homogeneous country like Denmark required some
explanation.

Although it was no surprise that a large city
like Copenhagen should have a relatively high
prevalence of hospitalised psychiatric patients, it
was not immediately apparent why the deviation from
the average figure should be so great. The age
distribution was unfavourable in Copenhagen, over
20 per cent of the population being over 65 years,
while the corresponding figure for the rest of the
country was about 12 per cent. In addition, the
City had a shrinking population, with healthy and
wealthy people tending to move out to the suburbs
leaving an older and more disabled population
behind. Furthermore, it seemed as if the uneven
distribution of psychiatric beds over the country
was related to the use of alternative institutions.
It was well known that some counties had a
relatively plentiful supply of beds in nursing
homes and this had a direct impact on the need for
hospital beds. This was the reason for the
disparity between Ringkøbing and Copenhagen.

The ministerial commission decided to
investigate the matter further. A special sub-
commission was formed with the purpose of comparing
Copenhagen, Ringkøbing and the county of Aarhus,
the latter having a bed ratio similar to the
national average when Copenhagen was excluded. It
was found that whereas Aarhus County had only nine
places in nursing homes per 1,000 population, the
corresponding figure in Ringkøbing was eleven. The
sub-commission visited nursing homes and inquired
how many of the residents were institutionalised
mainly because of mental disorder. In Aarhus the
proportion was 24 per cent; in Ringkøbing County no

less than 41 per cent. If the numbers of psychiatric inpatients and psychiatric patients in nursing homes were added, Ringkøbing had a bed ratio of 5.6 per 1,000 and Aarhus 4.3 per 1,000. As for Copenhagen the higher bed ratio could be explained chiefly by demographic factors.

It was natural to ask why the type of institutionalisation differed so much among the three areas. The difference between Ringkøbing and Aarhus could easily be explained. Aarhus had a psychiatric hospital in the centre of the county and in addition two psychiatric wards in general hospitals; access to psychiatric wards was therefore easy. In Ringkøbing, on the other hand, there was no psychiatric hospital and only a small psychiatric ward in a general hospital and the majority of psychiatric patients had to be admitted to a distant psychiatric hospital in the neighbouring county. The alternative of accommodating patients in nursing homes therefore seemed preferable. For Copenhagen the situation was different since the City had its own hospital system, including the mental hospital and psychiatric units; the state was therefore relieved of its direct responsibilities for mental health services in the Copenhagen area, merely reimbursing the city authorities for the cost of care. The result was that the City could expand its hospital system without imposing a financial burden on its citizens. On the other hand, if psychiatric patients were placed in nursing homes under the social welfare system, the City would only be reimbursed by the state for half the costs. It was therefore in the City's interests to create several large institutions under the hospital administration (called nursing hospitals) instead of building its own nursing homes.

The conclusion from this investigation was that the prevalence of mental disorder was probably similar in different parts of Denmark if age distribution and other demographic factors were taken into consideration. However, nothing definite could be said about the optimal combination of hospital and nursing home placements and the different counties have had to formulate their own policies, bearing in mind that other elements in the psychiatric care system could reduce the need for institutional provisions.

When the government guidelines were published the minister requested the counties to formulate their preliminary psychiatric plans and submit them to the ministry for comment by 1980. In 1982 counties were again asked to submit plans, this time for all types of hospitals. The results of this second submission were published in 1983. As regards psychiatry, the plans differ considerably among counties. One common feature was the emphasis on sectorisation which has been instituted, at least in principle, in all counties. Sector sizes vary from between 30,000 to 250,000 inhabitants, the larger sectors being mainly in urban areas. Another common theme was the emphasis on expanding outpatient services, with only a few counties intending to build new psychiatric units. Indeed, most counties planned to reduce bed capacity, partly as a consequence of modernisation of old hospitals.

PSYCHIATRIC PROVISIONS: TRENDS IN THE EIGHTIES

A general trend has been for counties with few psychiatric services to withdraw patients from establishments in other counties, quite often without providing adequate alternative facilities within their areas. An inevitable consequence has been the closing of wards and whole institutions which for many years have housed patients from other counties.

The number of psychiatric hospital beds has continued to decline since the state hospitals were transferred to the counties in 1976. For some patients, especially the elderly, accommodation has been provided in municipal and county nursing homes, and this has reduced overcrowding in hospitals. There has been a decrease of inpatient numbers in most age groups: a one-day census in 1977 showed there were 10,312 inpatients, in 1982 the corresponding figure was 8,824. During the same period the number of day-patients has increased from 1,829 to 2,259, a figure amounting to a quarter of the inpatient capacity. Admissions have only slightly decreased - from about 43,500 to about 40,500 per year - the decline in bed occupancy being explained by shorter stays of those admitted. This development is partly due to expansion of outpatient services and the work of the domiciliary psychiatric nurses employed by hospitals. These nurses also take part in the screening of patients referred for hospitalisation with the aim of preventing unnecessary admissions.

In 1982, 40 per cent of admissions were to psychiatric units in general hospitals, although the number of beds they contained amounted to only 15 per cent of the total, indicating that their focus is on acute work. Almost 80 per cent of beds are still in psychiatric hospitals, although they currently cater for only 53 per cent of admissions, equally an indicator of their role as providers of long-term care.

SPECIAL INSTITUTIONS

The first outpatient clinic for child psychiatry was opened in 1935, followed in 1944 by an inpatient department. Over the years a small number of child psychiatric departments have been established in different parts of the country, the largest one in collaboration with Aarhus Psychiatric Hospital. Current plans envisage that gradually all counties will at least establish outpatient clinics for child psychiatry.

The largest institution for epileptics has for a century been the private hospital 'Filadelfia' on Zealand. This hospital has also established a psychiatric ward and a sanatorium for neurotic patients. Three other institutions for patients with neuroses have been created in the private sector; their existence is now in danger as a consequence of the reluctance of the counties to pay for patients placed in institutions outside their area. In 1982 2.6 per cent of psychiatric admissions were to these sanitoria.

Most alcoholics are treated on an outpatient basis. Nevertheless, alcoholics constitute a large proportion of acute admissions. Some hospitals have special outpatient services for alcoholics, but there are also a great number of facilities for alcoholics in the private and voluntary sector. There are similar provisions for the treatment of drug addicts: many are admitted to hospitals, but most stay only for a short time. Some special agencies operate clinics for drug addicts, and a number of small hostels exist for these patients.

In the criminal law of 1930 the psychiatrist's role in the treatment of psychiatrically disturbed offenders was greatly extended. A special establishment was founded near Copenhagen and served for several decades as a model institution. During the 1960s and 1970s there was less confidence in the value of psychiatric intervention for these offenders and a radical revision of the criminal law reduced the role of psychiatry. Nowadays the special institutuion mainly treats patients who are so disturbed that they cannot be placed in ordinary prisons.

The ministerial report of 1956 stressed the importance of research and it recommended that a special research institute be founded at the Aarhus Psychiatric Hospital. This institute developed rapidly during the 1960s. Special departments of biological psychiatry, neuropathology, clinical psychology, genetics, and psychiatric demography were established, the last named containing the national psychiatric register which records all psychiatric admissions and discharges in Denmark. This register has been an invaluable aid to clinical and epidemiological research and has provided the basis for the planning of mental health services after decentralisation.

MENTAL HEALTH STAFF

In Denmark there are at present about 450 psychiatric specialists (8.8 specialists per 100,000 population). Since the beginning of the century psychiatry and neurology have been separate specialisms, although psychiatrists continue to have some neurological training. Of the 450 psychiatrists, 100 are in full-time office practice, 200 work full-time as hospital doctors, and the remainder have short-term or part-time positions. In hospitals about 50 per cent of the medical staff are junior doctors in training.

There is no basic qualification in psychiatric nursing but there are some postgraduate courses. As well as fully qualified nurses there are nursing aides, who in earlier times had only one year of training in a psychiatric hospital. A recent decision means that in future nursing aides must have the same training as aides working in general hospitals and, in addition, a year's training in a psychiatric hospital. Nursing aides can work in all kinds of psychiatric wards. However, most of them work in chronic wards or nursing homes, whereas nurses with a full training are the dominant group in acute wards.

Although social workers and occupational therapists have become a large and important group among psychiatric staff, there are no specialist basic qualifications. Within the training of psychologists there is a possibility to choose the sub-speciality of clinical psychology.

PSYCHIATRIC LEGISLATION

The legal situation of psychiatric inpatients is regulated by the 1938 law which stipulates that compulsory admission is only possible if the patient is psychotic and dangerous or where the chances of recovery will be considerably reduced without admission. Where an admission has taken place without these requirements being fulfilled, and if the patient demands it, discharge must follow immediately. There is not, and has never been, an initial period for observation. The patient can appeal the decision to the Ministry of Justice. The decision of the Ministry, which is always made on the basis of advice from the psychiatric section of the State Medico-Legal Council, can if the patient wishes be appealed to the courts. The law has functioned very well. It is concise and clear, and it gives good protection of the patient's civil rights. However, the increasing sensitivity of the public to questions of personal freedom has led to much discussion about a possible revision of the law. Recently a parliamentary commission has been appointed to investigate whether legal changes are desirable.

The number of compulsory admissions has declined steadily and now represent about three per cent of all psychiatric admissions. In contrast to some countries voluntary admission has always been possible, the only conditions being the production of a certificate from the patient's doctor and the permission of the medical superintendent of the hospital. Psychiatric offenders can be sentenced to detention in psychiatric hospitals and in these cases there is no requirement that the person must be psychotic.

CONCLUSION

Progress towards the establishment of a community-based psychiatric service has led to a reduction in bed capacity and an improvement in the range of services available to the patient at all stages of treatment. Yet the psychiatric hospital remains the impoverished element in the system. On the whole, the reductions in the number of admissions and inpatient beds have not been accompanied by improved working conditions in the psychiatric hospitals. The strained economic climate in Denmark, with drastic cuts in hospital budgets leading to reductions in staff, has resulted in a general situation in mental health care which cannot in any way be judged superior to that in 1976 when the counties took over. Some politicians hope that community work can largely be preventive, rendering most treatment, and especially expensive inpatient treatment, superfluous. Yet an efficient community service will require much additional manpower and no one can be certain that it will substantially reduce the need for institutions.

As this chapter has outlined, the plans of Danish local authorities vary considerably and the present picture is rather confused. On the positive side the present stage can be regarded as a period of experimentation. Such experimentation will, however, be rather meaningless if there are no serious attempts at evaluation so that different procedures can be compared, opening up the possibility of putting planning on a sounder footing.

BIBLIOGRAPHY

Betaenkning afgivet af kommissionen af 29. marts 1952 vedrørende Statens sindssygevaesen. Betaenkning nr. 165. (Report from the Commission of 29. March 1952 concerning the State Mental Health Service. Report No. 165) (1956). Statens Trykningskontor.

Betaenkning om grundlaget for planlaegning af psykiatrisk sygehusvaesen afgivet af et udvalg nedsat af indenrigsministeren. Betaenkning nr. 826. (Report on the Basis for Planning of Psychiatric Hospitals, Presented by a Committee appointed by the Minister of Interior Affairs. Report No. 826). (1977).

Betaenkning om Psykiatriens udvikling i Danmark i
    den naermeste fremtid afgivet af Dansk
    Psykiatrisk Selskab og Danske Psykiateres og
    Børnepsykiateres Organisation. (Report
    Concerning the Development of Psychiatry in
    Denmark in the Near Future, presented by the
    Danish Psychiatric Association and the
    Organization of Danish Psychiatrists and Child
    Psychiatrists) (1970). Sundhedsstyrelsen 18,
    225-248.
Dupont, A., Videbech, Th. and Weeke, A. (1974) A
    cumulative national psychiatric register: its
    structure and application. Acta Psychiatrica
    Scandinavica, 50, 161-173.
Gjerulff, Th. (1942) Lov om sindssyge Personers
    Hospitalsophold af 13 April 1938 med
    Cirkulaerer, Noter og Register. (Law of April
    13, 1938, concerning hospitalisation of
    mentally ill persons, with circulars, notes
    and reqister). Gads Forlag, Copenhagen.
Indenrigsministeriet (Ministry of Interior Affairs)
    (1977) Vejledende Retningslinier for
    planlaegning af psykiatrisk sygehusvaesen.
    Cirkulaere af 4.4.1977. (Guidelines for the
    Planning of Psychiatric Hospitals. Circular
    of 4.4.1977).
Indenrigsministeriet og Sundhedsstyrelsen (Ministry
    of Interior Affairs and National Health
    Service) (1983) Sygehusvaesenet 1978-1992.
    Planredegørelse 1983. (Hospital Services
    1978-1992. Statement of plans 1983).
Lindhardt, A. and Reisby, N. (1984)
    Distriktspsykiatriske projekter i Danmark
    udgående fra sygehusvaesenet. Beskrivelse og
    aktuel status. (District psychiatric projects
    in Denmark based on the hospital services.
    Description and current status). Ugeskrift
    for Laeger, 144, 1733-1740.
Nielsen, J., Nielsen, J.A., Kastrup, M. and
    Stromgren, E. (1981) The Samsø Project. A
    community psychiatric project in a
    geographically delimited population. Acta
    Jutlandica LV, Aarhus University.
Strömgren, E. (1958) Mental health service
    planning in Denmark. Danish Medical Bulletin,
    5, 1-17.
Strömgren, E., Kyst, E., Ryberg, I. and Weeke, A.
    (1979) Estimation of Need on the Basis of
    Field Survey Findings. In H. Häfner (ed.)
    Estimating Needs for Mental Health Care. A
    Contribution of Epidemiology. Springer,
    Berlin, Heidelberg, New York, pp. 37-42.

Weeke, A. and Strömgren, E. (1978) Fifteen years later. A comparison of patients in Danish psychiatric institutions in 1957, 1962, 1967, and 1972. Acta Psychiatrica Scandinavica, 57, 129-144.

Chapter Five

GERMANY: THE PSYCHIATRIC ENQUETE AND ITS AFTERMATH

Steen Mangen

The objective of recent mental health policies in the Federal Republic has been to transform the traditional practice of German neuropsychiatry, with its sharp division between inpatient and outpatient treatment, into an integrated system of care founded on the principles of sectorisation. This chapter assesses the achievements and problems that have occurred in implementing these policies in what is a pluralist system in terms of policy-making, financing and the administration of health services.

Before examining the major review of policy in the 1975 official commission of enquiry, the 'Enquete', a brief account is given of developments in German mental health care in earlier decades of this century. Then follows a description of the organisation and financing of health services, and a review of the existing psychiatric provisions which the commission sought to reform.

Twentieth-Century Developments

Until the late Sixties German psychiatry was comparatively little influenced by developments in social and community psychiatry occurring elsewhere in Europe and in the USA in the years after the Second World War. Yet Germany had not always been negligent of social models of care: In the Second Reich and in the Weimar Republic, for example, there had been successful boarding-out schemes in certain areas. Mental hygiene associations operated counselling services and outpatient clinics. Two celebrated services of this period are worthy of mention: at Gelsenkirchen an extra-mural clinic offering advice and care was established at the public health department and became a model for facilities elsewhere. So, too, was the 'Erlangen Model', in which the local mental hospital engaged in an innovatory after-care and domiciliary service. At Gütersloh hospital in the 1920s Simons gained an international reputation for his work in industrial therapy. There were experiments in patient-administered wards and a gradual move towards an 'open door' policy (Panse, 1964).

The Nazis swept away many of these innovations. As soon as they took power a decree was issued banning the teaching of psychoanalysis. A year later a new law was passed which took away the legal basis of many of the hospital extra-mural services and in 1935 the mental hygiene associations were forced to disband. In their place, the Nazis set about formulating their own policies on mental health 'care'. They were to leave a ghastly legacy: between 200,000 and 350,000 compulsory sterilisations; between 70,000 and 120,000 victims of euthanasia (Blasius, 1980; Dörner, Haerlin, Rau, Schernus and Schwendy, 1980). The Nazis left another legacy that has had enduring effects. Aryanisation policies meant that Jewish psychiatrists were dismissed. Others quitted Germany of their own volition, leaving behind their more conservative colleagues who were to become medical directors of the mental hospitals in the Forties and Fifties. Moreover, after the War the mental hospitals were one of the few sources of employment for large numbers of unemployed doctors who took up their new duties with varying degrees of commitment. It is partly for these reasons that innovations in psychiatric care occurring inside and outside hospitals in certain areas of Britain, France, Scandinavia and the United States gained little foothold in the young Federal Republic.

In post-war Germany the continuing institutional separation of university psychiatric clinics and mental hospitals, each serving distinct patient groups, dulled the interest of academic psychiatry in social and community mental health care. Chronic patients, the target group for many experiments in social therapies in other countries, were mostly accommodated in the large mental hospitals. In the teaching hospitals, with the accent on acute care, the neurobiological sciences have dominated research interests; psychoanalysis, reinstated after the War, has enjoyed a formal, albeit uncomfortable, academic co-existence in separate departments of psychosomatic medicine.

74

By the mid-1960s, however, there were clear signs of the beginnings of a process of change. One of the results of university reform following the student unrest of 1968 was the formal separation of neurology and psychiatry as academic disciplines, although one should add that training programmes for psychiatrists retain a large component of neurology. Modest steps were taken in some universities towards developing research interests in the field of social and epidemological psychiatry. These changes were contemporaneous with demands for the reform of the mental hospitals, which were fuelled by increasing media coverage of the scandalous conditions in which many patients were forced to live. 1970 was to be the year when psychiatric reform became a real possibility: the Congress of German Doctors, for the first time ever, devoted its annual conference to the problems of mental health; and the change of government in 1969, which ended the Grand Coalition, created a favourable political environment in which reform could at least be considered. For a variety of reasons politicians of all major parties in the lower house, the Bundestag, were agreed that something must be seen to be done. Accordingly, the appointment of a commission of enquiry (the 'Psychiatrie Enquete') in 1970 received all-party support.

In the next section the organisation and financing of mental health care in the Federal Republic is summarised in order to provide the context for the discussion which then follows of the major elements of the psychiatric system reviewed in the Enquete.

THE ORGANISATION AND FINANCING OF PSYCHIATRIC SERVICES

No one political authority in the Federal Republic of Germany is vested with the ultimate responsibility for (mental) health policy. In the German brand of pluralism, responsibilities for policy-making, service provision and liability for costs are distributed among a diffuse range of public authorities, state-regulated agencies and private bodies.

Policy-making

The 1949 Constitution provides for a federal structure in which major responsibilities for health and welfare policies are conferred on the eleven federal states or 'Länder' (including Berlin-West). At federal level the Ministry of Youth, Family and Health Affairs supervises regulations governing the health professions and standards of professional training. Most important in the present context is its responsibilities for administering the social assistance programme which, inter alia, finances most activities defined as 'social' rehabilitation. The Ministry of Labour and Social Affairs oversees the social insurance system which incorporates the various health and disability insurance funds. Regulations concerning medical and occupation rehabilitation are also under its supervision.

Federal ministries prepare 'outline bills' to assist the federal states in drafting legislation in areas for which they have political competence. This practice enables the federal government to promote its own views on policies and it also ensures a degree of legislative uniformity among the states. The exhortative role of the federal government extends, for example, to the commissioning of enquiries into the health services, where recommendations can have national implications, although the powers to implement them rest, in large measure, with the federal states. Although federal responsibilities for health care are limited in scope, they are important and have been increasing since the early Seventies, especially with regard to capital expenditure programmes and, more recently, cost containment measures. The 1972 Hospital Finances Act provided for a new system of investment and maintenance subsidies for building programmes where new beds conform to certain 'needs' criteria. Under this Act hospital investment programmes receive a 33 per cent federal subsidy with the remainder being obtained in approximately equal amounts from the other two political tiers: the federal states and local authorities. At the same time subsidies for operating costs were withdrawn, these costs now being disbursed by health and disability insurance funds, the social assistance scheme and patients themselves. One of the principal aims of the Act was to improve the distribution of inpatient services and eradicate local excess capacities.

Hospital needs plans (Krankenhausbedarfspläne) are prepared to advise state health ministers of the total authorised bed requirements in each medical speciality. Excess proposed or existing beds are ineligible for public subsidies. However, beyond authorising the withdrawal of these subsidies, the federal ministry has no direct means of enforcing bed closures, although it can claim success in its policy of phasing out small hospitals containing less than one hundred beds.

The 1977 Cost Containment Act represents a considerable extension of the federal role in monitoring health care expenditures. Under its provisions the federal ministry has been able to introduce criteria aimed at controlling increases in fees negotiated by the medical professional bodies and the insurance funds. Certain contributions to treatment and prescription costs were imposed on the patient. At the same time the federal ministry encouraged the state ministries to maintain a stricter control of increases in hospital daily fees they authorised. A central planning committee was appointed with the task of arriving at agreed levels of increases in fees and other charges. Membership is derived from the relevant federal and state ministries, local authorities, insurance funds, representatives of the hospitals, professional bodies and the pharmaceutical industry. The committee's recommendations form the basis of the contracts concluded between the insurance funds and the office practitioner associations or the public, private or voluntary bodies administering the hospitals. Further discussion of recent policies on the control of health expenditure appears in later sections.

At present, about 15 per cent of the costs of all inpatient services are met from public funds. It is generally predicted that public subsidisation of health care is set to rise sharply, especially with the projected increase in the numbers of elderly patients requiring some form of institutional care. Currently the federal government is considering proposals to introduce an additional statutory insurance to cover the costs of chronic care which should therefore reduce its own liabilities. These plans, in as far as they relate to mental health care, are discussed later in the chapter.

The federal states implement their own health laws as well as relevant federal laws. All the

states have a health ministry but its functions
vary as do the range of additional responsibilities
it undertakes, usually in the field of welfare or
employment policy. Within each of these ministries
there is a mental health directorate. Although the
federal states are entrusted with the task of
planning for the whole range of health services, in
practice their statutory planning duties are
confined to the preparation of hospital needs plans
which specify authorised bed capacities and are
drawn up after consultation with the insurance
funds, the associations of bodies managing
hospitals, and the local authorities. As already
mentioned the federal states provide a 33 per cent
subsidy of the costs of authorised hospital
building programmes. The state psychiatric
hospitals (Landeskrankenhäuser) are under their
direct administration and the laws on compulsory
admissions are also passed by state legislatures.
The principal organ of coordination of health
policy among the federal states is the standing
conference of state ministers holding the health
and finance portfolios.

Local authorities (Kommunen) are charged with
certain functions in health and welfare. However,
it is enshrined in German law that services in
these fields should be managed by voluntary
organisations (Freie Wohlfahrtträger). Public
authorities have the statutory duty to provide
funds for all or part of the building and
maintenance costs; otherwise, they are restricted
to a subsidiary role of direct administration of
services only in situations where voluntary bodies
are unable or unwilling to manage the required
facilities (Subsidiaritätsprinzip). In fact, the
only provisions that local authorities are
automatically entitled to administer directly are
those at the public health boards
(Gesundheitsämter) which provide preventive and
after care services for specific client groups,
including psychiatric patients. These important
services are discussed in the next section.

The numerous voluntary organisations involved
in administering 'medico-social' provisions are
organised at state and federal level in five
groups, some of which are denominational, component
voluntary bodies deriving part of their income from
the church tax paid by all employed persons unless
they specifically contract out.

Hospitals. Over half of all psychiatric hospitals are administered by the federal states, the remainder being operated by voluntary and private bodies. Although the situation varied widely among the states at the time of the Enquete, eight out of every ten beds were in state-run hospitals. There was - and is - a long-standing separation of university clinics and other psychiatric hospitals. These clinics have no catchment area obligations and generally provide acute treatment facilities. According to the 1973 Enquete survey the clinics accounted for 3 per cent of beds and 16 per cent of admissions (Enquete, 1975).

Outpatient treatment. General practitioners and specialists in office practice have for the past fifty years exercised near- monopoly rights in the outpatient treatment of the insured population (1). Before 1977 outpatient clinics did not exist outside the university psychiatric hospitals, where they were permitted for the purposes of teaching and research (2). It is one of the achievements of the Enquete that, for psychiatry at least, this restrictive practice was partly lifted. Office neuropsychiatrists work independently of - and, for the most part, in isolation from - the psychiatric hospitals. They are typically one-man enterprises and seldom offer domiciliary or emergency interventions. Furthermore, they have tended to congregate in large cities: the Enquete survey indicated that 60 per cent of practices were in conurbations containing only 30 per cent of the German population (3).

Certain psychiatric services are available at clinics at public health boards, which are agencies organised at local authority and regional level. These boards have general responsibilities for health protection and environmental health; they also have formal obligations to inspect medical and allied establishments, as well as a planning role in ensuring that the health needs of the area are adequately catered for. Most important in the present context is their role in providing a variety of preventive and after care services as one of their duties in the field of social hygiene.

The clinics have long been associated with counselling and after care for psychiatric patients, particularly chronic patients, as well as being the main agencies administering the compulsory admissions procedures. The health insurance laws have required that they restrict themselves to counselling and care and not engage in 'medical' treatment (typically the distinction has been the ability to prescribe medication). For many years, before the establishment of hospital outpatient clinics, the services at the public health boards were the only specialist outpatient facilities available in all areas, although, of course, neuropsychiatric office practices were available in the larger towns.

Other services. Day centres, advice centres, sheltered workshops, hostels and other residential provisions were thin on the ground at the time of the Enquete. German welfare law stipulates that the principal agents administering these services are the voluntary bodies. A review of current service provisions appears later in the chapter.

Paying for Services

The operating costs of inpatient and other institutional services are recovered by charging a daily fee (Pflegesatz) which the institution negotiates with the insurance funds and the social assistance schemes and which is ultimately authorised by the state ministry. Doctors in office practice receive reimbursement principally on an item-of-service basis. Separate sickness and disability insurance cover costs in most cases, the funds directly reimbursing the service provider. However, in mental health care the social assistance scheme plays an important role, since for any one medical condition insurance funds are liable only for the first 78 weeks of inpatient treatment in a three year period. Therefore, social assistance is the major source of funding for chronic inpatients, as well as for patients in nursing homes and hostels.

Sickness insurance. Over thirteen hundred sickness funds (Krankenkassen), variously organised at local, state and federal level, underwrite the costs of treatment and 'medical' rehabilitation. 99 per cent of the population has sickness insurance coverage. Of subscribers for whom health insurance is compulsory, 30 per cent are members of substitute funds in lieu of compulsory membership of a statutory funds. The remainder (who earn above a certain income threshold) have voluntary

80

private insurance. The statutory and substitute funds are friendly societies and their minimum liabilities are regulated by the 1911 Reich Insurance Order and its subsequent amendments. Beyond the statutory minimum coverage the funds are free to compete among themselves by offering extras.

Disability insurance (Rentenversicherung). Disability insurance is organised at state level for blue-collar workers and at federal level for white-collar workers. Liabilities include the award of disability pensions and the costs of 'occupational' and certain 'medical' rehabilitative services, where interventions are orientated towards the re-establishment of the individual's capacity to undertake open employment (4).

Social assistance (Sozialhilfe). In cases where liability is disclaimed by the sickness or disability funds, the costs of care may be underwritten by means-tested awards of social assistance. Provisions are regulated by the 1961 Federal Social Assistance Act and its revisions. To some extent the level of social assistance awards varies among the federal states.

Social assistance is administered by regional bodies (uberortliche Sozialhilfetrager) in the federal states and also by local authority bodies (ortliche Sozialhilfetrager). The former are largely engaged in subsidising services providing long-term care, such as homes, sheltered workshops and hostels. The latter subsidise the costs of counselling and preventive services and may also underwrite the costs of an individual's treatment.

The Federal Act specifies that social assistance should be a subsidiary award, forthcoming only in the absence of liability coverage under insurance. Apart from cases of long-term hospitalisation, eligibility for social assistance generally occurs when medical treatments no longer offer the chance of significant clinical improvement or occupational rehabilitation the prospects of the restoration of work capacity. Social assistance funds provide for the social re-integration of patients as well as underwriting the costs of preventive and counselling services. Thus, the investment and maintenance costs of most 'medico-social' institutions are derived in large measure from social assistance as, too, are the associated daily fees for patient care.

The Organisation and Financing of Psychiatric Care:
A Critique

Neuhaus and Schräder (1984) have provided a useful
summary of the advantages and disadvantages of the
German health care system. As positive factors
they cite the diffuse distribution of power shared
by many political and social agencies; the broad
incorporation of various groups in society in
health policy through the self-administration
principle of the insurance funds; the lower
bureaucratic costs accruing to the public sector
through the delegation of certain functions to the
insurance funds; and flexibility of patient access
to specialised medical treatment and the freedom of
patients to choose their doctors, including
specialists. Negative factors are an over-emphasis
of the interests of providers of care, especially
in terms of income; a relative neglect of
collective risks; and insufficient stress on the
quality of care.

Let us examine some of these factors as they
related to mental health care on the eve of the
Enquete commission in 1970, and, indeed, in the way
they continue to have an impact on the delivery of
psychiatric services. Firstly, the pluralist
policy-making system: on the positive side, the
division of responsibility may make it easier to
introduce innovative services, since service
providers may have recourse to several bodies which
underwrite costs. Furthermore, in a federal
system, it may be that innovations can be tested
more easily locally and only introduced at a
national level after they have proved their worth.
This is especially the case in respect of
psychiatric legislation or funding programmes for
'model' services. None the less, it would appear
that, on balance, negative aspects of the system
predominate, at least in regard to mental health
care. The division of policy-making powers between
federal and state authorities, as well as the
participation of the voluntary organisations,
medical associations, hospitals and insurance funds
in the decision-making process, means in effect
that there is no comprehensive, nationally-
determined mental health policy being actively
pursued by all actors in the system. Indeed, even
within the confines of the federal political
system, the stipulations of health and social
legislation can be contradictory at different
levels of government, despite the intentions of the
Constitution.

In terms of effective planning the political division has had an adverse effect on the research and intelligence base in the health services. Although hospital needs planning is well-developed, no effective machinery exists for integrating the planning of other mental health services, especially those in the medico-social field. This situation is exacerbated by federal welfare laws, the effects of which have been to introduce a large number of agencies administering services, public authorities being allocated the passive role of financial sponsor rather than active service provider. These agencies have been somewhat competitive in operation and have tended to specialise in the care of certain religious denominations, patient groups or types of provision. They have been particularly keen to protect their rights and privileges from encroachment by newer service providers. The large charities are most active where public subsidies are guaranteed; less interest is shown in new or experimental provisions, especially when they cater for 'unpopular' patient groups (Muller, 1981). Here the field is left to smaller and newly-founded voluntary bodies; but the small-scale nature of their undertakings has frequently resulted in problems of cost coverage, since their operating costs must be met by the fees received in respect of a relatively small number of clients. Whatever other benefits there may be, the system has not facilitated an optimum investment of resources across a broad range of services. Rather, psychiatric care outside the hospital is typified by a patchiness of supply, with duplication of some services (e.g. advice centres in large towns) and wide gaps in other provisions (e.g. sheltered workshops).

The system of social insurance also acts more as a constraint on attempts to improve psychiatric services than as a promoting agent of change. Liability for treatment costs is accepted by the sickness insurance funds only if the disorder conforms to the definitions of illness contained in the 1911 Reich Insurance Order. The criteria betray a marked bias for a somatic concept of illness, with emphasis placed on individual risk. It is 'sickness' rather than 'health' insurance. Furthermore, the funds have no statutory duty to cover the costs of treatment no longer having a reasonable chance of offering a cure or marked improvement in clinical state. It was only in the early 1970s that certain preventive measures, such as cancer screening, were added to the list of liabilities. It was not until the phenothiazines were introduced that the statutory sickness funds extended their liabilities to the treatment of psychosis. Only since 1971 have both the statutory and substitute funds covered the costs of psychotherapy (5). The investigation of liabilities is undertaken case by case and requires a large bureaucratic machinery - 70,000 people are employed by the funds (Leichter, 1979) - as well as consuming a large amount of clinical staff time.

In a similar fashion, the disability insurance funds accept liability only for occupational rehabilitation leading to restoration of capacity for open employment which, for many psychiatric patients has been a difficult case to establish. The division of responsibilities for cost coverage frequently results in competition among the different types of funds, each seeking to deny its liability on the basis of its interpretation of definitions of 'treatment', 'care' and 'rehabilitation' contained in the legislation. These conflicts stem from definitions of rehabilitation in the relevant legislation which are narrowly based on physical disorders, where it is easier to conceive of medical, occupational and social rehabilitation following one another sequentially, whereas in psychiatry the three measures (if, indeed, they are separable) occur simultaneously. The ultimate recourse is to protracted litigation, in which the final arbitrators are the state social courts. Some of the numerous instances of these conflicts in accepting liability for costs of mental health care are reviewed in a later section.

The practice of dividing patients into 'treatment' cases, with a right to claim against insurance, and 'care' cases, who must apply for discretionary awards of social assistance, has continued despite widespread criticism that it contributes to the discrimination of the mentally ill. Insurance funds are able to disclaim liability for the costs of chronic care. By practically recreating the category of the 'less eligible sick', the policy is a poignant reminder of psychiatry's close historical association with the poor law. One of its direct effects has been to hold down the fees that psychiatric hospitals have been able to negotiate to about half the level of those charged in general hospitals.

84

The German system of office neuropsychiatry has been criticised for failing to provide adequate provision of outpatient treatment, a service for which, until 1977, it enjoyed a near-monopoly. It is true that the system is popular with many patients, since they have direct access to office neuropsychiatrists and are largely free to change doctors at regular intervals. Yet the maximisation of patient choice is reduced by the spatial mal-distribution of practices. For a lot of patients outside the large towns there is no effective choice and, in practice, relatively few patients do change their specialist (Kaupen-Haas, 1969).

The method of payment of office practitioners has been the most frequently cited factor helping to sustain their narrow interpretation of the medical model. Item-of-service fees have always been considerably higher for technical procedures such as E.E.Gs than for more time-consuming interventions such as the recording of a case-history or psychotherapy sessions. The structure of the fee catalogue provides a disincentive to doctors to broaden their clinical approach: to receive maximum reward, a doctor must subjugate himself to the logic of the fee system, for he will be financially penalised if he wishes to devote more time to developing rapport with patients. On the other hand, he will be rewarded if he prolongs costly treatments or undertakes unnecessary but lucrative tests. The present fee catalogue may be one of the reasons why most psychiatrists in office practice have retained a large neurological caseload; the Enquete survey found that, in the average practice, about 40 per cent of consultations were for neurological disorders.

The strict separation of outpatient and inpatient treatment has undoubtedly created a structure which is fundamentally unable to guarantee a continuity of care and introduces substantial diseconomies through duplication of effort (e.g. expensive medical tests) and by affording patients, even those with minor disorders, the right to consult a specialist directly without first being screened by a general practitioner. The office practitioner's monopoly position in the outpatient sector has also led to unnecessary hospitalisation: especially before the establishment of psychiatric outpatient clinics (and still the case in other medical specialisms), patients referred to hospital by office doctors unable to provide the required outpatient treatment had to be admitted if the hospital was to be reimbursed by the sickness funds for treatment costs.

When the negative effects of the method of reimbursement are considered: a hospital daily fee which provides an incentive to prolong inpatient spells and maintain high bed occupancy rates, and a fee for each item of service which rewards the doctor according to the number and type of interventions he performs there must be real doubt that the system in the Federal Republic represents the most cost-effective means of delivering health care or of controlling health care expenditures. Rather it is a system which has given rise to a myriad of powerful conflicting interests, whose resolution depends on what Altenstetter (1974) has termed 'accentuated legalism' (6).

As the Enquete commission was to report, psychiatric patients have been one of the largest clientele most critically affected by the negative aspects of the system. The rigidity of the insurance schemes and the uncoordinated structure of planning and service provision have imposed major constraints on the development of an integrated and community-based psychiatric service. All these factors can have a detrimental impact on patients' access to treatment; there are many opportunites for patients to fall through the gaps in the provision of services. For others, problems in regularising liabilities for cost may lead to long-term mis-placement. The Enquete report tacitly - and at times explicitly - acknowledged that successful mental health reform on a national scale requires extensive and protracted re-negotiation of territory by each element of the psychiatric system. Its proposals are now summarised and are followed by an assessment of the report as a basis for planning.

THE ENQUETE REPORT

The Commission was entrusted with a wide brief: to report on standards of 'psychiatric, psychotherapeutic and psychosomatic care of the population' (7). Here, only the proposals concerning general adult psychiatry can be reviewed. The members of the Commission approached their brief with what one can only call a German relish for thoroughness. The task of data

86

collection and the processing of expert evidence and the position papers of the many interested parties was immense. The Enquete provided the occasion (never since repeated) for the collection and publication of an impressive range of statistics on German psychiatric services. In one way or another a thousand people participated: some of them experts from abroad, invited to report on the situation in their home countries. The Commission members took over four years to complete their task. The result of their labours is a report and accompanying literature amounting to over 3,700 pages.

The report, published in 1975, makes for depressing reading on the state of psychiatric care in one of the richest countries of the European Community. In the words of the Enquete: patients were living in 'impoverished and, in part, inhuman conditions' Thirty-five per cent of patients were housed on overcrowded wards in a way which flouted fire regulations; more than half were on locked wards. Over two-thirds of psychiatric beds were in hospitals with a capacity of more than a thousand beds. One-third of hospital buildings were erected in the last century. Typically, psychiatric hospitals had large catchment areas and were remote from the centres of population they served. In some cases staff ratios were too low even to maintain a skeletal service: there was, for example, only one psychologist and one social worker for every five hundred patients. Only 42 per cent of nurses had the full state-recognised training in which, in any case, psychiatry was a minor component; a mere six per cent of nurses had additional specific qualifications in psychiatric nursing. Conditions in the larger hospitals, administered by the federal states, were even worse: they accommodated higher proportions of chronic patients and more of the beds were located on locked wards. Moreover, patients there were frequently found to be engaged in essential hospital work under the guise of 'occupational therapy'.

The Commission was equally critical of the mental health services outside the hospital. It documented the serious deficiencies in preventive and rehabilitative services. Provisions such as day care, hostels and sheltered workshops were non-existent in many areas. The inadequate number of office neuropsychiatrists and the serious inequality in distribution of practices did not provide a basis on which their contract conferring monopoly outpatient rights could be fulfilled. Nor could they ensure a continuity of care: rather the reverse. The surveys reviewed by the Commission indicated that less than a third of patients, advised to do so, actually consulted an office practitioner on discharge from hospital. Thus, the available evidence suggested that the office psychiatrist practised in isolation from the inpatient sector with a distinct and separate caseload, only a minority of his patients ever being referred to hospital (Dilling, Weyerer and Lisson, 1975).

The Enquete proposed a wide range of measures to remedy the deficiencies so apparent in the prevailing system. Although the report contains literally hundreds of recommendations, the sovereign principles are the equality of status for the mentally ill and the physically ill, and the establishment of community-based mental health care. In the new psychiatry prevention was to take precedence over cure. Counselling and crisis intervention services, based in every locality and complementing existing provisions, were to be established to permit early recognition of mental illness and speedy clinical intervention. These services together with improved facilities for rehabilitation would, it was hoped, help in the planned de-institutionalisation of large groups of patients, with a transfer of emphasis away from the inpatient sector to care 'in the community'.

Within this framework the Commission envisaged a streamlined system of services in 'standard care sectors' (Standardversorgungsgebiete), each of which would serve on average a population of 250,000. Every sector was to conform as closely as possible to existing political boundaries and offer a wide range of general psychiatric and allied services. At the regional level, incorporating several sectors, there would be additional specialist services. The report reveals an unequivocal preference for psychiatric units at general hospitals to provide for the sector's inpatient needs. To ensure that these units could fulfil full catchment area obligations, it was recommended to plan for an average capacity of two hundred places, including facilities for day care.

The Enquete report is more reticent about proposals for the future of existing mental hospitals. It was recognised that, of necessity, these hospitals would continue to be an important resource in inpatient care; after all, there were at that time a mere 44 general hospital psychiatric units in the whole country, with a total of less than three thousand beds. Clearly, until adequate alternative provisions were established, the mental hospitals would have to remain. The members of the Enquete were mindful that future, and unforseeable, political and economic situations would determine the long-term fate of the mental hospitals. Wisely, perhaps, they chose not to speculate. However, they did recommend that the maximum capacity of the hospitals should be reduced to six hundred beds. To assist in the decline of hospital capacity, they advocated an acceleration in the existing practice of transferring chronic patients, judged to be no longer in need of active treatment, to a variety of nursing and residential homes. Furthermore, they argued that care of the mentally retarded should no longer be a function of the psychiatric hospital; they, too, should be accommodated elsewhere.

In the Enquete's view these measures, when taken together, would intensify the clinical role of the hospital in caring for those patients who were to remain. Hence, the Commission advised that the category of 'care only' patient should be abolished. The newly reformed hospitals would undergo internal sectorisation so that each unit would serve the inpatient needs of a 'standard care area' with, as yet, inadequate inpatient provisions of its own. Clinical work within the hospital was to be further intensified by sub-division according to clinical specialisms.

To protect the rights of psychiatric inpatients, the report suggests that the post of patient advocate should be created. Moreover, the members of the Enquete regarded it as imperative that existing psychiatric legislation should be reformed, with new laws giving priority to the prevention of hospitalisation by making provisions for crisis intervention.

The Enquete survey revealed that, in 1973, there were 1.8 beds per thousand population, then the lowest psychiatric bed ratio in the European Community (EEC, 1981). As no data on the differential need for places in various psychiatric facilities were available, the Commission sensibly did not commit itself to projecting future bed ratio requirements, arguing that total inpatient needs would be a function of the availability of alternative services.

The prime emphasis in the recommendations lies in the creation of a network of outpatient, day care and other community services within each sector. Here planning ratios are stipulated. In addition, in currently under-served areas, the establishment of community mental health centres is advocated, each with a drop-in advice centre, day centre, hostel and sheltered workshop.

The report was at pains to stress that the anchor of outpatient work in the sector would continue to be the office neuropsychiatrist and it was urged that steps be taken to ensure a minimum provision of one practitioner for every 50,000 people. However, in a bold move - and one which did not win the support of the entire membership of the Enquete - it was proposed that psychiatric hospitals should be allowed to establish outpatient clinics, not in competition, but complementary to the services of office psychiatrists. To further extend provision of outpatient facilities, the Commission recommended that mobile 'social psychiatric services', already in operation at the public health boards in some cities, should be established in all sectors. These services, the best of which already employed multi-disciplinary teams, would offer counselling and follow-up care, with the special role of caring for patients who do not readily attend for treatment. Furthermore, in areas with high rates of psychiatric morbidity their work was to be supported by 'psycho-social contact centres', which were to act as referral agencies for other services in the network.

The members of the Enquiry were conscious that the fate of many of their proposals hinged on securing coordination among the institutions operating and financing mental health services. Without such cooperation there would be no basis on which to attempt to plan future provisions. To strengthen the research and intelligence activities of public bodies, it was proposed that a national institute of mental health should be established. The process of creating mental health departments in state health ministries should be completed. Advisory committees to the federal and state ministries of health were to be appointed. At the sector level there were to be coordinating committees of service operators and professional agents, as well as a special mental health committee convened under the aegis of the local authorities. The Commission suggested that the legal, administrative and financial problems incurred in introducing innovatory provisions should receive full documentation in a research programme they proposed for 'model services' (Enquete, 1975).

The Enquete: A Critique

The report has been criticised for a narrow medical approach to psychiatric problems in which a prime goal is the integration of psychiatry into the rest of medicine (8). From some quarters comes criticism of the lack of consideration of the ontology of mental illnesses. Several commentators complain of over-reliance on technical solutions in which the focus remains the individual, reducing social problems to individual problems. (Kommer and Sommer, 1977; Wambach and Hellerich, 1980; Zaumseil, 1978). The emphasis placed on professionalisation did not please others. Riedmüller's critique is typical of those who would have preferred more priority being allotted to self-help and lay-help (Riedmüller, 1978).
There have been reservations, too, about the utility of the Enquete report as a basis for planning. Some fear that the very scope of the report, with its hundreds of proposals for a gap-less network of services, is one of its major disadvantages as a planning instrument. Since the Commission could not call on a large number of studies of the comparative effectiveness of different provisions - nor, indeed, on data on patients' attitudes to services - it gave less explicit order to its list of priorities than many planners would have liked.
Many of the criticisms of the Enquete are justified; others less so. One may question, for example, whether a government-commissioned enquiry is the most appropriate instrument for a critical assessment of the scientific status psychiatry. But an enquiry is a useful means by which proposals for organisational change can receive a public airing. The fundamental flaw of the Enquete - the result of a need to compromise to retain the semblance of consensus among the membership - is that it proposed mental health reform within an unreformed health care system. The compromise may have made political sense in the short-term, but it has seriously undermined attempts to introduce community-based psychiatry nationwide.

The Official Response

It was 1975 when the report was laid before a
parliament preoccupied with the oil crisis: not the
most opportune moment to win support for expensive
proposals. The federal Health Minister had her
reservations and made it clear that reforms could
only be introduced over a prolonged period.
However, to complement the crash programme
announced by the federal states to eradicate the
worst conditions in the mental hospitals, she
announced a federal programme to sponsor 'model'
services.

A planning consultancy had been appointed even
before the publication of the report to prepare a
strategic plan incorporating the Commission's
recommendations. This plan, published in 1978,
provides a range of projections on staff and
service levels for eight clinical areas. Three
planning periods are identified, extending to
beyond 2000 A.D. (Heinle, Wischer and Partner,
1978) (9).

It was not until 1979 that the official
federal and state government responses were
collectively published. The tone of the federal
government's statement was cautious: a period of
ten years would be required to assess adequately
the viability of the Enquete's recommendations.
The Health Minister expressed reservations about
some of the potential effects of sectorisation
which she envisaged would entail a centralisation
of resources in each sector to permit coordination,
at the same time as decentralising care. In this
regard, she regretted that the organisational,
financial and legal problems of enacting the
proposals had not been addressed in more detail in
the report. The federal contribution to attempts
at evaluating these problems was to be the funding
of a second five-year model programme to run from
1980/81.

There is in the Minister's statement a certain
urgency to stress that the major task of reform lay
not at the federal level but with the states and
local authorities. None the less, she was equally
quick to point out that the establishment of new
services could not enjoy an absolute priority over
existing provisions. Specifically, the building of
psychiatric units at general hospitals could only
be sanctioned if they conformed to planning needs
for new beds.

Although the federal states' reactions varied, a certain unformity of response was the more dominant feature. State governments were unanimously critical of the surfeit of recommendations in the report, many of which they regarded as nebulous or utopian. The idea of a national institute of mental health did not find favour; nor did the proposal to appoint mental health committees for each sector, the objection being that existing local authority health and social services committees already had a coordinating role and they could be used to strengthen attempts at informal coordination among service providers. The concept of sectorisation was accepted in principle, but most of the states felt it needed substantial modification, both in terms of size and structure. On the other hand, the view of some states was that insufficient value had been attached to existing services - notably office practitioners, clinics at the public health boards and facilities within the psychiatric hospitals - which rendered some of the envisaged provisions superfluous. Those states that made any reference to the strategic plan regarded it as too expensive to carry out, but they did announce their adoption of the recommended 'medium staffing levels', which in some areas had already been achieved, at least for nursing (Stellungnahme zur Enquete, 1979).

If the federal states' responses to the Enquete's proposals were broadly similar, in practice - in their psychiatric plans and in the funding of public and voluntary mental health services - they have parted company in the degree to which they have been prepared to put elements of the grand plan into operation. One predictor of this differential propensity, as we shall see, is the political composition of the state governments.

FEDERAL INITIATIVES: THE MODEL PROGRAMMES

The first model programme, 1976-1980, encountered problems quite early in its existence. The planning consultancy undertaking the scientific evaluation complained that many of the services were deviating from their allotted 'model' role. It soon became apparent that the programme would be of limited benefit: the services sponsored - thirteen in all - were often very small-scale operations, having little local impact and they were too widely dispersed over a range of services in different parts of the country to permit comparative evaluation.

In the second model programme the object has been to assess the degree to which present financial and organisational arrangements can provide a basis for the operation of sectorised psychiatry and to identify areas where the system needs amending. Accordingly, funds have been directed towards the creation of a network of services in selected sectors. The fate of this programme illustrates some of the political constraints in the German federal system when attempts are made at centralised coordination. Despite attracting all-party support in the Bundestag, the programme subsequently met opposition from CDU-ruled states. Their objection rested on the constitutional irregularities introduced by the programme, since it involved the federal health ministry in the affairs of the states and could thereby set a dangerous constitutional precedent. There was, in addition, a resentment that at the end of the five years when federal aid ceased state governments would be required to fund services created by a programme which they had not instigated. The programme has gone ahead in SPD-ruled states, whilst some of the CDU states have launched projects of their own.

Fourteen 'model' areas were chosen in six federal states. Conditions for participation were that inpatient capacities conformed to the Enquete recommendations and that a start at least had been made in developing outpatient and day care facilities. Also being promoted are special projects for the psychiatrically disabled as part of a separate federal programme for rehabilitation announced in 1980. To obtain funding the states were required to give assurances that subsidies would continue after the end of the programme in 1986. Priorities within the programme are the establishment of services outside hospitals, although 20 per cent of the budget may be allocated for improvements to the inpatient sector and for the creation of hospital outpatient clinics.

Accompanying research and evaluation is being undertaken and results will be available in 1987. Some periodical reports have been issued complaining of a chronic lack of direction at the sector level, with insufficient emphasis on coordination at the crucial initial stages. There are fears that the new services will not necessarily lead to an integrated network and that the identification of an appropriate and agreed means of financing the sector is still a long way off. As a stop-gap measure a working party of federal and state authorities has recently been set up to formulate interim financial regulations.

Currently, the most pressing concern of the model services is securing funding after the expiry of the programme. Many feel that the funding period - five years - was too short a time but, despite a recent collective statement from the participating states urging that the programme be continued, the present federal government, which came to power after the programme had begun, has been reticent about committing itself to funding beyond 1986. In spite of the original intentions, a large number of services are under real threat. In Berlin for example, only three of the nine sponsored services have, as yet, a guaranteed financial future.

STATE INITIATIVES: THE PSYCHIATRIC PLANS

Most of the federal states have now published their mental health plans for services under their direct responsibility or dependent on public subsidies. Perhaps because the psychiatric hospitals are under their direct control, there is a regrettable tendency for the plans to continue to conceive of the inpatient sector as the pivot of the new psychiatric system. In all of the plans the existing psychiatric hospitals are assured of a life extending well into the next century, although the states vary in their projections of the proportion of inpatient facilities that will continue to be located there. Although the hospital base is not being surrendered its size is being curtailed. In general the number of psychiatric beds has been steadily falling since the early 1970s - with marked variation among the states - and the more recent planning projections have been set some way below the ratios recommended in the 1978 strategic plan (10). Nevertheless, the crash programme of improvements to the old psychiatric hospitals, instigated by the states in the mid-1970s, continues to dominate budget policy, to the detriment of efforts to accelerate the establishment of alternative sector services.

95

The psychiatric plans of several states contain notable departures from the Enquete recommendations. The concept of the sector is in many cases far removed from the ideas put forward by the Commission. In some plans sector sizes will be significantly larger; in the Bavaria Plan, for example, one sector will contain the whole of Greater Munich (population over two millions). In other plans it is not envisaged that all sectors will provide the range of services recommended in the enquiry. Varying priority is attached to the ultimate goal of creating a full network of psychiatric units in general hospitals and, in any case, this is constrained by hospital bed planning criteria as discussed in an earlier section (11).

SECTOR SERVICES: DEVELOPMENTS SINCE THE ENQUETE

In this section a review is presented of some of the developments in service provisions identified in the Enquete as essential components of sectorised psychiatric care. Particular attention is paid to the enduring legislative and financial problems.

Inpatient services. In common with other countries in Western Europe, there has been a simultaneous decline in the number of psychiatric beds in the Federal Republic and an increase in the number of hospital admissions. Between 1975 and 1981 there was a decrease of 13 per cent in the number of psychiatric beds but an increase of over 20 per cent in admission rates. As stated earlier these trends vary considerably among the federal states. As a direct result of federal and state policies bed capacity in the large state mental hospitals has been reduced by one-third, although they are still a long way from achieving the target maximum of six hundred beds. Much of this decline is attributable to the transfer of elderly and long-term patients to other institutions, at a current rate of four thousand a year. The total psychiatric bed capacity authorised by the hospital bed plans in 1981 was just over 100,000 (approximately 1.6 per thousand population). Units in general hospitals account for only 5 per cent of the total (5520 beds), with a similar bed capacity in specialist hospitals. Three per cent of beds are in university hospitals (Statistisches Bundesamt, 1983).
96

Admission rates reveal a pattern similar to that of neighbouring countries: a sharp rise in the number of admissions of patients suffering from alcoholism or related disorders, now accounting for half of all admissions, accompanied by a decline in the number of admissions of patients with schizophrenia. Three-quarters of patients are discharged within three months and 90 per cent within a year of admission. There are no official statistics at the national level but Häfner and Klug (1982) have analysed data for old and new long-stay patients in the Mannheim case register area. They found that 61 per cent of beds were still occupied by inpatients of more than one year's standing. Between 1973-1976 there was a significant decline in the number of old long-stay patients, but this was partly matched by a smaller accumulation of the new long-stay. There were marked clinical differences between the two groups. If and when a balance will be obtained - and therefore stability in the size of the long-stay population - could not be accurately predicted.

The proportion of voluntary patients increased between 1975-1979 from 55 per cent to 63 per cent of the inpatient population. There have been increases, too, in the number of beds on unlocked wards. Hospitals have reported a substantial improvement in staffing: a 24 per cent increase in the number of medical staff and a 12 per cent increase in the number of nurses (Reimer, 1980). Currently, 59 per cent of nurses are qualified, although this percentage is lower in the state psychiatric hospitals (12). Specialisation in psychiatric nursing is not offered as a basic qualification, but there has been some increase in the minority of nurses who have completed the post-qualifying course in social psychiatry.

The Federal Republic has made considerable headway in improving the inpatient sector since the time of the Enquete survey. None the less, certain negative features remain and others have appeared in the intervening period. Some hospitals, for example, still serve catchment areas containing well over a million people, not the 250,000 envisaged in the Enquete. Medical directors have complained of the negative budgetary effects of the reduced bed capacity which push up operating costs per bed (Bundesarbeitsgemeinschaft, 1983). Psychiatric hospitals are now being pressurised by the insurance funds and social assistance schemes to convert inpatient wards into residential units

which would provide nursing care only and attract a
lower daily fee. As it is, at present, the
insurance funds indemnify the costs of treatment
for only one-third of patients in psychiatric
hospitals; the remainder are partially or totally
dependent on social assistance. Increases in the
daily fee therefore impose the greatest burden on
social assistance, but in the current economic
recession all underwriters are anxious to restrict
their mounting liabilities. In contrast to their
attempts to curb costs in acute medical services,
the transfer of chronic patients to less costly
institutional provisions is an attractive strategy
to them, since it can be put into effect without
enormous difficulties.

Psychiatric outpatients clinics. Since 1977, when
an amendment of the Reich Insurance Order came into
force, psychiatric hospitals have been able under
certain conditions to open outpatient clinics. The
creation of these clinics was one of the
recommendations of the Enquete that gained
immediate favour with the federal government.
However, the Federal Association of Office Doctors,
representing the interests of the office
neuropsychiatrists, pressed for and succeeded in
securing a restrictive policy. Only psychiatric
hospitals are automatically allowed to open
clinics. Yet these hospitals are not the most
suitable centres for outpatient services because
they are often in remote locations ill-served by
public transport. Specialist psychiatric hospitals
and psychiatric units in general hospitals wishing
to establish clinics must negotiate contracts with
the office doctors associations. Contracts are
forthcoming only if the number of practices falls
below the recommended planning ratio (1:50,000);
they are subject to three-yearly review and may not
be renewed if, in the intervening period,
sufficient numbers of psychiatrists have set up
practice locally.

In common with other new provisions outpatient
clinics have had problems in cost coverage. A
regulation which came into force in 1981 restricts
the level of reimbursement to 80 per cent of the
fees chargeable in office practice for the same
treatment. At present, outpatient clinics recover
on average only half of their operating costs from
the insurance funds and the outstanding sum must be
found by the hospital underwriters, which in the
case of psychiatric hospitals are most often the

98

federal state authorities
(Bundesarbeitsgemeinschaft, 1983).

Day Hospitals   Day care remains an inadequate
provision in the Federal Republic, although there
has been a considerable increase in the number of
places available since the late 1970s. Estimates
from one study suggest there are now about eighty
day hospitals providing a total of two thousand
places, corresponding to approximately two per cent
of the inpatient bed capacity. The average number
of places available in each unit is twenty. Most
patients are referrals from the inpatient services,
although, by 1983, one third of patients were
direct referrals.   About 60 per cent of day
hospitals offer occupational therapy, but only 21
per cent have facilities for industrial therapy
(Bosch and Steinhart, 1983).
     Once again day hospitals have experienced
difficulties in covering costs. In the early days
insurance funds were reluctant to accept liability
and, until 1984, many funds restricted their
indemnity of costs to patients receiving day care
immediately after inpatient treatment.   Recent
amendments of liability do not resolve problems in
offering a flexible day care programme. In most
cases the insurance funds still do not permit part-
time attendance, arguing that if patients do not
need to attend all the sessions they should be
treated as outpatients.

Social   Psychiatric   Teams   Outside   Hospitals
(Sozialpsychiatrische   Dienste).   The
multidisciplinary teams, mostly based at the local
public health boards, are primarily concerned with
the care of long-term patients. Despite the public
association with compulsory admissions, the
psychiatric services at the public health boards
have a decisive role to play in community care
since, apart from the hospital, they manage the
most disturbed and seriously ill patients and
provide a domiciliary service and, if need be,
visit the patient's workplace.
     The work of the teams varies. The best of the
larger services offer counselling and crisis
intervention, often in connection with new
psychiatric legislation. All the services are
involved in after-care, including domiciliary
follow-up. Some teams provide medical supervision
for homes and hostels and have been active in
promoting self help by assisting in the

establishment of social clubs and flat-sharing ventures for former inpatients. The principal groups among the clientele are chronic psychotics, addicts, alcoholics and the mentally retarded. Many services have now secured contracts enabling them to 'treat' as well as 'care' (the critical distinction is the right to prescribe) and be reimbursed by the sickness fund. Yet problems in cost coverage have arisen because the funds do not accept liability for all forms of intervention. There is also a complaint about the arbitrariness in accepting liability, the same form of intervention being reimbursed in some services but not in others (Kulenkampff, 1981).

One problem in expanding the network of social psychiatric teams has been the difficulties public health boards experience in attracting medically-qualified employees. In lower Saxony, for example, only one department in every five in the early 1980s had been able to engage a psychiatrist for the purpose of setting up a service (Bauer, 1982).

Residential and Rehabilitation Services. It is in these fields that services in the Federal Republic are the most deficient. Problems in securing funding have arisen because of a lack of agreement by the financial underwriters on the question of whether certain categories of establishment can be acknowledged as authorised services under present legal stipulations, the contentious issue again centring on the diverse definitions of rehabilitation.

It was not until 1969 that the costs of rehabilitation of the mentally ill became a statutory obligation of social insurance. The 1974 Rehabilitation Act makes sickness funds liable for the first time for the costs of 'medical' rehabilitation, though it does not specify the conditions an institution must fulfil to gain recognition. Consequently, the Act has not regulated the distinctions routinely made by insurance funds between different elements of rehabilitation: 'medical', 'occupational' and 'social'. One of the aims of the present federal model programme and the 1980 federal action programme for rehabilitation is to promote the extension of rehabilitation services by working out an agreed system of regulating liabilities. Working parties with representatives of all relevant bodies were appointed to study these problems. At the present stage of their work it would seem that a consensus has been reached on the categorisation of services and the forms of rehabilitation they should offer, but little headway has been made in respect of the ultimate acceptance of financial liabilities (Nowak, 1984).

Meanwhile, the protracted arguments among the funds and the social assistance schemes cause the greatest difficulty for hostels with attached workshops which offer a programme of rehabilitation falling between after-care, occupational training and social therapies. The problem for these hostels is that few of them can present a clear-cut case to convince disability insurance funds that they are primarily geared to restoring or substantially improving the employability of their clientele. For the sickness funds the issue is whether these establishments are more appropriate for inclusion as 'special institutions' under the Reich Insurance Order or as 'cure' and convalescent homes, in which case liability would rest with the disability insurance funds.

At present, the regional-level social assistance schemes are having to provide most of the funds for these establishments, as part of their duties as 'subsidiary' funders, prior to an ultimate agreement among all underwriters. 85 per cent of hostel residents receive social assistance support, although 60 per cent of residents must make a personal contribution to costs. Only in 4 per cent of cases do the insurance funds accept liability (Stroebel, 1981). Such heavy dependence on social assistance has negative consequences for both the client and the service. Clients are denied access to social insurance benefits to which they may have been contributing for many years. Instead, they must apply for social assistance benefits, the levels of which are lower than the corresponding insurance benefit and which, as means-tested awards, may impose partial or entire liability for costs of care on the individual or his family. The heavy dependence on social assistance funding has other negative effects on psychiatric patients' access to rehabilitation services. Stroebel's analysis of data on patients who are invalided out and receive early retirement pensions (Frührentner) clearly indicates that psychiatric diagnostic categories are over-represented. He argues that the social assistance authorities actively encourage these claimants to apply for Frührentner status as a means of reducing their liabilities in the funding of rehabilitative facilities (Strobel, 1983).

101

For the services themselves reliance on social assistance is no adequate solution. Funding of the investment costs is often insufficient, coming in the form of an initial award of public money, which is sometimes supplemented by funds from the organisation managing the service or even from the daily fee chargeable for each client, although this intended to cover operating costs. Many of these services are small-scale and in a financially precarious situation, especially in times of public expenditure cuts. Some of the rehabilitation hostels have complained that, to cover operating costs, they have been forced to change their policies and accept patients with poorer prospects of rehabilitation, but guaranteed support from social assistance. They have also had high drop-out rates among residents who must pay for themselves (Froese, 1977).

An unavoidable consequence of these kinds of constraints has been the limited development of rehabilitative services for the mentally ill. In the whole of the Federal Republic there is still only one establishment (in Heidelberg) which, as well as preparing psychiatric patients for outside employment, provides a job-finding service. Training centres and sheltered workshops for former psychiatric patients are in short supply. Moreover, a survey in Bavaria by the state health ministry indicated that only about ten per cent of trainees of general sheltered workshops are former psychiatric patients. Statistics on the number of ex-psychiatric patients in occupational training centres are not available, but the same source states that few are adequately geared to working with this client group.

A survey conducted in 1977 revealed that there were three thousand hostel places in the Federal Republic, a mere quarter of the number required to meet the Enquete's recommended ratio of 0.2 places per thousand population. The hostel places were available for a restricted client group. Almost three-quarters of hostels specifically excluded alcoholics and drug addicts. Almost half did not accept people aged over 45 (Stiftung Rehabilitation, 1979). Since then, more emphasis has been given to encouraging patients to move to single-room accommodation in ordinary houses or to shared flats. Dörner (1983) reports on an interesting project in which long-term patients at Gütersloh psychiatric hospital have been moving into informal residential accommodation. Prior to the move they receive social skills and 'survival' training and their relatives were contacted and involved in the programme. Of the 128 patients in the initial project, 62 per cent went to single accommodation or to shared flats and a small number returned to their relatives or entered half-way hostels. A part-time nursing post was funded by the social assistance authority to provide follow-up care. Client satisfaction with their new accommodation was rated as high and most were able to cope, but 63 per cent of the sample had no day-time occupation apart from housework, indicative of the comparative lack of day centre provisions in the locality.

Many patients have been moving out of hospital in quite opposite directions to those going to informal accommodation. In recent years one way that psychiatric hospitals have been able to intensify their clinical functions has been by transferring long-term patients to residential and nursing homes. With a current annual transfer rate of four thousand patients, it is estimated that there are now between 50,000 and 60,000 patients in these homes, as many as there are in chronic wards in hospitals. The growth of the homes sector has been rapid and unplanned. In the rush to convert old TB hospitals and hotels, and to transfer elderly patients to homes for the aged, little consideration has been given to providing accommodation in the patient's original home area. The situation has not been improved by the recent policy of public authorities to rely increasingly on homes in private ownership.

The quality of the environment offered in homes has been found to depend significantly on whether the psychiatric hospital has retained a clinical association. Where this is the case homes generally provide satisfactory conditions, but they tend to accommodate the least disturbed patients. In other homes almost three-quarters of the residents had no structure to their day beyond meal times; a third of them had no direct access to their personal possessions. These were the homes with the least adequate staffing levels, poor medical supervision and meagre rehabilitative services (Kunze, 1981).

Significant financial advantages accrue to the social welfare authorities by the transfer of patients to homes, since the fees paid to homes are below those the hospitals obtain for chronic 'care cases'. Moreover, the present fee system imposes a disincentive for homes to engage in active rehabilitative work that leads to functional improvements among residents, since the fees are calculated on the basis of the level of nursing care each resident requires. If residents in general improve and the need for nursing care declines, the daily fee may be reduced and the homes would then lose income; it is a further example of the potential penalties the present financial system may impose on services successfully carrying out their roles.

LEGISLATIVE REFORM: NEW LAWS ON COMPULSORY ADMISSION

New laws governing compulsory admission are being introduced by the individual states as a result of the recommendations of the Enquete. The legislation is an attempt to reduce the emphasis on control and public safety by promoting as the prime goal clinical measures seeking to avoid hospitalisation of patients. To assist this policy, the laws provide for an expansion of crisis intervention work undertaken by the social psychiatric services, most of which are based at the public health boards. The success of the legislation will partly depend on the degree to which the twin goals of care and control can be reconciled in practice (Reichel, 1980; Walter, 1981). The new laws increase the legal rights of patients. In future an application for compulsory admission may only be made by a doctor with clinical experience in psychiatry (not necessarily a qualified psychiatrist). A representative of the local court must visit the patient and, where relevant, his legal representative within seven days of admission to ascertain whether further detention is required.

It is, as yet, premature to assess the full effects of the new legislation on compulsory admission rates which, in most of the federal states have tended to be high. In the past, rates have varied considerably among the states according to legal provisions and the differential use of guardian ad litem orders. Official statistics are not available at the national level, but in some states it is estimated that as many as 40 per cent of current inpatients are compulsorily detained. Nowadays the number of new compulsory admissions is much lower: in areas where social psychiatric services have been active for several years the percentage varies between five and ten per cent of all admissions (Bauer, 1982).

CURRENT PROSPECTS

As the Eighties have progressed West German health and welfare policy has increasingly been dictated by the government's concern to control rising expenditures. A further Cost Containment Act was passed in 1981 in an attempt to curb medical and hospital fees; patient contributions were again increased. Within this overall strategy the intention has been that cinderella services such as psychiatric provisions should be given some priority. Yet, during the same period, the mental health services were hit by cuts in social assistance expenditure which has held down the daily fees obtained for chronic patients and has also reduced the amount of money health and social services have had available for rehabilitation. Further cuts in the benefits of patients receiving occupational rehabilitation were introduced in 1984, at the same time as additional cost containment measures were announced for rehabilitation centres.

As one solution to budgetary problems the federal states and the insurance funds are favouring a policy of establishing nursing and long-stay homes in the private sector. An important recent development is the proposal of the federal government to introduce an additional insurance scheme to cover the costs of 'care', with the aim of reducing the large amount of social assistance expenditure allocated to institutional provisions for the elderly and for patients in receipt of long-term care. Negotiations are still in progress but it would seem that currently preference is for a care insurance scheme administered by the sickness insurance funds, with an additional premium levied on the individual at a rate of one per cent of income. There would also be a personal contribution of up to 30 per cent of costs, but social assistance would be available for eligible persons.

In the present climate purely discretionary duties to fund services are the first to be limited or surrendered. Now several of the small undertakings begun in the mid and late-Seventies and heavily dependent on public subsidies are in serious financial difficulty and some have already had to close. Some of the psychiatric hospitals are also facing budgetary crises, in part a result of their success in reducing inpatient numbers, but also because of more general controls on the level of the daily fee. The bed occupancy rate not only determines the total income the hospital derives from fees, it is also part of the formula used to calculate staffing levels. Nurses' jobs are the most threatened and they cannot be guaranteed alternative posts in 'community care'. It is therefore understandable that some hospital staff and the management are eager to retain as many occupied beds as possible.

The current economic crisis is not one conducive to promoting effective cooperation among a diffuse group of services, some of which feel under real threat. A global budgeting system across the whole range of services might be a step forward but this is not seriously on the agenda, at least at present. In the meantime, developments continue to be uncoordinated, with a certain duplication of effort co-existing with large gaps in the provision of other facilities. It is true that in the ten years of official experimentation with 'model' services some progress has been made on the question of what is required in each sector, but no agreement has yet been reached on the vital issue of how to finance all the components of the mental health care system.

Critically, the Federal Republic has attempted psychiatric reform without a reform of the health care system as a whole. This, in retrospect, may prove to be the greatest handicap of all. The federal division of responsibilties in policy-making, with the additional need to negotiate with a diffuse range of service providers and underwriters of costs does not provide a suitable framework within which to plan for a comprehensive psychiatric service within each sector. The present system leans heavily on legalism and responds sluggishly to change. Important innovations in psychiatric care have been possible in some areas, where the cooperation and goodwill of local politicians and service providers and underwriters have been forthcoming. But in the country in general progress has been slower, particularly when demands for reform are perceived as threatening long-established and powerful positions. In these situations what seem like innocuous attempts to create new facilities such as a day hospital or a social psychiatric service can take on a deeper significance (13).

The move towards psychiatric reform in West Germany occurred later than in most of its neighbouring countries. At the time when reform of mental health services became a political issue, reports from countries with long experience of some form of 'community' psychiatry were already spreading disillusion about the standard of care received by many patients: the 'community' was being used as a dustbin, there was 'burden' on the family and a transfer of institutionalism to residential homes. It was a time, too, of a 'psycho-boom' of alternative therapies available in the large cities and on offer to all-comers. Community care was therefore only one of several slogans being brandished about in the early Seventies and, in a country where generations of psychiatrists have received a strong neuropsychiatric training, it was relatively easy for proposals for reform to become a polarising issue, perceived by some as a potential means of undermining medical expertise without having proved themselves an effective alternative.

NOTES

(1) For an account of how the polyclinics run by sickness funds were forced to close by the Nazis, see Hansen, Heisig, Leibfried and Tennstedt (1981) (eds). Some sickness funds again attempted to run clinics in the Allied zones of post-war Germany and in the early years of the Federal Republic. The sole survivor is in West Berlin. A law in 1955 re-instated the near-monopoly rights of office practitioners to provide outpatient treatment.

(2) Hospital directors have always been allowed an outpatient caseload but they have tended to restrict their practice to private patients (Michaelis, 1979).

(3) Since 1960 there have been no general restrictions on the locations in which new office practices might be created. In 1977 a planning procedure was established with the aim of achieving a more equitable distribution of practices. The

office practitioners representative associations and the associations of insurance funds at state level cooperate in producing a plan indicating where the areas of need are and the specialities in demand. In these endeavours they are assisted by their counterparts at federal level. The chief instrument used to direct doctors to under-served areas is a range of financial incentives. However, in particularly serious cases of overprovision the medical associations may restrict the issue of further licences to practice in those areas.

The recommended planning ratio for office psychiatrists is 1:50,000 population. In the Seventies the number of neuropsychiatrists increased by over 60 per cent and the planning ratio has now been met, although regional inequalities in distribution have not yet been overcome. In fact, the present ratio is 1.5:50,000 but this includes practitioners with a large neurological caseload. Currently 45 per cent of all psychiatrists are in office practice.

(4) In addition, there is separate industrial accident insurance. The Federal Institute of Employment Affairs (Bundesanstalt fur Arbeit) underwrites the costs of rehabilitation aimed at re-training for a specific occupation. Relatively few psychiatric patients are in receipt of these services.

(5) Discussions in the past few years on a 'Psychotherapy Law' which would have allowed direct reimbursement of psychologists by the sickness funds, have not made much headway. Fresh proposals are currently being prepared by the Federal Health Ministry. Psychologists may be reimbursed for the costs of interpretative psychotherapy if patients are delegated to them by a medically-qualified psychotherapist. Since 1981, the substitute funds have also directly reimbursed psychologists for behavioural psychotherapy.

(6) As an example of how fiercely interests are defended, see Safran (1967) who recounts how, in 1959, a relatively minor amendment to sickness insurance liabilities unleashed tremendous opposition from the funds and medical professional bodies which ultimately forced the resignation of the federal Labour Minister.

108

(7) The official title of the report is 'Bericht über die Lage der Psychiatrie in der Bundesrepublik Deutschland - Zur psychiatrischen und psychotherapeutish/psychosomatischen Versorgung der Bevolkerung'.

(8) It says much about the value then attached to 'multi-disciplinary' mental health care that all but two of the 26 members of the Commission were medically qualified. Despite the fact that the Enquete had been prompted by conditions in the mental hospitals, the membership was predominantly academic. Only four members worked in mental hospitals; seventeen had current or past associations with university clinics. There was only one member in practice as an office neuropsychiatrist.

(9) The eight clinical areas are: general psychiatry; child psychiatry; gerontopsychiatry; addiction; epilepsy; psychosomatic medicine; forensic psychiatry; and mental retardation. The 'medium staffing levels' proposed in the strategic plan have been adopted in state mental health plans. For acute and medium-term inpatient care the ratios provide for one psychiatrist for every twenty-five patients, one nurse for every three patients, and a social worker for every sixty patients.

(10) The strategic plan provides a range of bed ratios for different kinds of urban area. In addition, a variety of ratios is proposed, depending on the emphasis given to each form of care and level of provision. The following ratio was recommended for adult general psychiatry in a sector containing 250,000 people and located in an urban conurbation:
Inpatient (acute and medium-term) and Day Care Places: 0.7/1000
Homes and hostels: 0.55/1000

(11) On the basis of current hospital building plans Hafner (1980) estimates that psychiatric units in general hospitals will provide only 7 per cent of all psychiatric beds by 1990. The units continue to be built too small to undertake full inpatient obligations for the average sized sector.

(12) An unpublished survey by the Schleswig-Holstein Social Ministry of nine of the eleven states indicated that in 1980 there was one nurse for every 2.5 psychiatric inpatients and one doctor for every 24 inpatients (i.e. more than the 'medium staffing level').

(13) The Autorengruppe Häcklingen/Uelzen (1981) have published a detailed account of the tribulations of one social psychiatric service in Lower Saxony.

REFERENCES

Altenstetter, C. (1974) Health Policy-Making and Administration in West Germany and the United States, Sage Publications, Beverly Hills.

Autorengruppe Häcklingen/Uelzen (1981) Ausgrenzen ist leichter: Alltag in der Gemeindepsychiatrie, Psychiatrie Verlag, Rehburg-Loccum.

Bauer, M. (1982) 'Bundesrepublik Deutschland' in H. Waller (ed), Zwangseinweisungen in der Psychiatrie, Huber, Bern, pp.10-20.

Blasius, D. (1980) Der verwaltete Wahnsinn: Eine Sozialgeschichte des Irrenhauses, Fischer, Frankfurt.

Bosch, G. and Steinhart, I. (1983) 'Entwicklung und gegenwärtiger Stand der tagesklinischen Behandlung in der BRD' in G. Bosch and A. Veltin, Die Tagesklinik als Teil der psychiatrischen Versorgung. Rheinland Verlag, Cologne pp.11-36.

Bundesarbeitsgemeinschaft (1983) Psychiatrische Stationärbehandlung in der BRD: Stand und Entwicklung. Statement of the Bundesarbeitsgemeinschaft der Träger psychiatrischer Krankenhäuser, 24/11/1983.

Dilling, H., Weyerer, S. and Lisson, H. (1975) 'Zur ambulanten psychiatrischen Versorgung durch niedergelassene Nervenärzte', Social Psychiatry, 10, 111-131.

Dörner, K., Haerlin, C., Rau, V., Schernus, R. and Schwendy, A. (1980) Der Krieg gegen die psychisch Kranken, Psychiatrie Verlag, Rehburg-Loccum.

Dörner, K. (1983) Gemeindepsychiatrie fängt mit Langzeitpatienten an. Unpublished.

Enquete. (1975) Bericht der Sachverständigen Kommission über die Lage der Psychiatrie in der Bundesrepublik Deutschland – Zur psychiatrischen und psychotherapeutisch/psychosomatischen Versorgung der Bevölkerung, Drucksache 7/4200, Bonn. (An English summary has been prepared by Anne & Brian Cooper and is available from Aktion Psychisch Kranke, Postfach, D-5300 Bonn).

European Economic Community. (1981) Social Indicators for the European Community, 1960-1978, Commission of the European Communities, Luxembourg, EC/12/SER 18.

Froese, M. (1977) 'Komplementare Dienste fur psychisch kranke Menschen: ein Beitrag zur Konzeption und Kostenproblematik', Zeitschrift für Mitarbeiter in der Behindertenhilfe, 4, 26-39.

Häfner, H. (1980) 'Planung und Aufbau psychiatrischer Abteilung und gemeindenaher Fachkrankenhäuser seit der Enquete-Erhebung', in H. Häfner and W. Picard (eds) Psychiatrie in der Bundesrepublik Deutschland fünf Jahre nach der Enquete, Rheinland-Verlag, Cologne, pp.17-22.

Häfner, H. and Klug, J. (1982) 'The impact of an expanding community mental health service on patterns of bed usage: evaluation of a four-year period of implementation', Psychological Medicine, 12, 177-190.

Hansen, E., Heisig, M., Leibfried, S. and Tennstedt, F. (1981) (eds) Seit über einem Jahrhundert...Verschutte Alternativen in der Sozialpolitik, Bund Verlag, Cologne.

Heinle, Wischer and Partner. (1978) Planungsmaterialien zur psychiatrischen und psychotherapeutisch/psychosomatischen Versorgung der Bevölkerung in der Bundesrepublik Deutschland, Bundesministerium fur Jugend, Familie und Gesundheit, Bonn.

Kaupen-Hass, H. (1969) Stabilität und Wandelärztlicher Autorität, Enke, Stuttgart.

Kommer, D. and Sommer, G. (1977) 'Psychiatriereform und Perspektiven der Gemeindepsychologie', in G. Sommer and H. Ernst (eds), Gemeindepsychologie, Urban and Schwarzenburg, Munich, pp.259-279.

Kulenkampff, C. (1981) Modellprogramme des Bundes und der Länder in der Psychiatrie: Kritische Übersicht, Rheinland-Verlag, Cologne.

Kunze, H. (1981) Psychiatrische Übergangseinrichtungen und Heime, Enke, Stuttgart.

Leichter, H. (1979) A Comparative Approach to Policy Analysis: Health Care Policy in Four Nations, Cambridge University Press, Cambridge.

Michaelis, W-D. (1979) 'Niedergelassene Nervenärzte', in D.H. Friessem (ed). Kritische Stichworter zur Sozialpsychiatrie, Wilhelm Fink Verlag, Munich.

Muller, C. (1981) Psychiatrische Institutionen: Ihre Möglichkeiten und Grenzen, Springer, Berlin.

Neuhaus, R. and Schräder, W.F. (1984) Planung und Management in Gesundheitswesen der Bundesrepublik Deutschland. I.G.E.S. Papier Nr 84-43, Institut fur Gesundheits-und Sozialforschung, Berlin.

Nowak, M. (1984) Sozialrechtliche Aspekte der Finanzierung von komplementären Angeboten fur psychisch Kranke, Soziale Sicherheit, 8, 234-239.

Panse, F. (1964) Das psychiatrische Krankenhauswesen, Thieme, Stuttgart.

Reichel, W. (1980) 'Zwischen Polizeigriff und Hilfeleistung: Das Recht im Transformationsprozess', in M. Wambach (ed). Die Museen des Wahnsinns und die Zukunft der Psychiatrie, Suhrkamp, Frankfurt, pp.271-309.

Reimer, F. (1980) 'Die Situation der psychiatrischen Landeskrankenhäuser nach Abschluss der Psychiatrie-Enquete', in H. Hafner and W. Picard. (eds). Psychiatrie in der Bundesrepublik Deutschland Funf Jahre nach der Enquete, Rheinland-Verlag, Cologne, pp.23-28.

Riedmüller, B. (1978) 'Psychosoziale Versorgung und Systeme sozialer Sicherheit', in H. Keupp and M. Zaumseil (eds), Die gesellschaftliche Organisierung psychischen Leidens, Sukrkamp, Frankfurt, pp.59-89.

Safran, W. (1967) Veto-Group Politics: The Case of Health Insurance Reform in West Germany, Chandler Press, San Francisco.

Statistisches Bundesamt. (1983) Ausgewählte Zahlen für das Gesundheitswesen: 1981. Kohlhammer, Stuttgart.

Stellungnahme zur Enquete. (1979) Stellungnahme der Bundesregierung zum Bericht der Sachverständigen Kommission über die Lage der Psychiatrie in der Bundesrepublik Deutschland. Bundesministerium fur Jugend, Familie und Gesundheit, Drucksache 8/2565.

Stiftung Rehabilitation. (1979) Funktion und Bedeutung von Übergangswohnheimen, Stiftung Rehabilitation Heidelberg, unpublished.

Stroebel, H. (1981) 'Die Rehabilitation psychisch Kranker und Behinderter in Übergangseinrichtungen und die Einordnung in das System der sozialen Sicherheit', Die Rehabilitation, 20, 42-44.

Stroebel, H. (1983) 'Der psychisch Kranke in System der sozialen Sicherheit', in H. Jaunich and C. Kulenkampff (eds), Benachteiligung psychisch Kranker und Behinderter. Rheinland Verlag, Cologne pp.11-19.

Walter, M. (1981) 'Aspekte für eine Reform des Unterbringungsrechts', in H. Lauter and H-L Schreiber (eds), Rechtsprobleme in der Psychiatrie, Rheinland-Verlag, Cologne, pp.51-61.

Wambach, M. and Hellerich, G. (1980) 'Therapie-Reform als Versorgungsreform', in M. Wambach (ed), Die Museen des Wahnsinns und die Zukunft der Psychiatrie, Suhrkamp, Frankfurt, pp.200-228.

Zaumseil, M. (1978) 'Institutionelle Aspekte klinisch-psychologischer Arbeit', in H. Keupp and M. Zaumseil (eds). Die gesellschaftliche Organisierung psychischen Leidens, Suhrkamp, Frankfurt, pp.15-58.

Chapter Six

FRANCE: THE 'PSYCHIATRIE DE SECTEUR'

Policy, Finance and Organisation: Steen Mangen
History and Critique: Françoise Castel

With the passing of the 1838 Lunacy Act France
became the first European country formally to
institute the practice of 'mental medicine'. The Act
provided for the establishment of a national network
of asylums and defined a legal status both for the
insane and the doctors caring for them. This
legislation still regulates compulsory
admissions, and the mental health care system, to
a large extent, still functions through the old
network of mental hospitals, publically administered
and centrally supervised, with the dual aim of
providing care and support for the patient and
protecting society from the 'dangerous'. In France,
as elsewhere, attempts to remedy the worst excesses
of this system have followed two long-established
and distinct paths: the humanisation of conditions
inside hospitals and preventive measures 'in the
community'. The history of French psychiatry since
the 1950s, which is reviewed in this chapter, has
been characterised by efforts to seek an integration
of these two paths through the sectorisation of
mental health services.

The Birth of Mental Medicine

The beginnings of the fundamental change in the
relationship between lunacy and the state in
post-revolutionary France date from the Napoleonic
Code of 1804, which instigated procedures to
determine the mental incompetence of the patient and
to appoint a legal guardian. Two years later, the
Penal Code provided for the plea of not guilty in
respect of acts committed 'in a state of dementia'.
This definition of criminal insanity remains in
force today and the accused may be committed under

114

order of the prefect either to a special institution or an ordinary psychiatric hospital. The archaic language and the outmoded procedures, the object of mounting criticism in recent years, are likely to be reformed in the proposed general revision of the Penal Code.

More important as a general psychiatric law is the 1838 Lunacy Act which, when passed, was widely regarded as pioneering legislation and quickly became a model for other countries. It was, in part, the outcome of a lengthy investigation of the plight of the insane in which Esquirol himself had participated and he was instrumental in marshalling sufficient support to guarantee it a safe passage through parliament. The Act gave formal recognition to the concept of lunacy as mental disorder, rather than the product of moral weakness; it contained measures to safeguard against arbitrary incarceration; it charged the départements with the responsibility of erecting asylums to accommodate patients, many of whom were being imprisoned with common criminals; and it conferred professional competence on a group of doctors who henceforth, as 'alienists', became public officials, rewarded more for their skills as asylum administrators than for their clinical expertise.

The 1838 Act was as much concerned with planning as it was with legal safeguards. Each département was required to build a public asylum to accommodate certified patients or to make suitable arrangements with a neighbouring département. Alternatively, a private hospital could be licensed to undertake functions under the Act - the so-called 'hopitaux faisant fonction'. The costs of care became a mandatory part of the departemental budget, although patients and families made a contribution where their resources permitted.

This Act and the Royal Order of 1839 specified the principles of organisation and administration of the public asylums. Thus, mental health became the first statutory and catchment area responsibility in public health of the départements created under the 1793 Constitution. The Act and the Royal Order cemented the liaison between psychiatry and the law and established a distinct legal status for the alienist. The creation of public posts for psychiatrists, appointed by the Minister of the Interior and receiving a separate training in departemental asylums, was part of a process which was to isolate still further the fledgling discipline from the mainstream of medicine and from the universities, a situation which continued largely unchanged until the late 1960s.

The procedures for the certification of patients are carefully prescribed and reflect the Act's concern with preventing the arbitrary incarceration of the lettres-de-cachet, which were still in public memory only fifty years after the overthrow of the ancien regime. There are two forms of certification: 'placement d'office', an emergency committal of those who present a threat to public order or to the safety of others, which is authorised by the prefect (Prefect of Police in Paris); and the curiously-named 'placement voluntaire', which sanctions compulsory admission on petition of a relative or friend of the patient and requires a doctor's certificate. The emergency procedure, although not needing a psychiatrist's certificate by law, is invariably accompanied by one in practice. Within twenty-four hours of admission a clinical assessment must be submitted to the prefect, a further report being required after fourteen days. Thereafter, a statutory monthly assessment is written in a special hospital record. As an additional safeguard the Act provided for regular inspections of psychiatric hospitals. Patients also have the right of judicial appeal. Finally, the property of those patients who were not declared incompetent was protected for the length of their detention, a provision which, as discussed later, was amended in 1968.

From the beginning mental medicine was isolationist both in practice and outlook. Although Esquirol had warned of the dangers of removing patients to remote asylums and was aware that it often occurred on other than therapeutic grounds, the Minister of the Interior of the time had more pressing concerns. He was worried about the need to accommodate in the short term an estimated ten thousand 'dangerous' persons for whom no specific institutions existed and he was determined that the interests of public order should take precedence (Castel, 1981). So it was that the insane were allocated to institutions of their own, supervised by doctors who were required to live within the asylum grounds and who were as isolated from the outside world as those in their charge.

It was in the period of euphoria immediately following the enactment of the 1838 legislation that the first public asylums were built. For more than a century there were scarcely any significant reviews of policy. Acts in 1851 and 1873 permitted asylums to allocate up to one-third of their resources for extra-mural activities aimed at the social re-integration of patients; but rarely more than a tenth of the budget was ever spent for this purpose by any département and, instead, the money was channelled into the establishment of lunatic colonies (1).

The final decades of the nineteenth-century were a time of refinement in the classification of psychiatric disorders and, in 1879, the first chair of mental science was created. It was a time, too, of increasing segregation of asylum patients according to the chronicity of their disorders. Industrial therapy was introduced in this period and was rationalised in terms of the theory of moral treatment, although in practice it all too often led to the exploitation of patients on tasks essential for the asylum's upkeep.

Between 1890 and 1940 no new psychiatric hospitals were built, in part because of the withdrawal of central government subsidies. In the Twenties, however, there were some important developments both inside and outside the mental hospital: the social insurance regulations were amended to extend liability to treatment for mental illness; and in Paris Edouard Toulouse founded the first 'open' service for the treatment of voluntary patients, though these services were to remain exceptional until after the Second World War.

Clearly influenced by the American mental hygiene movement, Toulouse was also active in promoting his 'Societé d'Hygiène Mentale'. In 1929, he initiated the first outpatient consultations for 'mental hygiene' in the public dispensaries (dispensaires) for social hygiene which offered screening and follow-up treatment in cases concerning child hygiene, tuberculosis and syphilis. Initially, consultations were largely confined to children and it was not until the 1937 circular issued by the health minister in the Popular Front government that services for adults began in earnest. This circular, besides encouraging expansion of the role of the social hygiene dispensaires, gave offical support for the open ward system and for social casework with discharged patients.

The Second World War was to have a profound effect on French psychiatry. The analogy between wartime conditions in the mental hospitals and the concentration camps was all too brutally apparent: inpatient numbers fell from 115,000 to 65,000, half of this decline being directly attributable to deaths by mass starvation in hospitals desperately unable to feed those in their charge (Audisio, 1980; Murard and Fourquet, 1975). Yet a positive outcome could be salvaged from this horror: the experimental service created during the War at Saint-Alban in Vichy France by two psychiatrists, Bonnafe and Tosquelles. To avoid starvation among their already under-nourished patients, the two doctors, aided by a local group of Resistance workers, set about placing them in the surrounding neighbourhood. The patients were quickly integrated into the life of the small community and it was found that many of them were surviving better outside than inside the hospital. Most important, by making a positive contribution to the survival of the village, patients gained the acceptance of the local populace. These experiences brought home to some psychiatrists the need for long-overdue reform of hospital care. Thus, by the end of the War, there were already several experimental units offering 'institutional psychotherapy', services akin to the therapeutic communities then being established in anglo-saxon countries.

In 1945 an amendment to the 1838 Act at last gave legal status to voluntary admissions. The early post-war years were a period of great intellectual activity in some psychiatric circles, anticipating the new approaches to mental health care adopted in certain areas of France from the late Forties onwards. A series of debates were held between 1945 and 1947 - the 'Journées Psychiatriques' - in which influential and reformist psychiatrists argued the need for a comprehensive mental health service based on principles of the unity and continuity of care. A ministerial circular exhorting the use of both social therapies and trial leave was issued in 1952. In the early Fifties, too, several of the Saint-Alban psychiatrists went on to develop their concept of institutional psychotherapy from a Lacanian perspective. This psychoanalytic variety was initially practised at the La Borde clinic, which became the dominant reference point for those few services then aspiring to be dynamic and modern.

New mental hygiene services outside hospitals were also being established at this time in several parts of the country, often at the instigation of psychiatrists engaged in institutional psychotherapy. Part of what in France are termed 'extra-hospital' services, these innovative provisions did, in fact, have a considerable local impact by contributing to a sharp rise in the discharge rate, albeit accompanied by the 'revolving door' syndrome. The Fifties were also a period of refinement of the concept and practice of after-care, especially after the introduction of the neuroleptics. The need to follow up discharged patients in order to monitor their clinical state and review their psychotropic medication became generally recognised as good practice designed to prevent relapse and re-admission.

The organisation and financing of these new extra-hospital provisions were integrated into the existing prevention programme offering free services at dispensaires administered by the 'Office Public d'Hygiène Sociale'. The programme derived its budget from subsidies from the state, départements and communes (lowest-tier local authorities). In 1954 alcoholism was added to the prevention programme and special dispensaires were planned for the compulsory treatment of patients defined by special tribunals as being 'dangerous alcoholics' This policy has been regarded by the majority of psychiatrists as excessively repressive and, in fact, has rarely been applied (2). One benefit derived from it, however, was that it permitted additional mental hygiene dispensaires to be established. One year later, in 1955, psychiatric consultations at the dispensaires became an obligatory part of expenditure on the prevention programme.

Another significant event in the same period was the venture in community psychiatry conceived by a group of anti-Lacanian psychiatrists in the Thirteenth Arondissement of Paris. These doctors formed a private association under the terms of the 1901 Voluntary Associations Act, which has been a common means of administering health and social services in France. Originally the service operated entirely without access to inpatient beds at what had been the catchment area hospital on the outskirts of Paris. Need for inpatient facilities

119

became apparent in the early Sixties and a local inpatient unit was opened. Offering a range of day care and outpatient services, and with active community work, the Thirteenth Arondissement has served as a model and, over the years, has become something of a shop window of the best in French psychiatry (Mueller, 1982).

However, innovations in inpatient and extra-hospital care in the ten years following the War had a negligible effect on the majority of French mental hospitals. Policy change, when it did come, was in no small measure due to the efforts of a small group of hospital directors. These senior doctors who, since 1945, had promoted the ideals of Saint-Alban were politically influential, as their proposals for psychiatric reform appealed to civil servants in charge of the mental health department of the Ministry of Health. Acting largely on the directors' advice the policy of sectorisation of mental health services was officially adopted and a ministerial circular was issued in 1960. The text of the circular emphasised the importance of local, community-based services, but it also contained a series of new planning norms for the conversion of old mental hospitals and for the construction of new ones. Hospitals were to be built on 'village plan' lines, with the aim of fostering community life and avoiding an institutional environment. Thus, as regards the mental hospitals, the objectives of the circular were adaptation and humanisation, not mass closure (Murard and Fourquet, 1975; Koeppelmann-Baillieu, 1979).

THE MINISTERIAL CIRCULAR AND EVENTS IN THE SIXTIES

Although there was a growing current of reform in the years up to 1960, very little had in fact changed in the mental health care system nationally. There were still 120,000 patients housed in overcrowded mental hospitals, with an estimated over-occupancy rate of 40 per cent (Acker and Capelli, 1977). Some of the hospitals were huge and provided their patients with sordid conditions; one had well over four thousand beds and was reputed to be the largest in Europe (Panse, 1964). Typically, the chronically ill formed the majority of patients: those handicapped by social disadvantage, old age or mental impairment (3). Psychiatric units in general hospitals did exist,

120

but their total capacity was only 1,500 beds, almost all of which were in university hospitals with highly selective admissions policies. There were also beds in private profit-making institutions serving those patients able to pay the whole costs of their treatment themselves or through private insurance.

The public and voluntary (private non profit-making) hospitals were left with the bulk of inpatient work. Hospital directors were recruited through a national competition. A mere five hundred psychiatrists headed clinical teams: a ratio of one fully-trained psychiatrist for every 240 patients. Psychiatric training in these hospitals was clinically-based, whilst the small number of psychiatrists in training in the university hospitals received a more classical, neuropsychiatric education leading to the highly prestigious certificate of specialist studies (4).

This, then, was the situation in France on the eve of the 1960 ministerial Circular. It might therefore seem curious that the chosen vehicle for reform of such an impoverished care system should be an exhortative circular, not a mandatory law. The choice was deliberate: the minister of health was anxious to see a speedy implementation and did not wish to run the risk of failure of the policy to gain sufficient parliamentary support by opening up a wider debate on the more contentious issue of the reform of the 1838 Act. In the event, reliance on a circular impeded progress on implementing the policy and more than ten years elapsed before the process of enactment through a series of parliamentary decrees was completed.

To its credit the Circular contained many important innovations. The whole of France was to be divided into 750 geographical sectors in which clinical teams would be responsible for the mental health of the whole population, rather than merely having a narrower 'catchment area' responsibility for referred patients. Each multi-disciplinary team would coordinate services for a sector containing an average population of 70,000. Ideally, every sector would have its own locally-based inpatient unit, though the Circular acknowledged that, for a considerable time, the old mental hospitals would continue to provide the majority of inpatient facilities. The hospitals were themselves to be sectorised: groups of wards would serve a specific sector and provide about 200 beds, a norm based on the 1954 WHO recommended ratios. The Circular lists the mental hygiene dispensaire, the day hospital, the night hospital, and sheltered workshop as essential extra-hospital services in each sector. Dispensaires could be in separate accommodation or, preferably, would form part of a general clinic offering wider medical treatments. They would undertake the vital tasks of early treatment and counselling, domiciliary care, crisis intervention and follow-up care. It was planned that dispensaires should operate in every town with more than 20,000 people. By allocating clinical responsibility to one team the clear hope was that prevention, early treatment and follow-up could be closely, and locally, coordinated so that the patient would receive a continuity of care from a community-based service in which the psychiatric hospital would be merely one of many provisions.

What the Circular outlined, then, was a vast technocratic plan for a comprehensive and uniform service responsible for the psychiatric needs of the whole population. Although the document was unenthusiastically received by the rank and file of psychiatrists, support for the policy of sectorisation did gain ground among the less conservative elements of the profession in the early years. A series of meetings convened between 1964 and 1967 by the distinguished psychiatrist, Henri Ey, holds a special place in the history of sectorisation, since they reflect the aspirations of a large, if select, number of psychiatrists at that time. Ey gathered together psychiatric hospital directors, office psychiatrists, psychoanalysts, psychiatrists holding university posts and psychiatrists in training. The proceedings of the meetings were published in the three-volume 'Livre Blanc de la Psychiatrie Française' which records a remarkable consensus about future policy among the representatives from varied backgrounds in the profession who attended the meetings: approval of the sectorisation policy and demands for an acceleration in its implementation; demands for increased expenditure on mental health services; requests for enhanced status for psychiatrists in public service and an increase in their numbers in order to guarantee the success of the new policy; and the demand for the recognition of psychiatry as a specialism distinct from neurology. There were also recommendations for a fundamental change in the system of recruiting and training psychiatrists, with increased emphasis on the teaching of the social sciences (Livre Blanc,

1965, 1966, 1967).

These psychiatrists did not have to wait long for some official reaction. Early in 1968 an amendment to the 1838 Lunacy Act reached the statute book. Under its provisions, the denial of a person's right to control his own property, as well as withdrawal of other basic civil rights, were no longer to be determined by the mere status of being a psychiatric inpatient. Henceforth, all persons judged incapable of managing their own property, for whatever reason, could benefit from legal protection; whilst others, including certified psychiatric patients, retain their financial control. This departure from the 1838 Act is significant because it represents the first step towards what many see as the ultimate goal: a total de-specification of measures at present aimed solely at the hospitalised mentally ill.

The events of May 1968 were also to have an effect on psychiatry by bringing forward reforms already in the pipeline. A new statute conferred on psychiatric hospitals the administrative autonomy enjoyed by general hospitals. Psychiatrists in public service were granted a status equivalent to that of other specialists and were awarded a salary increase in return for introducing the traditional medical hierarchy, with the creation of posts for junior psychiatrists. Those hospital psychiatrists involved in sessional work at extra-hospital services were now to be directly reimbursed for these duties. Later in the same year came the formal separation of psychiatry and neurology as academic disciplines and the establishment of a common syllabus for all psychiatrists in training. And, for the first time, non-university hospitals were eligible for recognition as training centres in collaboration with the medical schools.

SECTORISATION AND THE MENTAL HEALTH CARE SYSTEM

The ministerial Circular had cautiously avoided the issue of the long-term future of the mental hospitals and gave few indications, beyond statistical norms, of how to plan sector-based inpatient provisions. Nor were additional funds allocated to create the required new extra-hospital services. Predictably, perhaps, the Circular generated a lot of discussion but comparatively

123

little in the way of concrete action. By the end of
the Sixties only a minority of départements had made
real moves towards instituting the new services.
Indeed, some départements had chosen to allocate
resources for the construction of new hospitals, to
the neglect of extra-hospital provisions. Most
départements had taken the Circular at face value:
an exhortative, non-binding measure without
additional financial support. Nor was this
situation improved by the inertia at the central
level which delayed the promulgation of the
necessary decrees of enactment.

By the late Sixties new constraints in the
form of public expenditure curbs were taking their
toll. Yet inadequate resources can offer only a
partial explanation of the relative failure of
sectorisation at this stage. Crucial internal
contradictions in the policy - which have never been
adequately addressed in official documents - have
made it the object of all kinds of compromises and
re-interpretations. Critically - and despite
official aspirations in the original and subsequent
circulars - the hospital has retained, indeed
expanded, its role and influence in the new system.
As we attempt to show in the following sections,
this hospital-centrism has been manifested in the
organisation and financing of sector provisions, as
well as in the structure of the new services and the
roles of sector team members.

The Organisation and Financing of Psychiatric Care

Policy-making

Central government responsibility for mental health
policy is vested in the Ministry of Social Affairs
and National Solidarity. The Ministry determines the
annual budget devoted to health and social services,
oversees policies and planning relating to the
psychiatric hospitals, supervises the social
insurance scheme, authorises the level of medical
fees, and decides the level of exchequer subsidies
to health care. To assist in the strategic
planning of services the health ministry has
delegated many of its functions to regional health
and social services administrations (DRASS) created
in 1977 under the regional prefects. However, most
important is the progressive delegation of major
areas of health policy to the 95 départements as
part of successive French governments' commitment
to decentralisation, culminating in the provisions

124

of the 1982 Decentralisation Act.

This Act and further enabling legislation now being passed represent the most fundamental reform of central-local government relations since the Revolution. The prefect, as appointee and representative of the state, loses many of his executive functions to the president of the elected departemental general councils ('conseils généraux'). In future the prefect, now known as the 'commissaire of the republic', will exercise a posteriori control over the départements by verifying the legality of proposals passed by the general councils.

The health and welfare responsibilities of the lowest-tier authorities, the communes, are not significantly altered by the reforms. The operation of the social insurance system also remains unchanged. Two acts passed in 1983 specify the redistribution of health and social services functions between the state and the départements which took effect at the beginning of 1984. Relevant details are given in the section on the financing of services. The departemental health and social services administration (DDASS), created in 1964 under the prefect, will continue to supervise public hospitals and private hospitals 'faisant fonction', as well as decide the level of inpatient fees. Until the end of the transition period in 1986 the presidents of the general councils will also have authority over the DDASS for those services which are to be transferred but which it is temporarily administering. Thereafter, the DDASS will continue as external services of the state administering those services remaining under the authority of the prefect.

Planning

Global economic and social planning goals are reviewed in the five-year National Plans. Earlier plans still have their effect on present psychiatric provisions. The Fourth and Fifth National Plans in the 1960s, for example, provided for an extra 20,000 psychiatric beds; and the Eighth Plan in the early 1980s was concerned with controlling health services expenditure by imposing stricter criteria in the 'health map' planning procedure.

The health map (carte sanitaire) was instigated in 1970 and extended to psychiatric services the following year. Its aim is to introduce a range of 'need' indicators into planning by relating the number of health provisions in each area to their respective utilisation rates. For this purpose statistics on hospital and extra-hospital activities are collected by the DDASS and forwarded to Paris. The resultant indicators of 'needs for services' are then used to allocate resources among the départements. The central ministry is also involved in the planning process through the directives it issues on such subjects as staffing and bed ratios. In this respect, it is worth mentioning that the first substantive planning directive on the staffing of sector teams was issued as late as 1974 (5).

The Plan d'Organisation Départementale (POD) translates the health map criteria into a specific plan for the département. However, the actual effect of this streamlined planning procedure on accelerating change in psychiatric services has been more modest than one might envisage. In most cases the PODs have not been backed up by adequate funding to permit the planned expansion of services. Furthermore, there is no legal provision to ensure that private profit-making hospitals are incorporated into the local plans, with the result that these institutions continue to be located according to considerations of profitability rather than in areas of 'need'.

Services

Hospitals are organised hierarchically according to their resource allocation and the level of specialist services they offer. In addition, in psychiatry, there is a further division between hospitals undertaking functions under the 1838 Act and those functioning independently of it. The former comprise: the departemental psychiatric hospitals managed by the DDASS and accounting for 70 per cent of public beds; private non-profit making hospitals 'faisant fonction' with a further 16 per cent of beds; and psychiatric units in general hospitals with the remaining 14 per cent. Since 1973 there has been a progressive internal sectorisation of hospitals in this group, with a revised planning recommendation of 100 acute/medium term beds per sector (0.7 beds per thousand population). In the second group are 138 private profit-making hospitals which, though typically small-scale, account for approximately 10 per cent of all psychiatric beds. Two-thirds of places in these and other private facilities have been created since 1963. Finally, there are also four special hospitals in which psychiatric offenders, violent patients and prisoners who develop mental disorders may be accommodated (6).

Extra-hospital services are managed by local authorities, or, less commonly in the case of dispensaires, by voluntary bodies under the provisions of the 1901 Voluntary Associations Act. Some mutual assurance societies also operate a number of services which enjoy a high reputation.

Patients are also free to consult general practitioners or specialists in office practice (7). Medical fees are negotiated by the doctors' professional bodies and the sickness insurance funds under the supervision of the health ministry. A minority of doctors practise independently of these arrangements (conventions) and patients who consult them must pay the entire costs of their treatment or obtain coverage through private insurance. For treatment by doctors in the conventions the patient is reimbursed the treatment fee, less a certain percentage ('ticket modérateur' system).

The Paying Agencies

Liability for treatment costs falls on the sickness insurance funds, the social assistance schemes of the state or local authorities (aide sociale), or the individual. Since 1978 the whole population has been included in the statutory insurance schemes which, inter alia, also provide cover for invalidity, accidents and industrial diseases. There are separate schemes for certain occupations, but 75 per cent of the population is covered by the general scheme which is administered at the local level (caisses primaires). Private insurance is also available and many people subscribe in order to cover the ticket modérateur which varies according to the disorder and the service consulted (8).

The prefect sets a ceiling for the daily fees ('prix de journée') chargeable in private hospitals. Formerly, inpatient and day care in the public sector were also reimbursed by a daily fee but this system is being replaced. Mental disorders are included in the category of 'long and costly' illnesses which, until recently, exempted the patient outside the private profit-making hospitals from any contribution to costs from the first day of treatment as opposed to the 31st day for other diseases (i.e. there is no ticket modérateur) Since 1984, in the university and specialist

127

hospitals, including psychiatric hospitals, the daily fee has been replaced by a global budget, variations of which have been the object of experimentation in several hospitals since 1979. Under the new system the hospital is guaranteed an annual budget within which it must operate, hospital revenues thus no longer being tied to bed occupancy rates. The global budgeting system is to be introduced in other hospitals and long-stay institutions in 1985. At the same time as instituting the global budget the government also levied a new 'daily surcharge' on all patients (except children in certain institutions) which is intended as a contribution to 'hotel costs'. The surcharge is an attempt at reducing the financial advantage accruing to patients receiving treatment in the 'long and costly' illnesses category compared to those who must pay the ticket modérateur. The net effect is to impose a contribution from patients in the former group, since for those in the latter the ticket modérateur is reduced by the full amount of the surcharge which they now pay.

Means-tested social assistance may be awarded in cases where insurance funds are not liable for treatment costs, or to cover the ticket modérateur or daily surcharge. The majority of recipients are inpatients of more than three years standing or those in certain long-stay institutions. In health care as a whole real expenditure on this form of social assistance, known as 'aide medicale', has been declining in recent years in line with the increase in the population having sickness insurance coverage (Waltisperger, 1984).

In 1980, about three-quarters of all health services expenditure was met by insurance funds or aide medicale; three per cent was met by the state or local authorities in the funding of the public health prevention programmes; and 23 per cent of costs were paid by patients themselves or reimbursed through voluntary private insurance.

At the same time as the global budget was introduced for hospitals, the whole system of financing extra-hospital services was reformed. Until 1984 these services were funded under the provisions of the 1955 ministerial decree incorporating mental illness into the mandatory budgets of the départements for the prevention programmes, which offered patients free treatment at the dispensaires. It was a complex system in which the state reimbursed the social assistance expenditure of the départements on a sliding scale

relating to three categories. The communes also
shared in the funding, again on a sliding scale.
Though not liable for the costs of preventive
measures or 'care' as opposed to 'treatment', the
sickness funds have contributed between ten and
thirty per cent of the budget in about a third of
the 95 départements.

In Group I of the budget were all the
preventive services, including the mental hygiene
dispensaires. State subsidies varied from 75 to 95
per cent of departemental expenditure, with an
average of 83 per cent. In the late 1970s it was
estimated that 40 per cent of Group I expenditure
was attributable to mental illness, alcoholism or
drug dependence. Group II attracted a state subsidy
of 50 per cent for expenditure on chronic care in a
variety of institutions, as well as placements in
hostels and rehabilitation facilities. More than
half of the budget of the entire programme was
devoted to the special social assistance scheme for
the mentally ill ('aide medicale aux malades
mentales') funded in this category. In Group III,
with a state subsidy of between 20 and 25 per cent
were all other forms of aide medicale.

The logic of state subsidisation was that
subsidies should be highest for services, such as
the mental hygiene dispensaires, which it was hoped
would contribute to a reduction in the demand for
inpatient and other costly institutional provisions.
Yet these subsidies did not prove the great stimulus
to local authorities to create the alternative
services; notwithstanding the considerable activity
in the Seventies, extra-hospital services were not
established in anything approaching acceptable
numbers. The enthusiasm and ability of local
authorities to contribute towards the cost of the
new provisions varied enormously. Despite state
funding of the greater proportion of costs,
sectorisation for some départements was regarded as
a heavy and sometimes unwelcome additional financial
burden. Many local authorities complained of the
unfairness of the formula used to calculate the
level of subsidies, which they argued did not take
sufficient account of their actual ability to
provide funds. Furthermore, as they pointed out,
calls were also being made on them to increase
their financing of other local services at a
time of considerable pressure on public budgets.

By the late Seventies it was generally
acknowledged that a funding system partially
dependent on the départements would be unlikely to

assure speedy progress towards a comprehensive service in the sector and would do nothing to reduce the substantial regional inequalities in the distribution of extra-hospital facilities. Supporting evidence came from official statistics: twenty years after the publication of the 1960 Circular the share of the mental health budget spent outside the hospital was extremely small - a mere 4.5 per cent of total expenditure on psychiatric personnel - while eighty per cent continued to be allocated to the inpatient sector (Psychiatric Hospital Directors Memorandum, 1981). But no one was arguing that this apparent advantage accruing to the inpatient sector accorded it a favoured position when compared to general hospitals: investment and operating costs of a bed in a public psychiatric hospital in 1978 averaged out at only 40 per cent of the costs for all bed categories (CERC, 1984). Clearly, psychiatry as a whole was a cinderella service.

In the redistribution of health service responsibilities in 1984 the government has taken control of the full funding of the prevention programmes for mental illness, alcoholism and drug dependency. Aide medicale and its special categories for the mentally ill and the disabled are now financed by the départements, including the costs of long-term hospital and other institutional care, the daily surcharge and relevant welfare benefits. The setting of tariffs and the supervision of nursing homes and other 'medico-social' institutions becomes the responsibility of the presidents of the departemental general councils. However, the state pays the social insurance contributions of patients in receipt of the various forms of aide medicale and is also financially liable for the operating costs of sheltered workshops, and for the costs of professional rehabilitation centres and attached residential services in cases where liability does not fall on the sickness funds.

As already indicated, the responsibilities of the sickness insurance funds have not been changed by these reforms. Indeed, the funds have been consistent in their resistance to attempts to extend liabilities to interventions bearing only a remote resemblance to the classical medical act . For the time being the paradoxical situation is likely to continue whereby the funds reimburse the patient 80 per cent of the costs of treatment by an office psychiatrist, whilst the dispensaires offering the same intervention under the label of 'prevention' receive at most a 30 per cent subsidy from them. However, it must be admitted, that since the proportion of staff time spent in extra-hospital work rarely strictly follows that agreed in the conventions, the funds are paying a hidden subsidy to the sector through their financing of inpatient treatment.

The new measures do at least remove the illogicality of the daily fee system by which any increase in extra-hospital activity leading to a decline in inpatient numbers would penalise the hospital budget and would ultimately reduce the amount of money the hospital had available for its staff to undertake extra-hospital work. However, the limitation of the present reform lies in its preservation of a triple system of financing psychiatric services, one in which the sickness funds are liable for the costs of hospital treatment, the state for extra-hospital interventions, and the départements for a large share of the financial responsibility for long-term care and rehabilitation services.

The government clearly intends that, as regards hospital and extra-hospital services at least, the present system will merely be a temporary solution to the financing of the sector. At present experiments in two psychiatric hospitals have been authorised, in which a global budget is allocated to finance both hospital and extra-hospital facilities. The total budget has been derived from contributions by the state and the sickness funds amounting to what each would have paid under present arrangements. The health ministry will examine the results in the two pilot areas in order to make further proposals for an integrated global budget for psychiatry, which it is projected might be introduced in 1986. One major constraint at the moment is the continuing opposition of the sickness funds to extensions of indemnity of extra-hospital work, a move which seems to have the support of some ministers in the government. Indeed, the funds are presently facing a serious financial crisis and are pressing for increases in the ticket modérateur as well as a more restrictive list of conditions exempting inpatients from contributing to treatment costs. Furthermore, some of the funds that have been contributing to the costs of the prevention programme are now reluctant to renew agreements. The signs are that the current system of financing the sector may continue well beyond the planners' target date.

Administering the Sector

The ministerial Circular introducing sectorisation did not amend the 1955 programme of subsidies. There was a clear intention - reinforced in the 1960s and by the 1972 model conventions - that communes and départements should be free to develop their own style of administering and reimbursing sector services. Three possibilities were outlined in 1972: local authorities could directly manage their own extra-hospital services; they could delegate this task to the departemental hospital; or they could contract out this undertaking to a voluntary agency. In the event the most common agreement has involved the hospital in operating extra-hospital services and providing the necessary clinical staff. A certain proportion of the hospital budget was reserved for these services and hospital staff were paid pro rata for their work there. Thus, from the start, sectorisation has been hospital-based in its organisation, financing and staffing. One of the aims of the new system is to reduce the hold this base has on psychiatric care; how far this will be achieved in practice remains to be seen.

In operation sectorisation has been a complicated, sometimes unwieldy system with a variety of forms of reimbursement depending on the type of service and its location. Moreover, some regional disparities persist in both the liability coverage of the insurance funds (e.g. the 'hospital-at-home' scheme) and in reimbursement arrangements. As a consequence a great deal of time may be taken up in identifying the paying agent and in calculating, for the purposes of their salaries, the proportion of staff time spent in hospital and extra-hospital work.

Despite the reforms, the sector is still seriously handicapped by being merely a geographical entity without an integrated budget. Nor does the sector team have responsibility for all the establishments in its area providing care for the mentally ill. Private profit-making services operate entirely independently. All too frequently other local services which should be closely coordinated with psychiatric provisions have catchment areas markedly different from the sector's boundaries. Sectoral 'mental health councils' were established in 1972 in an attempt to introduce an element of coordination into this diffuse system. One council was planned for every six sectors and membership is open to all those involved in providing mental health care. However, in general, the councils have not worked well; meetings are too infrequent, and participants too numerous to permit effective decision-making. In any case, the councils have only consultative powers and are increasingly being by-passed by sector teams in their dealings with public authorities.

SECTORISATION AND THE PSYCHIATRIC TEAM

A second circular issued in 1960 outlined plans for the modernisation of the old psychiatric hospitals, thereby assuring them a long-term future. So, as the only existing institution from which to launch the sectorisation policy, a hospital-based service has been practically unavoidable. Other provisions, especially day hospitals and night hospitals, have frequently operated as annexes of the main hospital; often day care is available only on an unstructured basis on inpatient wards.

From the beginning some clinical staff have paid mere lip-service to the ideals of the sector, preferring instead to retain as much of their hospital practice as possible. Whilst the improvement in the status of the hospital medical directors in 1972 was contingent on their initiating sectorisation, this has frequently been interpreted merely as the acceptance of catchment area responsibility for a sector, the introduction of mixed wards staffed by nurses of both sexes, and the undertaking of a weekly clinical session at a dispensaire for follow-up consultations. In this way some senior psychiatrists have been able to benefit from their new status without surrendering the privileges derived from their hospital roles. The profession as a whole has achieved considerable expansion in the years since sectorisation was inaugurated; in the Seventies, for example, the number of qualified psychiatrists quadrupled (Cellule Prospective, 1980).

On the other hand, the status of the psychiatric nurse has not been appreciably improved by the new policy. It is a measure of the low status of psychiatric nursing that the profession was not involved in the key discussions preceding the publication of the 1960 Circular. Moreover, in

133

comparison to general nursing, psychiatric nursing remained a low status occupation throughout the Sixties. It was not until 1972 that the length of training was brought into line with general nursing. The idea of a common nursing syllabus, which enjoyed a certain currency in the Seventies, was gradually revised and the new syllabus, introduced in 1979, has only a common first year. Although the number of fully-qualified psychiatric nurses more than doubled in the last decade - the present ratio is 107 psychiatric nurses per 100,000 population - they currently comprise only 22 per cent of all qualified nurses and regional inequalities in distribution remain.

Promotion in nursing continues to be achieved through hospital service and extra-hospital work is consigned to the minority who volunteer for it. Moreover, the fear of a loss of nursing role, the lack of qualifications in community work, and the threat of job losses in rural areas where the mental hospitals are located have made the psychiatric nurses trade union less than enthusiastic for a speedy implementation of sectorisation.

Clinical psychologists and social workers were too small a group in mental health care to have much of an impact on the sector policy in its early days. Social work training, in any case, has been neglectful of psychiatric casework. Clinical psychologists in France received a formal statute only in 1977, permitting them to be directly reimbursed by the insurance funds for their interventions. This has increased the number setting up independent practices, although by 1980 there were over 1200 psychologists employed by the DDASS in the field of mental illness (approximately 2 per 100,000 population).

Despite considerable increases in staff numbers, a lot of sector teams hardly justify their multi-disciplinary title. Many continue to be solely composed of the psychiatrist and several nurses who work within a hierarchical 'medical model' from a hospital base. So, too, is the concept of continuity of care illusory. In a common situation where the patient is seen by different agents according to whether he is in hospital or outside it, continuity of care loses its original meaning and is reduced to continuity of information passed on from one therapist to another.

Inadequate coordination between hospital and community-based staff frequently results in the failure to provide follow-up care for some patients.

In major cities, too, there is the additional problem of a large number of discharged patients who do not live within the sector area or who have no community at all to go back to. Deveau (1981), for example, in a study of hospitals serving Paris, found that almost one-fifth of the inpatients were 'hors secteur'.

The insufficient provision of day care and residential facilities has adverse effects, not only for patients who have already left hospital but also for those awaiting discharge. Thus, in many areas, the psychiatric hospital is still having to fulfil a welfare 'warehousing' function for a variety of socially disadvantaged groups, diverting effort from its role as a place of active therapy.

All these problems are exacerbated by the continuing focus on inpatient care in the training of psychiatric staff, to the neglect of community psychiatry which is narrowly interpreted in terms of the provision of after care.

Apart from these criticisms of financing and organisation, there are those who are sceptical of the very concept of the sector as a means of practising humane and caring psychiatry. They have argued that sectorisation merely streamlines psychiatry's traditional roles of care and control without addressing the issue of whether these two roles are reconcilable. For them sectorisation, by straddling the middle ground between the health and social services, runs the risk of extending coercive functions. Castel (1981), for example, has seen the policy as a re-organisation of psychiatric territory, consolidating the psychiatrist's role as expert in screening, control and normalisation, as well as maintaining psychiatry's segregative function. He acknowledges that the original proponents of sectorisation viewed it in terms of its preventive and caring functions, but claims they ignored its potential as a means of controlling large numbers of people through the 'management of risk': through the supervision of the 'at risk' population. For Castel the issue of psychiatry's relationship with the state is deeply problematic. It is the incompatibility of the therapeutic role and the coercive powers conferred on psychiatrists by the state, irrespective of the relative infrequency of their use, that for Castel is unresolved and which the work of the sector team, strengthened by the demands of the patient's family, neighbours, the police and local politicians, only serves to reinforce.

Evaluating the sector

These issues apart, what evidence is there for the effectiveness of the sector on its own terms? Empirical evaluative research of this field is not in plentiful supply in France and there have been remarkably few attempts at assessment of access to services or the quality of care they offer. One important study compared a narrow range of socio-clinical outcomes in a sample of patients in three sectors with varying availability of extra-hospital provisions. In general, results were similar in all three sectors. Outcomes were more positive for young psychotic patients in the sector with most provisions; but less positive results were obtained in this sector in the case of chronic schizophrenics and alcoholics. There was no direct link between the presence of a wide range of extra-hospital services and the decline in inpatient numbers observed, this being largely attributable to the transfer of elderly psychiatric inpatients to nursing homes. In terms of cost-effectiveness, the best-provided sector had the margin of advantage, though the researchers point out that in all three sectors the overriding financial considerations were the number and length of inpatient spells (RCB, 1975).

Epidemiological studies of a number of sectors have revealed sex, age and diagnostic differences in the clientele of inpatient and extra-hospital sectoral services. However, in the absence of data from private services, the degree to which there are significant disparities in class utilisation of various mental health provisions can only be conjectured (Casadebaig and Quemada, 1982).

Finally, there are official statistics of service inputs. Routine data on extra-hospital services are largely confined to the activities of the dispensaires. The statistics indicate that, in spite of the organisational and financial problems outlined above, there has been a substantial growth in the work of these clinics, albeit if some operate on a part-time basis. The most recent data indicate that there are almost three million consultations annually, representing a more than five-fold increase in the first twenty years of sectorisation. In comparison, the number of new patients has risen by 350 per cent. At present just under 40 per cent of patients are new referrals, an indication that dispensaires are working with a more chronic caseload than is likely

136

to be the case in office psychiatrist practices (MOH - SESI, 1983).

DEVELOPMENTS IN PSYCHIATRIC CARE OUTSIDE THE SECTOR

The past twenty years have seen the creation of mental health services which represent something of a break in the consensus on the sector policy; they have certainly contributed to the modification of its original field of action. These new provisions, and the veritable 'psycho-boom' in 'alternative' therapies, have made significant inroads into the pre-existing psychiatric system.

Child and Adolescent Psychiatry

In 1974 'inter-sectors' for child psychiatric services were formed, with approximately one inter-sector for every three adult sectors. The fact that there are no formal organisational links with the adult teams has proved a serious mistake. But it has been the proliferation of voluntary services, preceding and simultaneous with the creation of the inter-sectors, and the exclusion of the special educational agencies from their remit, that has had more serious consequences. Inter-sector teams frequently complain of being mere gatekeepers of access to the provisions of other agencies, rather than directly undertaking these services themselves. This situation has been made worse by the enactment of the 1975 Handicapped Persons Act, whose effects on adult psychiatry are discussed below.

Services for the Chronically Ill and Disabled

The Act governs the allocation of services for all groups of disabled people, including the mentally retarded and long-stay psychiatric patients. Its aim is to stimulate the establishment of additional rehabilitation services and long-term residential provisions. Special financial incentives have been offered to voluntary bodies to manage these services, indicative of a preference by government for the development of facilities outside the public sector. Under the Act, disabled persons who are incapable of living independently are to be transferred to special long-stay institutions. The Act provides for two tribunals. One, a 'medico-social tribunal', has the task of determining the degree of incapacity, the entitlement to disability pensions, and the institutional placement. For psychiatric patients, the tribunal may decide that the psychiatric hospital remains the most appropriate placement, or they may recommend a boarding-out scheme, other purely residential accommodation, or a place in one of the special homes now being established for the profoundly disabled who are considered incapable of benefitting from rehabilitation.

The second tribunal meets under the aegis of the Ministry of Labour, a fact reflected in the composition of its membership. Its function is to allocate patients capable of profiting from industrial rehabilitation to an appropriate training programme, either in an industrial training centre, where workers receive at least 70 per cent of the national minimum wage (SMIC), or to sheltered workshops where the wage is fixed at a minimum of 90 per cent of the SMIC. Hostel accommodation may also be allocated by this tribunal.

For both categories of patients there are improvements in benefits related to the national minimum wage. The parental contribution has been abolished in the assessment of entitlements. Relatives of patients are also eligible for increased attendance allowances. Yet the Act provoked hostile criticism from psychiatrists and their representative bodies for its concept of handicap as a fixed condition and for its nineteenth-century notion of 'curable' and 'incurable' disorders. The government subsequently attempted to allay fears by issuing a ministerial circular in 1978 acknowledging that psychiatric disability was not irreversible and advocating a close liaison between services for the disabled and the sector and inter-sector teams. But the mental health professions have remained uneasy: long-stay homes continue to be run with low staff ratios; they are too dependent on untrained staff and there is a lack of a medical presence. Coupier and his colleagues (1977) found that one of the main functions of psychiatric homes was as repositories for psychogeriatric patients, some containing as many as 400 beds. Facilities were often very poor: in their study, for example, only 14 per cent of residents were provided with any form of diversionary occupational therapy.

Both tribunals set up by the Act have been criticised for their lengthy bureaucratic procedures. Psychiatrists play a minimal role: only one member of the medico-social tribunal must be medically-qualified, and not necessarily a psychiatrist. Furthermore, patients and their families appear to be marginal participants in the decisions affecting their future. Sector teams, who are excluded from all these procedures, face a dilemma of either refusing to cooperate with the tribunals and risk denying patients their benefits, or of collaborating in a system which many see as imposing highly stigmatic labels and merely transferring patients from back wards of psychiatric hospitals to an exclusionary environment elsewhere. There has been criticism, too, of the preferential treatment accorded the voluntary bodies in managing services, a policy which has been attacked for its relegation of the public sector to the sidelines.

Faced with a meagre budget, sector teams have increasingly had to rely on voluntary provisions in order to meet their catchment area responsibilities. Prior to 1975, certain facilities were extremely scarce: there were, for example, only fifty sheltered workshops in the whole of France. Progress towards establishing the ranges of services envisaged in the Act has been uneven. One survey of 73 départements revealed that in 23 there were no proper psychiatric rehabilitation or residential services, not even hostel accommodation (Reverzy and Dameron, 1979). Admittedly the Act has provided a fillip in the development of group homes and sheltered accommodation; on the basis of a limited national survey it was estimated that by 1980 there was a total of about 3000 places in various kinds of establishments. The average size of the units in the survey was ten places and most relied on a 60 per cent government subsidy (Reverzy and Decraene, 1980) (9).

No clear ministerial guidelines have been issued for the financing of these services, which have multiplied without any real coordination. Many are small-scale and with a budgetary status that can best be described as fragile. A number of facilities have encountered problems in gaining full recognition from public authorities which have frequently awarded subsidies on an ad hoc basis, reviewed case by case, rather than guaranteeing them a degree of financial security. Some of the voluntary organisations managing these services have preferred to forego public funding in order to retain their independence and freedom of action; other services, such as some of the sheltered workshops, have amalgamated to form larger units in an attempt to overcome financial difficulties (Audisio, 1980).

Psychotherapy

The fashion for psychoanalysis among psychiatrists and the general public in the 1960s and 1970s, combined with the reform of psychiatric training, had the effect of expanding the market of the office practitioner with an additional analytic qualification. However, by the late 1970s the increase in the number of office practices had begun to surpass the demand for psychoanalysis. Many of these psychiatrists were therefore obliged to return to a more medically orientated practice to attract a clientele, a move reinforced by the strong recovery of interest in biological psychiatry, itself in part a reaction against the influence of social and psychotherapeutic models in the Sixties. The general return to medical objectivism which, in fact, was never surrendered by academic departments, has been to some extent inspired by modest advances in biochemical and genetic research. It is now beginning to re-establish its primacy in sector teams which, with the mass transfer of chronic patients to other institutions, are currently undergoing a process of clinical re-orientation.

Psychoanalysis has also had to contend with competition from the 'human potential' therapies primarily attracting a 'normal' clientele. These therapies are extending psychiatry to new groups in the population and are helping to modify the field of psychological medicine.

SECTORISATION: CURRENT PROSPECTS

A government-commissioned report, published in 1980, disclosed that, of the 1200 projected sectors, only in 911 was there a senior psychiatrist to head the sector team. One hundred sectors had no team at all; neighbouring sectors were having to provide clinical cover as best they could. Furthermore, the range of extra-hospital provisions remained too narrow in many areas and only a minority of sectors could be judged as having adequate facilities, even on the modest criterion of there being a full quota of dispensaires. The outcome, as the report points out, was that these facilities had not made any significant impact on reducing admission rates, but had become juxtaposed provisions, to a large extent serving a distinct clientele. The report concluded that, when account was taken of the large numbers of patients being transferred from the responsibility of the sector teams, the 'psychiatrie de secteur' was a long way from achieving its original goals.

According to the report, a serious problem delaying progress has been the serious over-capacity of inpatient services. The effects of earlier building programmes were beginning to catch up: 33,000 beds had been created between 1960 and 1972, many against the advice of the health ministry. According to the 1980 health map indicators, there was an average excess bed rate of 40 per cent; on these criteria some hospitals had almost double the number of beds they required. Such a situation had naturally encouraged conservative discharge policies: there was every incentive to maintain a high occupancy rate since, at that time, the hospital budget was derived from a daily fee charged for each occupied bed. The absurdity of the situation was not lost on the authors of the report: whilst sector teams had an explicit policy of preventing unnecessary admissions and shortening inpatients spells, hospital administrators had quite contrary preoccupations. It was their view that this financial impasse, combined with the lingering reticence of some départements to see a real expansion of services at a time of constraint on the public purse, would ensure that progress towards full sectorisation would continue at a slow pace.

The change of government in 1981 provided a fresh opportunity to take stock of official mental health policy. Within a few months of taking office the new minister of health announced a series of discussions on future policies, and a commission was appointed to review mental health legislation. The minister declared his intention of directing a massive transfer of resources away from the psychiatric hospitals and into extra-hospital services, a process which was to be assisted by the plans then being formulated for the decentralisation of political power.

Decentralisation legislation relating to the health and social services came into force at the beginning of 1984, at the same time as the global budget system replaced the daily fee in major hospitals. In future, responsibility for psychiatric extra-hospital provisions will rest with central government and the départements will provide the greater part of aide medicale funding of other services. These reforms, involving the large-scale transfer of resources between the various tiers of government, have not been carried out without accompanying problems. The government underestimated the 1984 extra-hospital budget by fourteen per cent, which led to reports of an immediate fall in the activity of the sector teams and a decline in staff numbers brought about by the non-renewal of short-term contracts. Part of this deficit was subsequently restored, with the promise of a real budgetary increase in 1985. Hospital managers, too, have complained of a shortfall in their budgets since the introduction of global budgetting; they fear this will not be fully compensated by the government's extra-ordinary allocation, late in 1984, of a sum amounting to one per cent of the budget for the hospital sector.

A solution to the over-capacity in psychiatric inpatient services is proposed in the Ninth National Plan (1984 - 1989). Within the planning period 12,000 unoccupied beds are to be phased out and 28,000 beds presently occupied by elderly and other long-stay patients are to be replaced by places in residential and community services. 7,500 beds are to be modernised.

At present, one of the government's prime concerns in health affairs is cost-containment. Since the mid-1970s expenditure on health care in France has been increasing at a rate significantly in excess of GDP, although rigorous financial control and rationalisation in 1982 and 1983 produced the smallest increase in the health budget since 1970. An unprecedented austerity programme, was announced in 1984 with huge cuts in public expenditure, a policy which finally signalled the end of communist participation in government. 'Medico-social' establishments, such as nursing homes or certain kinds of rehabilitation centres, which have low occupancy rates will be reduced in size or closed. There are fears among psychiatric staff that, under prevailing economic conditions, savings derived from the closures and transfer programmes in the hospitals will not be passed on to community-based services. There is also the suspicion that global budgetting will be used more as a means of enforcing curbs on expenditure than as a way of ensuring an integrated and flexible budget for the whole sector. Furthermore, some commentators

142

are predicting that the recent reform of the medical career structure, with the merging of the two grades of junior hospital doctor, will lead to a reduction in the number of junior psychiatrists in the public service.

Late in 1984 the government made its first official collective statement on policies for the future of the psychiatric services. It reinforced its espousal of sectorisation, but stressed that there should be integrated teams, not, as at present in many areas, separate teams for inpatient and extra-hospital work. Within the general policy of restructuring services priority is to be given to provisions for the elderly mentally ill.

Whatever the priorities for the psychiatric services, and despite the progress that has undoubtedly been made in reducing regional inequalities, there is an urgent need for an infusion of funds, not merely a redistribution of the mental health budget. The financing of psychiatric services has always fared unfavourably when compared with physical medicine and this imbalance is unlikely to be redressed by the reforms introduced in the 1980s. But the prospects of substantial additional funding are scarcely propitious. In times of serious economic recession governments will not be eager to attach great priority to areas of social policy so low in public consciousness as mental health. So it is that the most disabled patients are being transferred to new institutions in the voluntary sector, a process in which psychiatrists in the public services are being relegated to a marginal role. Other groups of patients prefer to consult psychiatrists in office practice; still others, mentally ill or not, resort to the myriad of psychotherapies now on offer. Some of the mentally ill are never treated or fall too easily through the gaps in service provision.

To the sector, once to be all-encompassing, there remains a considerably reduced field of action. And, with the office practitioner siphoning off the more affluent patient, it is easy to understand how some clients will regard sector services as second class. In the midst of the clamour for position in the new psychiatric system efforts at social and occupational rehabilitation, never as advanced here as in anglo-saxon countries, run the risk of being dissipated in the face of complex bureaucratic procedures and must, in any case, be reassessed in terms of the viability of their goals in an era of chronic recession.

Though France has its share of exemplary services showing what can be done - sometimes because of, sometimes in the absence of sectorisation - many within the psychiatric professions are becoming increasingly disillusioned with the global strategy, feeling that its grand designs for nationwide provision are unrealistic, at least in the short run. Others, perhaps in the minority, entertain more fundamental doubts, arguing that the ambiguities of the goals of the 'psychiatrie de secteur' have not, indeed, cannot be resolved.

Whatever the feeling inside psychiatry, mental health is not a major political issue in the country as a whole. The vote for the 1838 Act was preceded by impassioned debate in both parliamentary chambers and aroused widespread interest throughout France. That level of public and political interest has never since been rekindled.

Françoise Castel's contribution has been translated from French by Steen Mangen. Tragically, she did not live to see the final edited version. In amending and adding to her text, every effort has been taken to preserve the full sense of her argument.

NOTES

1. The two colonies in France, Dun-sûr-Auron (founded in 1891) and Ainay-le-Chateau (1900) in fact represented more of a deportation of patients from overcrowded Parisian asylums than an attempt at new forms of care 'in the community'. Although now entitled 'psychotherapeutic centres', they have remained a form of custodial welfare institution. Ainay-le-Chateau has at present over 1100 clients, the overwhelming majority men, most of whom are boarded out among five hundred families.
2. A similar regulation for the compulsory treatment of drug addicts was introduced in 1970 but, again, has rarely been applied.

3. In France at this time there were scarcely any specialist services for the mentally retarded. Services have subsequently been set up, assisted by the provisions of the 1975 Handicapped Persons Act. Many of the existing facilities are undertakings by voluntary bodies sometimes formed by the patients' families.

4. Certificate d'Etudes Specialisées (CES) de Neuro-psychiatrie. Academic departments of psychiatry have retained their neuropsychiatric orientation, several of the chairs of psychiatry being occupied by neurologists even after the formal separation of the disciplines in 1968.

5. The recommended ratios are given below; in parentheses are the average complements in 1976 derived from a ministerial survey of 143 sectors in nineteen départements.

Staff per extra-hospital sector team:

Senior psychiatrist:	1	(0.88)
Junior psychiatrists:	4 - 5	
Qualified nurses:	7	(2.7 - 3.2)
Social worker:	1	(1.02)
Medical secretary:	1	(0.97)

6. In addition there are twelve regional medico-psychological centres (CMPRs) in prisons which have been established since 1977. See Information Psychiatrique, 1983, Vol. 59, No. 2 which is devoted to a discussion of these centres.

7. From 1960 onwards there has been a growing trend for newly-qualified psychiatrists to set up in office practice, so that currently almost 60 per cent of all psychiatrists are office practitioners, although some of these have sessional contracts in hospitals. Based on present inadequate data, it would seem that the role of the office psychiatrist is selective in terms of the clientele served; certainly office practices are mainly in the higher income areas of large cities.

8. In 1983 only 28 per cent of expenditure by the sickness funds (caisses primaires) involved a ticket modérateur.

9. In 1981 there were over 48,000 places in all forms of sheltered employment in France (10.3 per 100,000 population). However, this takes no account of the clientele. Some indication of the proportion of places taken up by former psychiatric patients may be obtained from the results of a survey in the Rhone-Alpes region where, in 1979-1980, almost 13 per cent of cases coming before

the industrial rehabilitation tribunals (COTOREPs) were classified as being disabled through mental illness (Santé et Sécurité Sociale, 1984, 3).

REFERENCES

Acker D & Capelli D (1977) La gestion des institutions dans l'organisation du secteur psychiatrique. Université de Dijon, Docteur de IIIe Cycle

Audisio M (1980) La psychiatrie de secteur: une psychiatrie militante pour la santé mentale. Éditions Privat, Toulouse

Casadebaig F & Quemada N (1982) Morbidité psychiatrique differentielle selon le type de prise en charge par le secteur. Social Psychiatry, 17, 7 - 11

Castel R (1981) La gestion des risques: de l'anti-psychiatrie a l'après psychiatrie. Éditions de Minuit, Paris

Cellule Prospective ((1980) La politique des soins en psychiatrie: bilan et synthèse. Ministère de la Santé et de la Securité Sociale, Paris

CERC (1984) L'Hôpitalisation en France: synthèse des études de CERC sur le coût d'hôpitalisation. Centre d'Étude des Revenus et des Coûts (CERC), Paris

Coupier J-P, Houser M & Reutsch G (1977) Hospice ou hôpital psychiatrique: ou est passé l'asile? Information Psychiatrique, 53, 953 -959

Deveau A (1981) L'Hôpitalisation psychiatrique. École Nationale de la Santé Publique, Rennes, Docteur de IIIe Cycle

Inspection Générale des Affaires Sociales (IGAS) (1978) Les établissements sanitaires et sociaux: Rapport 1977-1978, Ministère de la Santé, Paris

Koeppelmann-Baillieu M (1979) Gemeindepsychiatrie: Erfahrungen mit einem Reformmodell in Frankreich. Campus Verlag, Frankfurt

Livre Blanc (1965-1967) Livre blanc de la psychiatrie française. Volumes 1-3, Édition Privat, Toulouse

MOH - SESI (1983) Annuaires des Statistiques Sanitaires et Sociales: 1982-3. Service des Statistiques, des Études et des Systèmes d'Information (SESI), Ministère de la Santé, Paris

Mueller C (1982) Les institutions psychiatriques: possibilités et limites. Springer Verlag, Heidelberg

Murard L & Fourquet F (eds) (1975) Histoire de la psychiatrie de secteur ou le secteur impossible ?. Recherches No. 17

Panse F (1964) Das psychiatrische Krankenhauswesen. Thieme Verlag, Stuttgart

Psychiatric Hospitals Directors (1981) Mémorandum sur la situation de la psychiatrie publique. Gestions Hospitaliers, 203, 123-136

RCB (1975) Le financement de l'activité extra-hospitalière en psychiatrie de secteur. Ministère de la Santé, Paris

Reverzy J-F & Dameron J-F (1979) Guerisons, soins, appartements thérapeutiques et structures intermédiares. Information Psychiatrique, 55, 353-382

Reverzy J-F & Decraene B (1980) Ou en sont les structures intermédiaires ? Information Psychiatrique, 56, 977-987

Waltisperger D (1984) L'Aide Sociale. Données Sociales. Institut National de la Statistiques et des Etudes Economiques (INSEE), Paris, 215-219

Chapter Seven

PSYCHIATRIC CARE IN IRELAND

Dermot Walsh

From the close of the Middle Ages until 1921
Ireland was an integral part of the United Kingdom
of Great Britain and Ireland. During this time
Irish matters were regulated by the London
Parliament, except for a period of autonomy between
1782 and 1800, when a separate Irish Parliament sat
in Dublin. This Parliament ceased to exist on the
passing of the Act of Union in 1800 and Irish
affairs were once again managed by Westminster. In
1921 the Irish Free State, the forerunner of the
modern Ireland, was established when 26 Irish
counties seceded from the United Kingdom. The
remaining six counties form the Province of
Northern Ireland and continue to be part of
Britain. Historically, then, most legislation
governing social affairs in Ireland was either an
extension or modification of English legislation.
    Early legislation for the relief of the sick
and destitute poor was enacted in a series of
statutory provisions dating from 1700, which may
collectively be called the Poor Law. These laws
were consolidated in the Poor Relief (Ireland) Act
of 1838, itself modelled on the 1834 English Poor
Law Amendment Act. Earlier, however, various
institutions such as infirmaries, fever hospitals,
dispensaries and, at the very beginning, houses of
industry (or workshouses) and foundling hospitals
had been set up to provide for the various
categories of the needy. Among their number were
the insane for whom, in 1728, cells were provided
in the Dublin house of industry. Similar provision
was made in houses of industry elsewhere by an Act
of 1772. However, the most concerted provision of
institutional care for the mentally ill took place
in the private sector. For example, in 1745,
Swift's Hospital, a charitable and private

148

institution, was established in Dublin. It was endowed in the will of the celebrated Jonathan Swift, Dean of St. Patrick's Cathedral in Dublin, his beneficent act being immortalised in the following lines:

> He gave what little wealth he had
> To build a house for fools and mad;
> To show by one satiric touch,
> No nation needed it so much

Other private but smaller madhouses were established later.

By the early years of the nineteenth century the number of pauper lunatics had increased to the point of civic embarrassment and it was realised that the problem could no longer be contained by ad hoc provision of accommodation in workhouses. As a consequence, a House of Commons Select Committee on the 'State of Pauper Lunacy in Ireland' was set up in 1804 (other reports followed in 1812, 1841, 1855 and 1859). In 1810 a Parliamentary grant was awarded for the building of an asylum in Dublin. This, the Richmond Asylum, opened in 1815, was the first district lunatic asylum in Ireland. The Lunacy (Ireland) Act of 1821 was 'an Act to make more effective provision for the establishment of asylums of the lunatic poor and for the custody of insane persons charged with offences'. The result was a national system of district lunatic asylums funded by local finances and administered by district boards.

In the 1850s lunacy had become so prevalent and such a serious matter of administrative and social concern that the office of National Inspector of Lunacy was created. The Inspector had a duty to submit an annual report to the Lord Lieutenant (chief administrative officer of the British Crown in Ireland) and to investigate and report on all matters of discipline arising in any district asylum. Successive reports of the Inspectors of Lunacy throughout the nineteenth century have a very similar ring: the most persistent message is concern about the constant increase in the prevalence of lunacy. No sooner was one lunatic asylum built than it was full to capacity, necessitating the creation of neighbouring or auxiliary institutions. In the late nineteenth century successive censuses of lunatics carried out by local police administrators established that lunatics were to be found: in

149

district lunatic asylums; in poor houses; in brideswells or gaols; and 'at large'. The grand plan of Victorian policy was to have all lunatics in the latter three categories appropriately accommodated in district asylums. By 1900 this had largely been accomplished and 0.5 per cent of the Irish population was to be found at any one time in a district lunatic asylum (1).

This situation was to remain virtually unchanged for the first half of this century. District asylums were full to capacity; they were isolated institutions with virtually no links with the rest of medicine and were subject to separate administrative and legislative provisions. Moreover, there was a fundamental distinction between private institutions and the district asylums. Here, too, there was little interdependence or communication; the better off went to private hospitals and the poor and 'chargeable' patients (so called because their keep was 'chargeable' to the rates of the local authority maintaining the institution) went to the district asylums. Indeed, separate legislative procedures existed for the two groups, so that, whereas two certifying doctors were necessary before a person could be received into a private hospital, only one was required in the case of a 'chargeable' patient admitted to the district asylum.

In the years following the establishment of the Irish Free State there was a growing recognition in political quarters of the situation in the asylums, together with a desire for a closer association of psychiatric and general health services. As a step in this direction, the responsibilities for the mentally ill, then dispersed among several central authorities, were transferred to the Ministry for Local Government and Public Health in 1924. In the same year the government commissioned an inquiry into the 'relief of the sick and destitute poor, including the insane poor'. Its brief, in that part relating to the insane poor, was 'to enquire into the existing provision in public institutions for the care and treatment of mentally defective persons' (2) and to 'advise as to whether more efficient methods can be introduced, especially as regards the care and training of mentally defective children, with due regard to the expense involved'. The Commission's report was published in 1927, and, despite the marked emphasis on the 'mentally defective' in the terms of reference, most of the report concerned the 'insane'. In general the Commission found that most of the existing accommodation for the insane was quantitatively and qualitatively inadequate. It made a number of proposals concerning additional accommodation, recommended the treatment of some acute cases in general hospitals and strongly advocated the introduction of voluntary admission for public patients, hitherto not permissible under existing legislation. Some of the recommendations of the Commission, notably voluntary admissions, were later enshrined in the Mental Treatment Act of 1945, which regulated the compulsory admission and detention of patients in mental hospitals.

Despite the advice of the 1927 report, treatment continued to be almost exclusively on an inpatient basis and, by 1950, no outpatient, or other facilities had been developed. Indeed, it was not until 1958 that the number of patients in Irish mental hospitals reached its peak at 21,000, representing 0.7 per thousand population. And there were marked regional disparities: in Sligo and Leitrim, for example, the psychiatric inpatient ratio was as high as 1.3.

Public and governmental disquiet at the very high numbers of psychiatric inpatients, both in absolute terms and relative to most Western countries, and the generally poor conditions obtaining in the mental hospitals, induced the government to appoint a commission of inquiry in 1961.

THE COMMISSION OF INQUIRY ON MENTAL ILLNESS

Central and local government, the legal profession, psychologists, nurses and psychiatrists in practice in Ireland and Britain were all represented on the Commission. It was, and still remains, the only serious formal examination of Irish mental health services since the report of the 1924 Commission. The members of the Inquiry:

> 'visited all the district, branch and auxiliary mental hospitals in the country. Some buildings are new or comparatively new, but most were erected between 1820 and 1900 and are clearly a legacy of the days when the emphasis was on security measures and on custodial care. In many cases praiseworthy efforts have been made to improve old

151

buildings and some have been brought up to a good, or reasonably good, standard; others have been sadly neglected. In the Commission's view a large number are unsuitable in design and lack the facilities necessary for the proper treatment of patients' (Department of Health, 1966).

Data available to the Commission on outpatient services indicated that attendances had risen twelve-fold in the decade since 1956 and totalled almost 84,000 in 1965, the number of out-patients increasing from under 3000 to over 25,000 in the same period. These changes; in service usage had occurred at a time when, in the Commissions view, staff ratios for all mental health professions were inadequate. Proposals for a comprehensive reform of psychiatric services were based on the principles of 'community care', active treatment and early discharge of patients. The Commission envisaged that there would then be a considerable reduction in the numbers requiring long-term residential care. Emphasising the impossibility of making firm projections, a target figure of a reduction of 5000 places was tentatively suggested and it was judged that about 10,000 beds would be required for long-term patients, at least in the foreseeable future.

The Commission also endorsed the role of general hospital psychiatric units as the most appropriate locus of short-term inpatient care as well as aiding the integration of psychiatry in general medicine, a process it regarded as essential for the provision of good service for the mentally and physically ill. This policy was seen as helping promote what has come to be called 'liaison psychiatry', since these units would provide psychiatric expertise to the rest of the general hospital. In planning the units a preference was to be given to self-contained accommodation in which a 40-bed unit serving a catchment area of 50,000 people was regarded as the minimum for effective functioning. On average the Commission recommended a ratio of between 0.5 - 1 acute psychiatric unit bed per thousand population.

Before advocating these developments the Commission had reviewed the arguments for and against these acute units. Among the counter-arguments was the elitist situation that might be created by these units and the demoralising effect that this would have on the mental hospital, which

152

might come to be regarded as a dump for chronic patients. However, although acknowledging this difficulty, the members of the Inquiry did not address themselves as to how it might be overcome. Indeed, the Inquiry report is notably weak on both the relationship of short-term to long-term care and the operation of the principle of continuity of care. It is quite clear that the Commission saw short-term and long-term care as essentially separate and functionally independent: for chronic patients there was an implicit acceptance if not reinforcement of segregation from acute patients, with little commitment to developing a specifically local-based service. The purpose of long-stay units was to provide activity through occupational therapy and recreation; all patients, except those prevented by physical illness, were therefore to be engaged in some form of suitable activity, the provision of which was regarded as 'one of the most important and essential aspects of therapy and constitutes the greater part of the work of nursing and other staff'. Industrial therapy units, orientated towards the rehabilitation of long-term patients, were to be encouraged and it was suggested that some of these units should be developed outside mental hospitals with a view to providing industrial retraining for open employment. In some units hostel accommodation was to be provided by the hospital. In addition the Commission made specific recommendations relating to other sheltered employment and job placement services.

COMMUNITY SERVICES

For the Commission the success of community-based services depended on the existence of complementary provisions and most notably specialist outpatient psychiatric clinics. These clinics were to be given a high priority in the health authorities' programmes and were to involve the whole mental health team. Domiciliary consultations by psychiatrists were also to be encouraged so that general practitioners would have ready access to specialist assessment of patients in their home settings. Day hospitals were to be provided at general hospital short-stay units and at psychiatric hospitals. As a guiding principle the day hospital was to be able to provide all the therapeutic facilities of the parent hospital. It was also felt important that specialist support be given to families receiving a discharged patient back in the home.

The contribution of hostels and other sheltered accommodation was acknowledged but the Commission stressed the importance of adequate supporting community services before hostels could be developed on an extensive scale. The report also contains a warning against the use of hostels as second-class hospitals for patients requiring inpatient care. Accordingly, the Inquiry advised that a number of hostels should initially be provided on an experimental basis in large centres of population.

Among other matters, the Commission expressed concern that all possible steps should be taken to preserve the individuality and identity of patients; it felt that the existence of very large hospitals, large dining halls and institutional clothing, was inimical to this goal. The role of private psychiatric hospitals was also reviewed and it was accepted that, provided they were adequately staffed and equipped and operated an outpatient service, they had an important contribution to make.

THE LAW AND MENTAL ILLNESS

The Commission examined existing legislation relating to psychiatric patients, principally the 1945 Mental Treatment Act and its subsequent amendments. Under this Act committal by judicial order was replaced by medical certification alone. Two categories of compulsorily detained patients were created: 'temporary' patients, including addicts, who were judged to require treatment for less than a six-month period, and 'persons of unsound mind' who were likely to require treatment over the long-term. 'Temporary' patients may be detained for six months initially and the reception order can be extended for a further eighteen months (six months for addicts). 'Persons of unsound mind' may be detained indefinitely.

The Commission took the view that the cumbersome formality surrounding the admission and discharge of voluntary patients should be reduced and admissions put on a similar footing to those to general hospitals (3). The six-month certification

154

period for 'temporary' patients was considered
excessive and it was recommended that the initial
period of compulsory detention be limited to
fourteen days at the end of which the patient
should either be discharged, have his status
changed to informal, or be detained for a further
period not exceeding six weeks from the date of
admission. Thereafter, further extensions at three
monthly intervals were recommended, up to a period
not exceeding 12 months. Two authorised medical
officers, one of whom should be an approved
psychiatrist, were to record separately the reasons
necessitating each further period of detention
beyond the initial fourteen days.

Other recommendations of the Inquiry.

The Inquiry expressed a very positive attitude
towards the role of the voluntary sector, albeit
with recognition of the need for support and direct
involvement of mental health specialists.
Recommendations were also made about services for
children and adolescents, the aged, alcoholics and
drug addicts, epileptics, persons in custody,
homicidal and violent patients, psychopaths, and
sexual deviants. The role of prevention, training,
education and research, as well as issues related
to service organisation and legislation were also
considered.
    As one of its most important and far-reaching
suggestions th Commission advocated the
establishment of a small but permanent planning
body which would formulate policy proposals and
offer advice in the field of mental health:

'The present is a period of change in the
field of psychiatry.... many concepts and
procedures are still in a state of evolution
and new ideas are being tested continually.
The Commission has recommended a pattern of
services, based on current knowledge, but this
pattern must be kept under review. In
addition, the recommendations are confined, in
many instances, to the main concepts and
principles involved: detailed information on
implementation and on some of the technical
aspects will be required from time to time.
The Commission's proposals involve fundamental
changes in existing services and the
establishment of new services: there will be a
great need to ensure that all these services

155

are co-ordinated with each other and with other health services. The Commission considers it very desirable that there should be an expert body to advise the Minister on these matters. It recommends that a National Advisory Council should be established which, on its own initiative or at the request of the Minister, would provide advice on any matter relating to mental health services'.

Unfortunately, such a body has never been created, although the government made a modest move in this direction by establishing a planning unit in the Department of Health. A working party is currently engaged on producing a discussion document on the future of the mental health services.

THE ORGANISATION OF SERVICES

At the time of the Commission's report the administration of psychiatric services was the responsibility of county authorities, and the financing of services fell on the county rates (local taxes) with an equal amount being contributed by central government. In practice this system of finance led to regional inequalities, especially in the west of Ireland where counties had to rely on poorly-developed services and where many of the psychiatric needs of the population went unmet. This situation was exacerbated by the fact that these were the counties deriving the lowest rate incomes and, since government gave only a pound-for-pound subsidy, the problem was perpetuated.
    During the 1960s the administration of the health services was reformed and the district mental hospital boards, owing their origin to the 1821 Lunacy Act, were abolished. In their place local health authorities were created with the remit of managing all local health services including the district psychiatric hospitals. At the same time financial reliance on central funds assumed increasing importance and psychiatric hospitals became relatively less dependent on the resources of the counties. The effect has been to reduce markedly regional imbalances in resource allocation. In 1970, in a further reform, the administration of health and social services was

entrusted to eight area health boards responsible for populations varying from 1.25 million to under 200,000 people. Each of these boards administers three nationally-determined health programmes: a community health programme, including general practitioner services; a general hospital programme; and a special hospital programme, largely concerned with hospitals for the mentally ill, the mentally handicapped and the elderly. Private GP health care is largely independent of all three programmes and accounts for over 60 per cent of all GP consultations (4).

No clear distinction was made between mental health responsibilities in the community care and special hospital programmes. However, in practice, community psychiatric services have been developed within the latter programme, with virtually no input from the former. The effect has been to maintain the isolationist position traditionally occupied by the psychiatric services.

THE FINANCING OF HEALTH SERVICES

Until 1953 patients in psychiatric hospitals were required to make a means-tested contribution towards the cost of their care. Since then, the regulations for psychiatric hospitals have been the same as those in general hospitals. Under current legislation there are three types of reimbursement status for patients. Persons below a designated income have 'full eligibility' to free medical treatment, including prescriptions and medical appliances. These 'health card holders' constitute about 35 per cent of the population. Those who earn below a certain income threshold, which is reviewed regularly, pay an earnings-related subscription for which they obtain 'limited eligibility'. They are entitled to free inpatient and outpatient treatment in public general or psychiatric hospitals and receive a partial refund of the costs of medication. Those 'limited eligibility' patients who make private arrangements with consultants during their treatment must pay their own medical fees. 'Limited eligibility' patients are entitled to join the voluntary health insurance scheme (VHI) to obtain coverage for services to which they have no free entitlement. VHI is a non-profit making scheme, created in 1957, which has monopoly rights in private health insurance and is, to a large extent, underwritten by the state. In total, over 85 per cent of the population have 'full' or 'limited eligibility' coverage (Hensey, 1979). Persons above the threshold for 'limited eligibility', which has been increasing in real terms in recent years, are encouraged to join VHI and the scheme now provides coverage for over half-a-million people. Since doctors treating VHI patients use hospital premises and involve other health staff employed by the state, there are good reasons to believe that VHI benefits from an hidden public subsidy.

Almost 95 per cent of the costs of health care in the public sector are met from general taxation, with the 'limited eligibility' subscriptions making a small contribution. Although psychiatric patients occupy 35 per cent of Irish hospital beds, only 12 per cent of current health services expenditure is allocated to the mental health sector, a proportion which represents a small decline since the late 1970s. There is a general feeling among the mental health professions that Ireland, like most other developed countries, spends a disproportionate amount on acute general hospitals and their associated technology and neglects the problem of caring for the chronically ill. In this context, it is worth remembering that Ireland is relatively one of the biggest health care spenders: in 1980 8.2 per cent of GNP went to the health services. There is a feeling in certain quarters that the value obtained is not commensurate with the expenditure.

Acute general hospital care, the greatest consumer of economic resources in the health service, has largely been provided in the voluntary and independent sector, in some cases for almost two centuries. Some of these acute general voluntary hospitals are still automonous and frequently act in competition with other general hospitals and with the rest of the health services. The result is a system inimicable to efficient utilisation of available resources. A small number of these voluntary hospitals are politically very powerful and contain on their staffs the majority of medical teachers and other persons employed in the medical schools. As a result the hospitals can command a disproportionate share of financial resources. A further consequence is that medical undergraduate teaching has been predominantly determined by people working in institutions lacking an orientation and commitment to community care. This may no doubt be related to the fact that Ireland has a very high proportion of beds per capita, in general as well as in psychiatric hospitals.

DEVELOPMENTS IN THE IRISH MENTAL HEALTH SERVICES SINCE 1966

In the time since the report of the Commission was presented to the Minister of Health in 1966, most of the improvements in service provision that have occurred have not been a consequence of ministerial intervention. Indeed, there has been no sustained activity by central government with the aim of implementing the Commission's recommendations. However, some of the eight health boards have independently published their own policy documents (Brown and Walsh, 1966; South Eastern Health Board, 1982).

As already indicated the peak of psychiatric admissions was reached in 1958 when there were 21,000 inpatients. Since then there has been a continuous annual decline, so that by 1981 the numbers had fallen to approximately 14,000. Moreover, whereas in 1960 four psychiatric hospitals had populations of over two thousand, now only one contains more than a thousand patients. A policy of catchment area sectorisation has been introduced. Thus, in the eastern health board, where there was formerly one large hospital for a population of over a million, there are now eight sectorised services, each with its own small inpatient unit. As a result, the parent hospital, which in 1960 had over two thousand patients, now has slightly less than a thousand. Similar sectorised services have been created in the southern and western health board areas. These developments have been made possible only by a significant reliance on disused tuberculosis sanitoria and a small input from psychiatric units in general hospitals. There are about ten of these units in the country; some are teaching units, provided in newly-built general hospitals and contain up to 50 beds, others are units that have been built in association with non-acute general hospitals and use psychiatric hospital staff. These latter units tend to have far less autonomy and function as extensions of the psychiatric hospital. Some of the more autonomous general

159

hospital units have catchment area responsibilities; others do not. In total there are approximately 350 beds in general hospital units; in 1980 they accounted for 15.4 per cent of the total of 27,098 admissions.

Since 1960 there has been a considerable proliferation of out-patient clinics throughout the country, so that now no town with a population of more than a thousand lacks a psychiatric clinic which operates weekly or fortnightly. Some catchment area teams may be involved in as many as fifteen clinics per week. Unlike in some other EC countries there are no institutional or financial inducements either for the health authority or doctors to undertake outpatient care. However, the need to see discharged patients fairly regularly is acknowledged, and in rural areas, where transportation difficulties pose major problems, it is much easier for patients to come to these clinics, which for the most part are held at health centres in towns distant from the parent hospital.

Health board psychiatrists in rural areas have few private patients. Private consultations do take place in larger cities but are relatively uncommon in other urban centres. In any case, they are less prominent a feature of Irish psychiatry than elsewhere. Some outpatient psychiatric clinics are operated in voluntary acute general hospitals in Dublin; most of the psychiatrists operating these clinics work in private psychiatric hospitals. The clinics have little raison d'etre , as they are not integrated in the area psychiatric services and many of the general hospitals involved have no psychiatric inpatient beds.

It has been the health boards rather than the voluntary sector that have been responsible for building day hospitals, day centres, hostels and group homes, but developments have been slow and uneven. Whereas some psychiatric teams have access to a range of community services that can compare with the best anywhere, the general picture is not so favourable and there are still some areas which have minimal provision. Since services, in general, are organised and run by a chief psychiatrist, sometimes called the clinical director (in essence synonymous with the old medical superintendent), much depends on his initiative. And at this level a recruitment problem exists: traditionally it has been difficult to attract medical staff of the highest calibre to the psychiatric services, although this situation has improved greatly recently. These difficulties are particularly in evidence in rural areas.

PRIVATE HOSPITALS

Private hospitals, often run by religious orders, are still a potent force in Irish psychiatry. They cater for both private patients and patients with 'limited eligibility'. In addition, the larger private psychiatric hospitals also provide catchment area services on a contractual basis and admit 'full eligibility' patients. They are reimbursed for this work by the patient's health board. Private hospitals provide about 1200 beds and in 1980 accounted for 17 per cent of all psychiatric admissions. Forty-four per cent of these admissions were for alcoholism, which nationally is the main diagnostic category among male psychiatric inpatients. Some of the private hospitals have developed specialist treatment programmes for this condition.

THE MENTAL HEALTH TEAM

(a) Nurses

Up to 1960 medical and nursing staff were the only professionals engaged by the psychiatric services. Psychiatric nurses had typically only a two-year specialist training and, compared to general nurses, enjoyed poor status. In the past twenty years, however, this situation has greatly improved. Many more fully-trained general nurses have entered psychiatric nursing and a high proportion of nursing staff in the mental health services possess both general and psychiatric nursing qualifications. Furthermore, moves are already in train to establish a common nursing syllabus in which psychiatric nurse training would be an integral part.

None the less, there remain some practices supported by the nurses' trade unions which interfere with the continuity and quality of patient care. These include rostering schedules where nurses work a day-on day-off shift, and unions still object to female nurses working on male wards and vice-versa. This has severely

161

militated against patient welfare, particularly on male wards. Promotion by seniority irrespective of merit has been another stumbling block perpetuated by the unions. However, it should be said that these practices are now under review and look likely to be discontinued in the foreseeable future.

Community psychiatric nursing (CPN) has been of increasing importance since the 1960s. These nurses work in a variety of locations: in the patients' homes; in outpatient clinics and in hostels; and provide a very successful service by maintaining the link between the patient's home and the hospital. One difficulty of expanding CPN services operated by hospital psychiatric nurses is that public health nurses working in the community as part of the community care programme tend to be excluded. There is a general feeling among psychiatrists that the specialised approach is the more useful, since psychiatric nurses know their clientele intimately and, as they work in hospital-based services, they have the appropriate links for the easy transfer of patients between the hospital and the community. At the same time there is also a suspicion that, if left to the wider community care programme, psychiatric patients would be neglected in favour of other, more 'interesting' cases.

(b) Psychiatric Social Workers

There are currently about 50 psychiatric social workers employed by the Irish psychiatric services. One problem in the reorganisation of the health services has been that social workers, no doubt influenced by the Seebohm Report in the United Kingdom, have opted for a generic rather than specialised caseload and are largely based in local area offices rather than in psychiatric hospitals. This has militated against the specialist role of the psychiatric social worker, with doubtful utility to the psychiatric services. Furthermore, certain clinical directors, misunderstanding the professional role of the social worker, have tended increasingly to rely exclusively on community psychiatric nurses.

(c) Clinical Psychologists

The role of clinical psychologists within psychiatric teams has evolved slowly over the last

162

15 years. Until comparatively recently there were no full training courses for clinical psychologists in this country. Now psychologists are increasingly being employed by the health services, but their concern with professional autonomy may prove difficult to accommodate within the traditional psychiatric team structure. Although the majority of clinical psychologists work within health board and voluntary psychiatric services, a few are now beginning to engage in private practice.

(d) Occupational Therapists

Occupational therapists have progressively been employed in recent years in psychiatric hospitals and day centres, whereas twenty years ago their posts were virtually non-existent.

(e) Psychiatrists

Prior to 1960 there was only one part-time chair in psychiatry. Since then departments of psychiatry have been established in all five medical schools, though none of the professorships is full-time. Psychiatry as an undergraduate subject is now firmly established as a compulsory part of the medical curriculum. The same cannot be said for pre-clinical behavioural sciences which are still neglected in favour of the physical sciences; nor does there appear to be any serious attempt on the part of medical faculties to improve this situation.

The unified postgraduate psychiatric training programme was set up about 10 years ago to train medical postgraduates. The training is of two types: the first lasts for a year and is directed at those requiring some experience in psychiatry which is now seen as an essential qualification for entry to general practice; the other is for medical graduates intending to specialise in psychiatry and is a three-year programme after which the student takes the specialist examination of the Royal College of Psychiatrists of the United Kingdom. In this context it is worth pointing out that there is no nationally - established body of psychiatrists in Ireland; Irish psychiatrists belong to the Irish Division of the Royal College of Psychiatrists. This has positive and negative consequences: Irish psychiatrists are associated with a major organisation with a long tradition and history of improving professional standards and with a high standard of examination for membership. On the other hand, the administrative and legislative basis of Irish services differs from those of the United Kingdom and therefore much of the professional debate within the Royal College on British mental health services is irrelevant to the Irish situation. Membership of this organisation also removes responsibility for autonomous academic and professional development from within, so there is always the feeling of having someone else doing one's thinking for one. One of the consequences of this is that research output from academic and other departments has been meagre. The recent foundation of an Irish Journal of Psychiatry with the objective of stimulating research in Ireland must therefore be welcomed.

(f) The Psychiatric Team and Primary Health Care

One of the most salient features of Irish health services compared with those, for example, of the United Kingdom is the relatively minor involvement of general practitioners in psychiatric care. There is good evidence from Irish case register studies that, once a patient enters the specialised psychiatric care in Ireland, he is less likely to be discharged than is the case in Britain. This may arise for two reasons: either general practitioners are less prepared to provide psychiatric care or the psychiatric services are less willing to discharge patients. In practice, both factors probably operate. The system of financing Irish GP services in the public sector by reimbursement for item-of-service inevitably increases demand without necessarily improving health. Furthermore, psychiatric items-of-service take more time to administer and many doctors may regard them as less renumerative and attempt to limit their involvement with a psychiatric caseload. There are also clear indications that in Irish psychiatric services, there is a marked tendency to hold on to clinical caseloads; for example, community nurses may continue to visit patients, who in other health care systems might be returned to GP or public health nurse care. Whether in the long run this 'tenacity' is better for the psychiatric patient is an open question and one that needs investigation.

LEGISLATIVE PROVISION FOR THE MENTALLY ILL

The 1945 Mental Treatment Act still regulates compulsory admissions and other matters of concern to the psychiatric patient. New legislation in the form of the Health (Mental Services) Act 1981 has been passed by parliament but has been unfavourably received by the psychiatric profession and is currently being reviewed by the Department of Health. The new Act incorporates some of the recommendations of the 1966 Commission report and simplifies admission procedures. The distinction between private and 'chargeable' patient will be abolished and, at least in theory, patients will be offered greater safeguards than under the 1945 legislation. The requirements for compulsory admission have been made more stringent. Two doctors' certificates will be required in most cases (there are to be some exceptions yet to be specified). Previously two medical certificates were required only in the case of private patients. Other than for a short period a patient may not be detained in institutions outside the area in which he normally lives. The Act also extends the range of institutions which will be subject to compulsory registration and routine inspection.

In each health board area a psychiatric review board is to be appointed with three members, at least one of whom must be a lawyer. Their brief is to review the need for further detention of all patients compulsorily detained for two years or more. This will be a regular two-yearly procedure. In addition, every patient will have an automatic right of communicating complaints to the review board and have the right of legal representation. It must be admitted that the Act is not as far-reaching as reforms in some other countries, where consent to treatment is required in the case of patients who are compulsorily detained. The legislation specifies that these matters should be managed by the Medical Council, which is the registration and disciplinary body regulating the medical profession in Ireland. This council, however, has recently indicated its unwillingness to intervene in the doctor's freedom to treat, even in the case of compulsorily admitted patients (5).

In fact, the legislation was unfavourably received both before and after it reached the statute book. The Irish division of the Royal College of Psychiatrists has complained of a lack of prior consultation at the drafting stage. Psychiatrists are unhappy that no minimum standards of care in psychiatric institutions are laid down. Nor do they like what they see as too restrictive a terminology used to establish criteria for compulsory admission, although they have welcomed the abolition of certification of addicts. The Irish division felt that obtaining two doctors to certify a patient would frequently be impractical, especially in rural areas. Among other complaints, the most significant are the criticism of the constitution and role of the review boards, the necessity of furnishing regular reports on each long-stay patient, and the need to obtain the sanction of the Medical Council to administer certain treatments. At the present time the Act is being revised with a view to amending the composition and function of the review boards and abolishing the requirement for certification by two doctors.

Child Psychiatric Services

Up to 1960 there was only one child guidance clinic in the whole country. Currently there are four separate services in the Eastern Health Board area, some of which provide an extensive range of facilities. There are also services in Cork and Galway. Some team members also work outside their immediate catchment areas. Nevertheless, there is still inadequate provision of child psychiatric services in rural areas. Central government and the health boards are committed to a policy of developing child psychiatric services in areas so far unserved.

Other Specialised Services

There is a central hospital for the psychiatric offender operated by the Eastern Health Board. In the Dublin area, where services have been almost entirely sectorised, there is a central secure unit for psychiatric patients who, for a short time during their illness, need secure accommodation. Specialised services for those suffering from alcoholism or alcohol-induced disorders have been developed over a long period within the private sector. Other specialised treatment services are provided by health boards and voluntary agencies. In general, the Irish approach to alcohol-related problems is somewhat outdated in that the

166

conventional treatment model is predominantly espoused and the prevention of alcohol-related problems is still very much under-developed. What steps have been taken reflect the easy options: i.e. the health education approach, to the exclusion of legislative and other control measures. Drug addiction has become a considerable problem among young people in city centre areas, particularly in Dublin, and specialised treatment agencies have been established in the last ten years.

The Public, Voluntary Agencies and Mental Illness

In common with other countries, the public image of mental illness in Ireland has been unfavourable. In the last twenty years considerable changes have occurred, particularly in urban areas. One product has been the founding of the Mental Health Association at national level, with local branches throughout the country. More recently the Schizophrenia Association has been formed by relatives of patients.

Notwithstanding these developments in the prevailing economic climate, the psychiatrically ill have to compete with other patients for diminishing financial resources. In spite of its improved public image mental illness is still not an important issue politically and there is a feeling among the mental health professions that psychiatric care is not getting its fair slice of the national health economic cake.

THE FUTURE OF IRISH PSYCHIATRIC SERVICES

An official working party on the future of psychiatric services was set up in 1983 but has not yet reported. However, if its public statements can be relied on, the future of Irish mental health care would seem to be in the direction of increased emphasis on community care with a continuing run-down of existing beds in the old mental hospitals. Inpatient accommodation will be located in units attached to general hospitals, although some psychiatrists may doubt the necessity of proximity to general hospitals and see a possible ambiguity of role: i.e. does the unit service a general hospital or a catchment area, and does such a unit establish a demand that is hitherto unmet or help generate unnecessary admissions of those who would not have been hospitalised? Whatever the case, it is clear that the model for the future is the small independent unit serving a defined population. This will take a considerable time to achieve and, in many parts of Ireland, the end of the large mental hospital as the cornerstone of psychiatric services is not yet in sight.

NOTES

(1)   Up to the 1930s some 'harmless lunatics' remained in county homes (i.e. former workhouses established under the Poor Law).

(2)   The term 'mentally defective' included the mentally disordered as well as the mentally handicapped.

(3)   For example, voluntary patients are required to give three days notice of their intention to discharge themselves. Since the 1950s voluntary patients have comprised the large majority of patients. In the late 1970s 85 per cent of psychiatric inpatients had informal status.

(4)   Most people are not eligible for free GP treatment. For a discussion of eligibility in health care see the following section.

(5)   The full text of the act is published in the International Journal of Health Legislation, Vol 32, No.4, 1981, 713-730.

REFERENCES

Browne, I. and Walsh, D. (1966). The Future of the Psychiatric Services in the Dublin Area. Dublin: Eastern Health Board, (Unpublished).

Department of Health. (1966). Commmission of Enquiry on Mental Illness. Stationery Office, Dublin.

Hensey, B. (1979). The Health Services in Ireland. Institute of Public Administration, Dublin, 2nd Edition. (See also Gormley, M. (1980). Guide to the Irish Health Services. Emerald Publications, Galway).

South Eastern Health Board. (1982). Psychiatry Services: Report of Sub-Committee. Kilkenny: South Eastern Health Board.

Chapter Eight

THE ITALIAN PSYCHIATRIC REFORM

Shulamit Ramon.

This chapter describes the recent psychiatric reform in Italy, arguing that it has a distinctly different character from the psychiatric systems of the rest of Europe. Officially the comprehensive reform of Italian mental health services dates from the 1st of July 1978, when Law No.180 came into effect (Basaglia, 1980). However, the passing of this Law was the culmination of a process which started in 1963 and which will be described below. The Law has been elegantly summarised by Mosher (1982):

1. Inpatient care:
   a. No new patients may be admitted to large public hospitals.
   b. Until 31 December 1980 ex-hospital patients may be readmitted voluntarily. No patients may be admitted after 1 January 1981.
   c. Construction of new psychiatric hospitals is prohibited.
   d. Psychiatric wards in general hospitals are allowed; they can have no more than 15 beds and must work together with community mental health centres.
2. Involuntary commitment:
   a. Compulsory evaluation and treatment should take place in community-based facilities.
   b. Compulsory admission to a general hospital ward may take place if:
       1) urgent intervention is required;
       2) the necessary treatment is refused;

3) community treatment cannot be opportunely implemented; and

4) two doctors and the mayor or his designate deem care and rehabilitation necessary.

c. Independent judicial review is required at two and seven days.

d. Patients and relatives may appeal the decision to the mayor.

e. These standards must be applied to patients at present involuntarily in mental hospitals.

f. The constitutional rights of involuntarily admitted patients must not be violated.

3. Miscellaneous:

a. Community-based facilities will be responsible for a prescribed geographical area.

b. All facilities will be staffed by existing mental health personnel.

c. As of October 1, 1980, medical and social welfare monies will be pooled and distributed on a per capita basis within each region.

This Law differs considerably from other European mental health legislation in its goal of completely restructuring the existing organisational framework and, equally important, of guaranteeing the employment of existing personnel.

For the originators of the Italian psychiatric reform the <u>restructuring of the organisation of services</u> has been a vital factor. The new framework of services is aimed primarily at the desegregation of the mentally ill, the mentally handicapped and physically handicapped: i.e. people with a problem which is socially perceived as a personal handicap. This goal is to be achieved by the closure of mental hospitals and by ensuring that the style of life of clients will be maintained at the same level as that of ordinary people. Concomitantly there is an attempt to move away from the hegemony of medically-trained staff to the sharing of power and responsibility by all professionals involved. The hospital base of the psychiatric system will be replaced by a network of community mental health centres (CMHCs). CMHCs are preferred to hospitals because they can be more informally maintained and their use is less stigmatising for clients. In addition, community

171

services facilitate multi-disciplinary approaches and avoid the unidirectionality of clinical practice typical of large total institutions.

The restructuring of services and clinical practice is a mammoth task. Moreover, there has been a reform in child psychiatric services including legislation, passed in 1977, for the closure of publically-owned special schools. In order to ensure <u>the protection of the employment of existing personnel</u> the regional laws require the re-deployment of staff in the newly-created CMHCs and guarantee that no one will be made redundant as the result of the reorganisation. These formal statements stand in contradistinction to other Western governments' manifest aims to reduce public expenditure, where one of the goals of every restructuring of services is to reduce the workforce. The Italian logic is to redistribute effort and resources: while staff will be relieved of most of the custodial and 'hotel' tasks, the job of resocialisation, the provision of consistent support, and work with new categories of clients who would begin to use these services require at least the same number of employees, albeit in new roles. Moreover, policy makers recognised the detrimental effects on the chances of success of the reform if they were to antagonise the very group who were to carry it through. In a society where unemployment was growing and where the chances of re-employment elsewhere were slim, there was a willingness on the part of officialdom to concede that people would resist working themselves out of a job. Furthermore, it was anticipated that there would be enough opposition to reform from certain professional circles, some right-wing parties and relatives of patients fearful that there would be a reduction in the quality of care, as well as among the general public, without, in addition, alienating mental health workers en masse.

The Focus on Treatment

The principle that treatment can be the only reason for compulsory admission is not unique to Italy, but it is still a minority stand in Europe. It assumes that only the need for treatment can justify the deprivation of freedom. If a person is regarded as 'dangerous' his management should be the responsibility of the judicial system, not the psychiatric services, though psychiatric teams should work closely with the legal professions in the case of people who are dangerous and also judged to be in need of psychiatric intervention.

Italy has no special hospitals for offenders who suffer from mental disturbance. Instead, it has six psychiatric prisons where people with fixed prison sentences can be given treatment. These institutions are not included in the provisions of the 1978 Law, although currently there is an attempt to formulate new legislation that will introduce a certain conformity with the Mental Health Act.

The separation of judicial intervention from mental health care marks a departure from the inherent logic of psychiatric thought and developments throughout Europe in the post-war period, in which mentally disturbed offenders were automatically included within the remit of psychiatry, even though frequently clinical diagnosis and clear treatment programmes could not be specified.

The circumstances under which the new Law reached the statute books exemplifies the complex nature of Italian political processes. After more than a decade of largely successful experimentation with mental health reform in several parts of Italy, those closely involved with these experiments began an energetic campaign for a mandatory policy of nationwide reform. Their case was taken up by the Radical Party, one of the small left-of-centre parties, which, on its own, did not carry sufficient political weight to bring about legislation. However, the Italian constitution provides for a public referendum for any proposal supported by the signatures of more than 500,000 citizens. Once this number of signatures had been collected the ruling coalition, headed by the Christian-Democratic Party, felt that it might become a political embarrassment to allow the law to be proposed via a referendum rather than by the government. The coalition government therefore adopted the proposal as its own piece of legislation and it was comfortably passed by parliament, since it attracted opposition support.

ITALIAN SERVICES PRIOR TO THE 1978 REFORM

The first national psychiatric legislation after the unification of Italy was passed in 1904 and came into force five years later. The Italian provinces were given responsibility for providing and supervising public asylums and an inspectorate was appointed within the Ministry of the Interior. The Act was inspired by the French Law of 1838 but it was, if anything, more rigid and more narrowly custodial in orientation, being principally concerned with 'dangerosity' and the maintenance of public order. The legislation provided only for compulsory admission: in the sixty years that this restriction applied those patients who were successful in obtaining voluntary treatment were admitted to private hospitals or university clinics.

Although the Act stipulated that certification should be authorised by the local magistracy, in practice the emergency committal procedure, which was free of this requirement, was almost exclusively applied. Medical directors of the asylums exercised great power, with the magistrate merely rubber stamping their decisions. Concern for the protection of society soon gave way to the practice of accommodating a wide assortment of marginalised groups and, in the thirty years after the passing of the Act, the asylum population more than doubled, reaching 95,000 by 1940.

In the fascist era a considerable amount of new construction was undertaken in the asylums. Another legacy of this period - and one surviving until 1968 - was the order of the Minister of Justice that all compulsory admissions should be entered in the criminal record of the individual (Balduzzi, 1981).

The period of ideological reconceptualisation following the defeat of the Fascists and the end of the War created an intellectual and political atmosphere which was relatively receptive to the ideas of a social model of psychiatry, as part of a larger and broadly socialist oriented movement. Nevertheless, these political changes were slow to filter through into psychiatric practice: although shortly after the War the asylums became 'psychiatric hospitals', the segregation of patients according to the duration of their disorders intensified, with detrimental effects on the standard of care offered to chronic patients. After a decline during the War and for some years afterwards inpatient numbers began to rise steadily, increasing by 24 per cent between 1950 and 1963, the peak year, to reach a total of almost 92,000.

The hospital remained practically the only psychiatric resource available, the majority of these institutions being owned either by provincial or local authorities. There was also a number of private institutions, of varying size, many of which were owned by the Church. Some authors have argued that, at this time, the quality of psychiatric care in Italy was amongst the worst in Europe (De Plato and Minguzzi, 1981). Italian hospitals were heavily overcrowded and often insanitary; staff ratios were low and the majority of the nurses untrained (Cerletti, 1961). In the years before the reform children from the age of three years could be hospitalised along with adults. The majority of patients were admitted for a variety of psychiatric, neurological and social reasons. Once inside they were likely to stay for a long time: some studies quote an average length-of-stay of fifteen years (e.g. Adamo, 1982).

The first real signs of change appeared in the early Sixties. During this period the group committed to more radical reform, later known as 'Psichiatria Democratica', took shape. There was some increase in parliamentary interest in mental health issues, but the official response when it came in 1968 was disappointing. An amendment to the 1904 Act for the first time formally permitted voluntary admissions to public psychiatric hospitals. The article of the Penal Code requiring registration of all compulsory admissions in criminal records was also abolished. Otherwise, the original legislation was left intact, including the focus on dangerosity. Although the amendment provided for the internal sectorisation of psychiatric hospitals – each unit to serve a defined catchment area - and the Italian government has since then been officially committed to a policy of community care, the creation of the required new outpatient and day care services was extremely slow and developments were restricted to some general hospitals or academic psychiatric departments. As late as 1973, for example, only thirteen community mental health centres existed in the whole country (Zanetti, 1974).

PSICHIATRIA DEMOCRATICA (PD)

The movement for reform which originated in the early 1960s was initiated by a group of

175

psychiatrists, social workers and sociologists. The senior members of the group had been active in the anti-fascist underground during the Second World War and all members expressed a preference for a broad socialist perspective, in which psychiatry was regarded as requiring urgent and radical reform. For the members of PD psychiatric hospitalisation was the outcome of segregation and institutionalisation; there was no need for these hospitals, and especially for the locked wards they contained. These symbols of institutionalism and incarceration were to be the prime targets for abolition. The PD regard the medicalisation of madness and, in particular, medical dominance as harmful, though they concede that there is a positive role for medically-oriented interventions such as psychotropic drugs. Instead, the PD argue that all patients are capable of living outside hospital if they are given sufficient support and social rehabilitation and if their self-respect is fostered. For the majority of patients individual psychotherapy is viewed as inappropriate since it involves the privatisation of symptoms and ignores the fact that the root of many personal problems lies in the breakdown of collective living. Counselling is not ruled out, however, and, in fact, is frequently practiced. Essential for patients' successful rehabilitiation is acceptance by the community; hence the attempts to effect a change of public attitudes are regarded as being as important as direct work with patients. Normalisation is seen as the essential means by which the public's image of mental disorder will improve. People with handicaps, including psychiatric problems, should therefore remain within the ordinary institutions of everyday life (school, work, etc.), even if the initial cost is high, since the main issue which needs to be remedied is the misery of living which unites all patients. The primary aim of any intervention should be the restoration of the ability to live with others and the attainment of a higher degree of self-sufficiency.

In the PD's campaign for organisational reform there were three guiding principles: de-segregation of the mentally ill and re-integration in the community; a more equal distribution of power among staff in multi-disciplinary settings; and greater flexibility of therapeutic role according to the specific needs of individual clients, rather than to pre-determined standards of any one professional group. In their arguments for a change in professional relations PD was conscious that professionals are not neutral but that their choices of strategies and policies are a function of prevailing ideologies and political views.

The conceptual framework developed by PD has been influenced by four theoretical approaches; the deviancy school of mental illness; the concept of the therapeutic community; marxism; and existentialism. The impact of the deviancy school is easily recognisable in the adherence to the view that segregation, and not the psychiatric condition itself, is what creates the gulf between the mentally ill and society. It is the majority's fear of the potential violence of the minority that leads to dissociation. An attempt to implement the principles of the therapeutic community are in evidence in PD's early work. Since the social unrest in Italy in 1968, however, PD has been disillusioned with this model and has discarded it. The disappointment with the therapeutic community occurred when the internal democracy gradually established in the hospital at Gorizia (Görz), which was the first institution in which the ideals of PD were applied, failed to result in a collective effort to establish shared goals. The limitations of the model manifested themselves most critically in relations with local government bureaucracy and with the general public. PD members at Gorizia gradually realised that this approach recognised only a limited number of conflicts and did not prepare people for life outside the institution. Furthermore, the therapeutic community seemed to be in conflict with the marxist understanding of reality.

The type of marxist literature and practice which the group found useful was mainly concerned with collective consciousness and motivating groups towards political action. Thus, Gramsci's emphasis on the need to dismantle capitalism's cultural hegemony received particular attention (Gramsci, 1971), since it attempts to deal with a key issue for the group, namely how to change social and professional attitudes towards the mentally ill. Marxist thinking is reflected in PD's approaches to the reorganisation of psychiatric services, with more sharing of power both among therapists and between therapists and clients, in the mounting of a positive collective consciousness, in action inside and outside the hospital, and in the methods adopted to provide support for patients whilst simultaneously preventing the fostering of dependence.

The existentialist perspective has been much less in evidence than either the deviancy school or marxism. But in both of these latter approaches the PD has concentrated on issues which have an existentialist flavour: the identity of a person labelled a deviant, the search for individual identities within collective living, the fear of subtle violence, the fragile borderline between rationality and irrationality, and the fate of the powerless. The PD accepts the anti-psychiatry critique of mental illness and established psychiatry. So far, however, PD has not produced its own theory of mental illness; PD members openly prefer to stay uncommitted to a particular aetiology or one model of understanding, a preference that is closely related to their goal of a 'total service' system.

The process of local reform initiated in the 1960s and 1970s by PD members in certain towns in north and central Italy follows a broadly similar path (see, for example, I Tetti Rossi, 1978):

1) Negotiations with the local authority aimed at securing cooperation in allowing the hospital to become open, the residents to move freely in the city and to provide the necessary resources, such as day allowance, alternative accommodation, initial employment opportunities and, ultimately, the creation of alternative mental health centres (CMHCs).

2) The act of opening the hospital doors followed preliminary work with both patients and staff in collective daily meetings on the aims and practice of this move.

3) At the point of opening up the hospital some of the residents would already be organised into small working groups carrying out defined tasks in the hospital, for which they were paid the minimal wage acceptable to the trade unions.

4) Later, all of the people being prepared for leaving the hospital would be members of small 'resocialiation' groups.

5) Community mental health centres should have been created before this stage, but often the impetus to establish them came only when ex-patients were actually living in the community.

6) Patients leaving the institution departed individually but went to live with others who had already completed the same process of re-

integration. The new accommodation varied, depending on availability as well as on the person's capacity for independent living. Thus, many elderly people went to small old peoples homes. In some places hospital buildings were converted into apartments where ex-patients could live in varying degrees of sheltered accommodation. Although, normally, people share a bedroom in this type of housing, the accommodation retains the atmosphere of a private dwelling in the way it is internally organised. The fact of sharing a living space and, at times, household duties diminishes the level of isolation of the person who has just come out of the hospital.

7) Only at the end of the first period outside the hospital would attempts be made to find suitable employment or vocational training. The PD have stressed how much is at stake in this initial period: how anxious the ex-patient is; how often he/she will be prescribed drugs at that point even after a long period of living without chemotherapy. Consequently, an observer can sense the tension among the staff when someone leaves the hospital and moves into the community, as well as the high degree of staff involvement with that person. The rest of the residents are not forgotten at this stage, since it is well remembered that the delicate balance achieved in the group home may be destroyed easily unless adequate support is given.

This, then, was the programme of activities of PD which have helped to pave the way for psychiatric reform in Italy. In terms of PD's relationship to the mental health professions as a whole, it must be acknowledged that membership is restricted to a minority. The PD movement has no official standing and its influence is maintained by the strength of the leadership of its members who have been working for the reform since 1963, as well as by initiatives of individual new members. The education of the majority of the staff in the principles of the reform, and efforts to sustain them in the face of criticisms the new system receives, are informal and somewhat marginal activities.

Services for Children

A similar transition process takes place in regard to children with a handicap who are on the point of entering school (Vislie, 1981).

Special schools have closed down in several areas of Italy (mainly in the centre and the north) since 1974, a process which was initiated by a large-scale OECD-sponsored project. As with the legislation on mental illness the closure of public-owned special schools, provided for in legislation passed in 1977, came after a period of experimention with such possibilities in different parts of the country. Children with psychological, mental and physical handicaps are now taught in ordinary schools. Those with a known problem are located by staff at the pre-nursery stage, where they and their families are given encouragement to join ordinary play-schemes and guidance on how to promote general learning abilities in a child with a specific disability. Prior to the date of entering the school (i.e. at the age of three for the infants school) negotiation will take place between members of the CMHC team, the headmaster and the teacher in whose class the child is likely to be placed. These talks are aimed at reducing the school staff's anxiety and at preparing for a relatively smooth path by showing where the difficulties lie and by planning and arranging for means of either overcoming or mitigating them. When judged necessary a support teacher will be individually attached to the child in addition to the weekly visits by the CMHC key worker.

Parents are supported at home by the CMHC but they are not invited to attend meetings at the school. It is typical of the reform policy that the role of the professionals is not limited to the transition period; usually support will continue as long as it is perceived as necessary by the staff and the clients. The lack of opposition to integration strongly indicates its <u>preventive</u> potential. Tomorrow's adults are learning to live together with children who are different from the majority.

THE STRUCTURE OF THE NEW SERVICE

(A) The Italian Health System

Until the enactment of Law 833 in 1979 instituting the national health service the Italian health care system was insurance based. Before their abolition, approximately two hundred sickness funds provided cover for about ninety per cent of the population. Those who were not members of these schemes or who were ineligible for other reasons, such as the chronically mentally ill, could apply for means-tested social assistance which was administered by the provincial authorities.

The decision to establish a national health service was taken for a number of reasons: central government wished to extend compulsory insurance coverage to the entire population, partly as a means of reducing expenditure on social assistance; there was a desire to take action to eradicate the significant inequalities in the distribution of services; and, perhaps most important, the central ministries were anxious to have more effective means of controlling health expenditure, which in the mid-Seventies had been rising at annual rates in excess of twenty per cent, although the proportion of GDP devoted to health care, at around five per cent, was one of the lowest of the EC countries.

Health care is now financed by insurance contributions to the National Sickness Fund which, in effect, is a supplementary earnings-related tax. In addition, the national health service is supported by general taxation.

Doctors work for the national health service under contract. For general practitioners remuneration on a capitation basis has largely replaced item-of-service fees, although the latter system still functions in private practice. Hospital doctors are salaried staff. Access to medical specialists is by referral from general practitioners except in the case of psychiatrists, to whom patients have direct access at community mental health centres. Doctors under contract to the national health service are also permitted to engage in private practice. Public hospitals are allocated an annual cash-limited budget, but private hospitals continue to receive a daily fee for each occupied bed. Private practitioners and private hospitals also undertake work under contract to the national health service.

The Ministry of Health retains supervisory functions in health care but major responsibilities have been devolved to the twenty Italian regions. However, central ministries authorise capital expenditure in the health service and new hospital building must conform to the quinquennial hospital bed plans the regions are required to submit to Rome. In psychiatry, where no new hospitals are permitted, these central powers take the form of sanctioning new psychiatric beds being created in general hospitals. Revenue budgets are also decided centrally and are then allocated to the regions for further distribution to the lower-tier health authorities.

The Italian health service is characterised by a large degree of decentralisation. Until the creation of the national health service the 94 old Italian provinces exercised limited functions in health care, notably related to their duties to provide welfare and after-care services for psychiatric patients. These responsibilities have now been transferred to the other health authorities. The regions, with populations varying from 100,000 to eight millions, have major powers in health policy, including supervising the training programmes of the health care professions. They manage national health service provisions and also administer the health insurance fund and social assistance programmes. Although the regions receive their budget from central government, they are largely free to decide how it is spent. Every region periodically produces forward plans but, unfortunately, they do not give much indication of the extent to which past targets have been met. Plans produced by the lower-tier authorities must be approved by the regions and conform to the strategic goals in these plans.

The regions maintain a tight control on the next administrative tier: the localities (Unità Sanitaria Locale-USL) which have populations varying from 40,000 to 200,000. Each USL is responsible for the management of specialist services including the psychiatric services which, with the creation of the national health service, are now part of the same administrative unit as other medical specialities. To assist in the administration and planning of psychiatric services the USLs have established mental health departments: the Servizio d'Igiene Mentale (SIM). Each USL exercises a certain degree of financial authority: for example, it may decide how to allocate the budget between the hospital and community services. Below the USL are the district units which serve a maximum population of ten thousand and are responsible for general services, including primary care, family advice centres, pharmacies and certain domiciliary services. All USL administrators are elected to serve for a period of five years.

(B) Psychiatric Services

The maximum number of health care staff in each district of ten thousand people is set at six doctors, four social workers, four psychologists and twelve nurses. Doctors tend to work individually rather than in group practices.

Social work services form another section of the health service, though they are funded by contributions from central government and the regional and local authorities. However, in some areas the social workers have chosen to work inside the psychiatric services rather than in separate departments.

The main establishments of the new psychiatric services are the community mental health centres (CMHCs). These operate as walk-in centres without the need for a prior appointment or referral by a professional. The centres are open for ten hours a day and have emergency cover for the rest of the time. In several areas the centres have a small number of beds (six to eight) (Gallio, 1982). The personnel of the centres normally includes psychiatrists, nurses, psychologists and social workers. In some places speech therapists and physiotherapists are also in attendance. Some areas have an integrated adult and child service while in others adult provisions are located within the psychiatric services and child services are operated by the municipal authority. No psychiatrists and nurses work in these child services, though they may be asked for consultation and support at times.

University clinics continue to operate in certain areas. In contrast to the CMHC's emphasis of offering a walk-in service, the clinics tend to work on a referral and appointment basis along psychotherapeutic lines with people recovering from acute episodes or those suffering from mild disorders. Relationships between these older-established services and CMHCs of very recent origin have not been easy. The university clinic at Verona offers an interesting exception since, unlike other university psychiatric services, it has accepted catchment area responsibilities and provides both acute and long-term care (Berti-Taini et al., 1982).

The general hospital's role in the new psychiatric services takes two forms: the legally-approved number of beds may be located there, either in a ward or distributed among the general wards; or the hospital may operate an emergency psychiatric service. Where CMHCs have their own beds the local general hospital only operates the emergency service.

So far in the psychiatric reform the relationship between the general hospital, the CMHCs and the directorate of the mental health services has frequently been uneasy. The quality of this relationship does vary and depends largely on the type of collaborative arrangement agreed and its effectiveness. For example, where CMHCs offer prompt consultation and readily assume responsibility for their clients there is less friction than where such support is not so forthcoming. In this respect it should be emphasised that, as yet, many CMHCs are poorly equipped. Staff do not have individual offices or even desks, though there are usually interview rooms and a room for medical examinations. CMHCs typically have no secretarial support, and administrative and clerical tasks are performed by the therapists with the active help of clients. Other factors which are critical in determining the relationship between different elements of the psychiatric service are the personalities, perceived therapeutic roles and seniority of the staff, especially in the hospitals. The more senior the personnel the less kindly they take to changes which have neither been initiated nor are fully controlled by them. This understandable reaction is most likely to be manifest among nursing staff who have to maintain discipline and a sufficient degree of order to ensure the smooth operation of the institution. It is too early to decide whether the frictions are merely teething problems associated with any innovation or are of a more serious nature.

Private psychiatric hospitals and private 'office' practitioners continue to exist though no comprehensive statistics on their activities are rountinely published. My impression is one of a decrease in private inpatient numbers and an increase in consultations with office psychiatrists. With the introduction of the reform those regions and USLs which have been the most committed have preferred to own the available provisions in their area and not make use of private services on a contractual basis. In the south, however, regional administrations have been less enthusiastic about initiating the reform and continue to rely on provisions in the private sector. At the same time, since the introduction of the national health service, which completes the process of abolition of sickness insurance schemes and makes health care free at the point of consumption, people may have become more reluctant to enter some of the low-quality private institutions. Among middle and higher income groups, however, there seems to be an increase in consultations with office practitioners, especially those engaged in psychoanalytic psychotherapy.

The CMHC: its work and clientele

Collective work is viewed as a key factor for a successful service. The frequency of formal team meetings varies from daily in CMHCs with inpatient beds to weekly in other centres. The degree of informal collaboration among the staff is also very high. Formal supervision is avoided and relatively little is recorded in case notes. The staff tend to work in pairs, especially on domiciliary visits which account for about three-quarters of the total number of patient contacts (where centres have beds the number of domiciliary visits is lower). In domiciliary care, as well as non-urgent work, nurses and social workers are the principal agents, whilst psychiatrists are largely engaged in consultations at the centres and in crisis intervention (De Salvia 1982:180). The number of joint interventions varies from between a third and a half of all encounters (De Salvia, 1982; Lanteri 1982:288). The remainder of CMHC work is largely taken up by commitments to inpatient work in general hospitals or preventive work in family advice centres.

CMHCs set out to offer a service which caters for the totality of a person's needs rather than narrow psychiatric problems. In their work the centres do not differentiate, to any significant degree, between potential stages of care such as assessment, clinical treatment and rehabilitation. Instead they offer an eclectic therapeutic approach and provide support, counselling, medication and help in securing accommodation, education and employment. An extremely important and innovative part of their role has been advocacy work, which has included forging links with the media and local and national organisations. Of particular interest is the publicity they have been able to generate for 'de-institutionalisation ceremonies' of groups of patients about to leave hospital and for the public meetings on mental health which are part of their preventive campaign.

Only a few studies have given a systematic description of the work of the CMHCs. The most frequently occurring intervention appears to be clinical assessment and advice, followed by counselling, medication, social work assistance and hospitalisation (Telleschi 1982:412). In this respect it should be emphasised that psychotropic medicine, though continuing to be widely used, is given in the majority of cases in small dosages by international standards, even to patients receiving inpatient care in the old hospitals. The peak points of drug prescriptions are at the time of discharge from hospital and at subsequent crisis points, including re-admissions (Schittar et al., 1982). Electro-convulsive treatment and psychosurgery are not offered by the new services.

Referrals to the centres come from a variety of sources, but primarily they are made by the clients themselves or by the emergency services. Referrals by the family and the police are the next most important but account for less than a half of the referrals from the first two sources (Gallio 1982:262). Diagnostic data indicate that, in the first two years of the reform there was an increase in the number of referrals among clients with schizophrenic psychoses but a decline among those with severe cyclothymic disorders (De Salvia, 1982; Mistura, 1982; Righetti, 1982). The principal age-groups served are clients between 29 and 59 years. Numbers of female and male patients are roughly equivalent, in contrast to other Western countries (De Salvia et al., 1982; Gallio, 1982). Typically clients are poorly educated. A third of the male patients are employed; another third are in receipt of invalidity or retirement pensions. About 15 per cent are officially unemployed (Righetti, 1982; Petruzzellis, 1982).

THE EFFECTS OF THE REFORM

The psychiatric reform is taking place within the context of the creation of a national health service, a process which has been subject to considerable organisational and professional constraints. Thus, a comprehensive evaluation of the new mental health services will need to incorporate this wider dimension; and, since the

186

new health service was created less than five years ago, there is no significant empirical research on which to draw. One clear input criterion is the current geographical distribution of the newly organised mental health services. The evidence is that the reform has been more frequently and thoroughly introduced in northern and central regions. Some interesting innovations have occurred in the south, but generally the health authorities there have tried to stall the reform. The reasons for the sluggishness of reform in the south are complex, but the different political structure and the relatively heavy reliance on private psychiatric institutions which, in turn, try to protect their vested interests are certainly crucial factors (Piro 1982).

Three outcomes seem essential in any evaluation of the psychiatric reform: the effects of the reform on the clients; the response of professionals; and the reaction of the local community. At present research on these issues is meagre and the material that exists is largely drawn from official statistics or case studies derived from clinical records, rather than being the product of well-defined and systematic evaluative studies. Available data are mostly concerned with the effects on the clientele and, given the above restrictions and the small-scale of most of these studies, the implications tend to be rather speculative and the scope for generalisation at the national level is limited.

(a) The effects on the clientele

Some of the more robust data are the hospital inpatient statistics. All of the published statistics show a considerable reduction in numbers of inpatients in the post-reform period: from 54,000 in 1978 to 36,000 in 1982 (Montezemolo, 1983; and see the regional analyses in De Salvia et al., 1982). Significantly, too, this decline in inpatient numbers holds for private institutions (Simons 1980). The number of compulsory admissions has declined dramatically in the five years since the passing of the reform law in 1978; nationally the numbers fell from 31,000 in 1977 to 12,000 in 1979, and, in the case of Trieste, one of the pioneering centres of the reform, there have been only twelve compulsory admissions in the period 1978-1982 (Gallio, 1982). On the other hand, there have been wide local variations in the numbers of voluntary admissions, some areas reporting substantial increases (Bussolari, 1982; Righetti, 1982; Casagrande et al., 1982) whilst others a continuous decline (Attenasio et al., 1982). These regional disparities in voluntary admissions appear, inter alia, to be a function of the availability of the new inpatient units, the lack of places of refuge in the community, the availability of crisis intervention services, and patients' readiness to enter hospitals voluntarily. Average lengths of inpatient stays have also been reduced considerably; currently the mean stay is between fifteen and twenty days (Bottaccioli, 1982). There appear to be marked variations in the ratio of first-to-recurrent admissions: of the four published studies, Mistura (1982) reports a 1:1 ratio, Telleschi (1982) a ratio of 2:1 and Gallio (1982) and Righetti (1982) a ratio of 1:2. These are local studies and variations may be related to differences in the time-scale of closing the old psychiatric hospitals and the availability of new beds in CMHCs or general hospitals.

There is no evidence that the decline in compulsory admissions or the closure of psychiatric hospitals are leading to an increased use of the six prison hsopitals for psychiatric offenders. Nor is there evidence of an increase in the suicide rate among former psychiatric inpatients (CNR, 1981). The massive transfer of chronic inpatients to large hostels, nursing homes and old peoples homes, which has been a policy in certain EC countries, has not occurred in Italy. Most Italian ex-patients are either living in small-unit accommodation converted from hospital property, or in shared flats, or with their families in their home areas.

A number of former patients work together in cooperatives created during the period of dehospitalisation. These cooperatives receive contract work from public authorities and are engaged in cleaning, gardening, kitchen work and printing. The importance of this experience for ex-patients cannot be overstated; it is crucial for self respect, development of the capacities for mutual support and for independence. The cooperatives offer more flexible work than jobs in outside employment: there is an understanding reaction when a member is unwell; equally emphasis is put on personal responsibility toward the group and the importance of the consistency of the work experience (Gallio, 1982).

Some clients of the CMHCs receive financial assistance, either in the form of a monetary benefit or subsidised or free meals or accommodation. Only one study of financial assistance has been published and this refers to the clientele of the Trieste service. Of the 3000 clients seen by the community services in the city just over one-third were in receipt of some form of financial assistance, but only 20 per cent of the clients were totally dependent on these benefits (Mauri, 1983).

From the material available the effects of the reform on clients are varied. Reliable evidence on some of the qualitative aspects is missing. Yet the overall impact of the reform seems to be positive in that living conditions have improved materially and socially, avenues for new and more enriching opportunities have been opened up, and clients are treated with respect. Where the services function adequately clients receive continuous support. Issues such as the balance between organised activities and allowing clients to settle down to the routine of everyday life are open to debate, although the Italians clearly favour the latter option. The two major groups to benefit most from the reform have been the people already in psychiatric hospitals and mentally handicapped children.

Case Descriptions. Two vignettes will be presented: one of an adult and the other of a child. They represent a variety of issues, problems and methods of work. However, it is not claimed that they are typical of the client population. Usually case studies are unlikely to be accurately representative of a client group, as they tend to offer a holistic - and hence unique - picture of the person in his situation. Rather, the value of case descriptions lies in their contribution to the understanding of causes, processes, methods, outcomes and community reactions.

'I' is a fifty year old man of a peasant family. He emigrated to France where he married and had a son. Following the breakdown of his marriage he came back home and soon afterwards entered the psychiatric hospital (in 1963), diagnosed as suffering from paranoid schizophrenia. A series of recoveries, discharges to the family and readmissions followed until the death of his mother in 1970, when he came to hospital ostensibly as a permanent patient. In 1973, after an intensive period of work with him by a doctor and a social worker he started to work in the ex-patients' cooperative and to live in sheltered accommodation on the hospital site. However, during this period he was sent to a psychiatric prison as a result of a past episode of violent behaviour. His workmates together with the local newspaper mounted a public campaign to release him. This led to a reduction in his sentence from two years to six months. Upon leaving prison 'I' refused to go back to the hospital, instead demanding to be rehoused on his own. During the period of searching for adequate and permanent accommodation 'I' was in intensive contact not only with the community service but also with the mayor who acted almost as a mother substitute. Recently 'I' moved to a house in a nearby town. The area is new to him and the local psychiatric service is his only social resource (Bondioli, 1982, 52).

'S' is a seven year old boy who attends the first year class of the nursery school (i.e. four years below his age). He is the only child of middle aged parents of a poor working class background. Following a normal birth there were considerable problems in feeding and he used to cry endlessly. His mother suffered from eczema which made nappy changing an ordeal. His father had an industrial injury followed by an operation and a period of unemployment when 'S' was one year old. The mother then went out to work while 'S' was minded in a private nursery. He cried there so much that the mother had to take him back home where he was looked after by his grandmother, who was described as cold and dominant. 'S' came to the attention of the psychiatric service only at the point of entry to obligatory education (i.e. when he was six years old).

'S' looks like a five year old child, small, thin and with beautiful black eyes. At the beginning he refused to enter school and would continue to cry the whole day. Later his behaviour alternated between being aggressive or terrified of the other children. A period of intensive work took place with the mother on her own whilst another worker was engaged with the child. The ordinary teachers were also involved. Today, a year later, 'S' comes willingly to school. He plays with the other children, although he is still a little apprehensive about being touched by them. Nowadays, 'S' sings, eats, smiles and rarely cries.

He still says little and only now has begun to make some of the most basic logical connections. Intellectually his performance is still far from that of an ordinary seven year old, though mental retardation has been ruled out. The service has now to decide whether he should stay for another year in the safe environment of the nursery school or be moved to an elementary school (Arezzo Childrens Service: history recounted by the psychologist in charge).

(b) The response of professionals

No systematic study has been carried out on the impact of the reform on its executive force: the professionals. The total number of staff hardly changed between 1978 and 1981, although psychiatrists, nurses and social workers moved from the hospital base to the community services operated from the CMHCs. The statistics that are available indicate a small increase in the number of these three groups and a considerable decline in the number of administrative and technical staff (Gallio, 1981; Ruccia, 1982). When compared with the pre-reform period, the reduction in the number of lower-level administrators is even more pronounced.

Professional roles have changed considerably from those of the pre-reform era. The traditional division of labour is maintained in so far as only a doctor may prescribe medication, only a social worker will deal with financial assistance, and only psychiatrists are the official directors of a service. Every staff member, however, is involved in providing emotional support and counselling, in home visiting, in work with relatives, and in contacting other agencies on behalf of the client. As team leaders, psychiatrists tend to assume more of the public relations function and initiate contacts with the higher echelon of the local government administration. When on a home visit it is natural for any staff member to help in carrying out manual tasks if this is seen as therapeutic (e.g. cleaning, peeling potatoes etc). It is also natural for clients to answer the phone in a CMHC, to eat at the same table as the staff and to remain in the rooms where staff do their office work. The fact that there are no private offices, combined with the absence of secretarial support or a formal appointment system, encourages a highly informal and collective existence for everyone: staff and clients. Some staff members not only attend meetings at their centres, but also a large number of meetings devoted to more general issues, including relations with the administration of the health service and joint meetings with trade unionists on the operation and defence of the reform.

These new and evolving roles have been the product of a long process of inter-professional collaboration and the shared experience of de-institutionalisation. Current newcomers to the community services have not benefitted from that experience, and the various meetings and joint work may in part overcome this deficit but, in my view, are not an adequate substitute for an organised training programme. It is psychiatrists and nurses who have had to undergo the most radical modifications of their traditional roles. While nurses stand to gain in power and prestige from the reform, the opposite may be true of psychiatrists who have had to adjust to a situation where their authority and expertise are constantly challenged. It is scarcely surprising that the major professional opposition to the reform has come from within medicine. In some cases mere lip-service has been paid to new roles and, at best, the letter rather than the spirit of the reform has been put into practice. In these situations conflicts, ostensibly focused on leadership styles and personality clashes, conceal profound ideological and methodological disagreements. These issues are unlikely to be explicitly aired at routine staff meetings, though they are discussed at Psichiatria Democratica meetings. Those doctors most likely to be disenchanted with the reform have tended to opt for further professional training and a move into university clinics or private practice, a trend which has been accelerated by the very limited opportunities for promotion within the national health service. Other dissenters - and these include nurses as well as doctors - have sought to cling on to as much of their traditional roles as they can.

Power relations within a staff group tend to be more egalitarian than they used to be, although formally each CMHC is headed by a psychiatrist. This state of affairs is partly reflected in salary scales where differentials among the various disciplines are considerably lower than, for example, in Britain.

The position of psychoanalysts vis-a-vis the reform is of particular interest since they represent an elite within psychiatry. The reform generated considerable hostility among psychoanalysts, since its originators stated their explicit preference for a social and collective therapeutic model. Analysts who have been prepared to work within the new system have had to respond to all the needs of the clientele, many of whom have not traditionally been served by psychoanalysis. Again, there has been some move away from public service and into private practice; others have taken up work as emergency psychiatrists in general hospitals and, thus, remove themselves from a chronic caseload. At the same time, however, there is a movement within child psychiatry to use more family therapy and psychoanalytic concepts.

The effects of the reform on professionals are much more varied than on the clients. For some, the Psichiatria Democratica movement has become almost a way of life; for others, the reform has meant considerable change in outlook and role. Yet, for others, the impact has been small in so far as the reform has not been internalised or it has led to the wish to withdraw from public service. The main shared impact has been the requirement to consider seriously one's views on and attitudes toward the mentally ill, mental illness, professionalism and society.

(c) The reaction of the local community

In those regions where reform occurred prior to the legislation in 1978, there was no sign of widespread public protest. Active minority engagement for reform coexisted with majority indifference. The members of PD realised therefore that they had to win community support to implement their ideas. To this end they opened up a debate on psychiatry at several levels: discussions with local political parties of both left and right; negotiation with the local and regional health administration; the initiation of public events, such as celebrations of the opening up of the hospital and promotion of public performances by patients; the involvement of all the media in the campaign; and maintaining dialogue with groups and individuals who were critical of, or who had had bad experiences of the new services. The PD movement did not attempt to organise relatives, ex-patients and other interest parties into voluntary support groups, since such activities are not a tradition in Italy. On the other hand, PD sought an international platform for its work and is a founder member of the international network for alternative psychiatry (Reseau International).

Italians have tended to assume that services which they pay for directly are likely to be superior to those provided as of right. The old insurance schemes reimbursing health care agents on a fee-for-service system no doubt encouraged this view. Despite a certain preference for private medicine, this is not within the reach of the majority of the population. This majority, then, accepts the reform as a necessity, though a degree of scepticism remains. The general public meets former patients of the mental hospital in coffee bars and on the street; at times some ex-patients get drunk and quarrelsome and complaints about these incidents are made to the mental health services and receive serious attention (for an example see Ramon, 1983). On the whole the prevailing attitude is one of treating ex-patients like everyone else, depending on the specific context of social relationships.

A few relatives' organisations exist, some of which oppose the reform on the grounds of inadequate provision for 'dangerous' patients. Not surprisingly, they are centred in cities with a well-developed private sector and a weak and poorly-staffed public service, of which Rome is the prime example. So far these organisations have not made positive proposals for change, apart from their wish to see the return of locked hospital wards. Other relatives' groups support the reform in principle.

How much does the service cost the community? Very little has appeared on the financing of the new services. Trieste has published the details of its budget for 1970-1977, the number of staff during 1969-1981, and the cost of welfare benefits for clients for 1981 (Gallio, 1982). The figures do not take account of the rate of inflation (which is higher in Italy than in most other European countries) or for what it would have cost to continue to maintain the old psychiatric hospitals. The findings show an increase in wages despite the overall decrease in the number of employees (from 544 to 477), an increase in maintenance costs for existing premises, and a decrease in the amount spent on drugs, welfare benefits and capital investment.

194

Costing calculations from Ferrara show that maintaining a patient in a psychiatric hospital is considerably more expensive than a comparable bed in a general hospital or his upkeep in a group home (Missiroli, 1984). Recent information from Bari demonstrates that keeping a patient in a private psychiatric hospital is three times more expensive than his maintenance in a public psychiatric hospital. Similarly, a place in a private group home is more expensive than a place in an equivalent public establishment (Canosa, 1984; Di Noya, 1984).

Currently there are three levels of public debate on the reform. The first is concerned with the issue of whether the Law should be modified (for a summary of the proposals see Cravedi, 1982). Those asking for modification would like to re-introduce open psychiatric wards in general hospitals, coupled with small units for the chronically ill outside the general hospital. This lobby is formed by right-wing political parties, as well as 'traditional' psychiatrists and relatives' organizations, and includes the current Minister of Health. Those opposing such a move come from the majority of the mental health service employees, the trade unions and the left-of-centre parties. The debate so far has taken the form of a series of public meetings and petitions, as well as the lobbying of parliament. The second level of the debate is focused on the future of the now largely empty premises of the old psychiatric hospitals. In one town there has been a successful conversion of a hospital into a secondary school while, in another, an attempt to create a technical college failed. Elsewhere proposals range from establishing a community centre to the provision of public housing. Although these debates do not attract a large audience, the very fact that they form a legitimate part of party politics, and that the health service is being made accountable to the citizens in a direct way, should be welcomed. Debate at the third level is concerned with the joint impact of the creation of the national health service and the psychiatric reform. The former is, of course, of more widespread relevance for all Italians. The health service is still in its infancy and has not yet succeeded in recruiting sufficient numbers of GPs committed to it, as distinct from those who have been attracted for the financial incentives it offers. Hospital-based physicians are currently in a state of near-open rebellion against the community orientation of the reformed health service and are locked in direct confrontation with many regional health authorities.

In this present climate the Italian psychiatric reform has tended to become the scapegoat of doctors, the administration and the general public. I believe that the reform is no longer judged mainly on its own merits and limitations, but on whether it lends support to a particular position vis-a-vis the general health service. The impact of the psychiatric reform defies simple conclusions: naturally it has greater significance for patients and those directly involved with the mentally ill. These people are to be found among its most ardent critics and most devoted defenders. The majority of the population stays silent and largely indifferent.

THE CURRENT BALANCE OF THE REFORM

A combination of factors were crucial in promoting innovation and reform of the mental health services; this fortunate combination may be peculiar to Italy, but none is in essence unique to this country. Necessary but of themselves insufficient conditions were the poor state of the mental health services and the lack of an alternative plan for reform from the psychiatric establishment. The existence of an enthusiastic professional movement with a detailed programme of reform, the strong autonomy of the Italian regions, and the desire of the socialist regions for radical experimentation in social policy, including mental health care, were both necessary and sufficient change-promoting factors.

(a) Positive outcomes

1. Psychiatric services in large cities have shown they can cope without psychiatric hospitals. Such a situation has not created havoc, nor has it posed a threat to the community. Trieste, for example, has existed for several years with only 1.3 beds per 100000 population, none of which is in a locked ward. A similar picture emerges in other cities (Mauri, 1983).

196

2. The material conditions and the quality of life of patients have demonstrably been improved.

3. New clients are not exposed to the risk of long-term stigmatisation of having been in mental hospitals.

4. The degree of informality, flexibility and attention to the totality of the person's needs which characterizes the new services commends itself in terms of accessibility, care and respect for clients.

5. The attention now paid to social factors in the aetiology of psychiatric disorders, and in clinical practice, redresses the previous imbalance in which the relevance of these factors was underestimated. However, this has not led to the neglect of psychological, biochemical and organic factors.

6. The genuine respect for ordinary people's values, even when dissenting from them, facilitates the gradual acceptance of the reform by the majority of the population. A key factor here has been the regular contact professionals have with a wide range of groups in the community.

7. The comparative costs of the reform have yet to be fully assessed. The new services may not be cheaper to run, at least in the short-term, but it is doubtful whether they are more expensive than maintaining the hospital-based system, many of whose institutions would have required massive repairs and refurbishment.

(b) Remaining problems

1. The reform has not spread evenly throughout Italy and the southern regions remain less enthusiastic than the rest of the country. The recession means that it will be all the more difficult to overcome this resistance. Furthermore, economic cuts have been imposed nationally and are taking their toll in terms of plans to reduce staff ratios and the failure to create sufficient places of temporary refuge and permanent accommodation for ex-patients. There continues to be inadequate investment in industrial rehabilitation and vocational services.

2. The present attitude of hospital-based physicians towards the concentration of all paramedical services such as speech therapy in

the general hospital. In some places the
insistence that clients will only be seen in
the hospital or that people will be treated
only if medical needs have been identified
amounts to an attempt to impose the return to
a hospital-based service instead of a
community health service. It also limits the
accessibility of the service and reintroduces
the dominance of medical power.

3. The politicisation of the whole administrative
    structure leads to lengthy decision-making
    processes in which the quality of the service
    suffers, or, at times, to decisions solely
    motivated by political considerations.
    Although this politicisation can have positive
    aspects in making services more accountable to
    elected representatives, the right balance has
    yet to be found.

4. There are disturbing signs that some national
    politicians, responding to public criticism of
    the national health service, are prepared to
    sacrifice psychiatric reform for the sake of
    pacifying opponents of the general health
    reform.

5. The reform can only progress in line with the
    public's response to it. The need to generate
    positive reactions from the community has been
    recognised by PD since its early days. The
    price to be paid is a slower pace of change
    than many reformers would like. Furthermore,
    there is an essential dilemma, as yet
    unresolved, of turning a blind eye to the
    central issues in the lives of many clients by
    asking them to conform to a life-style which
    may be the primary source of their
    difficulties. In this respect it is
    interesting - and curious - that PD has not
    been active on issues such as the position of
    working class women in Italy or the isolation
    of many ex-patients from basic social
    networks.

6. The desire to move away from formal
    professionalism and the fear of privatisation
    of clients' problems has created an ambivalent
    attitude to various forms of psychotherapy.
    There is a noticeable reluctance to
    acknowledge these therapies as being distinct
    from common-sense approaches. This has led to
    a failure to examine whether all the methods
    being employed are mutually consistent, or are
    in consonance with the manifest values of the

new services. Furthermore, there is a neglect of formal training of new staff in these therapies and, therefore, a danger that the benefits to be derived from such interventions are not being fully exploited.

7. A related issue to the one raised above is the prevailing attitude to family members of adult clients. They are expected to support the client and to be able to carry on with their life as usual, despite the fact that they are in a crisis too. In a well-functioning service family members will be supported during the intensive crisis period to enable them to maintain a positive atmosphere for the client. However, these relatives are rarely considered in their own right, in comparison to the parents of a handicapped child who are approached more as persons than just as parents. The reasons for this omission do not lie in the theoretical approach, which actually emphasises the need to work with the whole primary unit. It seems that the identification with the index client is probably the main factor which limits the perception of family members as persons in need in their own right. In addition, family members are often reluctant to accept such intervention since it puts them on a par with the patient.

8. The unevenness of the spread of the reform throughout the country and the decentralisation typical of Italy had a beneficial effect at the initial stage of the reform in facilitating experimentation. Two main deficiencies are apparent now: a system which prevents the repetition of mistakes from one place to another is desperately needed, but is virtually non-existent; and, as already mentioned, the reform has been more successful in the north and centre than in the south of Italy, due primarily to differences in social structure. People who live in the south, however, judge the reform by its local results.

Conclusions

Though the national reform was instigated only in 1978, the reform movement is now well into its second decade and there is a need to sustain enthusiasm for what is becoming routine work.

Given the inevitable variations in service provision and practice, new ways will have to be found of maintaining the unity of the movement. The untimely death in 1980 of the man most closely associated with the reform, Professor Franco Basaglia, has brought forward a crisis in leadership. At present, PD has created a collective leadership which is primarily addressing itself to marshalling support to resist the modification of the reform law.

Despite the considerable difficulties which confront the Italian psychiatric reform, I believe its strategy and the positive outcomes already achieved offer several lessons for other European countries. Italy has shown that it is possible not only to close down hospitals, but also to provide a community service respectful of the needs of its clients. It has shown how crucial it is literally to empty the hospital in order to forestall its gradual re-establishment by all those who only superficially share the stated aims of de-institutionalisation.

Such policies require the existence of:

1. A radical professional movement supported by politicians, at least in one part of the country, who are committed to wide-ranging social reform.

2. The key role of adequate organisation and relationships with local, regional and national power groups must be fully recognised.

3. New and often unconventional alliances are possible.

4. There needs to be a critical evaluation of the role of professionals; a reluctance to confront this issue can prevent professional groups from creating fruitful alliances.

5. A multi-disciplinary professional movement is an absolute necessity.

6. There must be a clear vision of the future, coupled with well-defined plans and a collective will to carry them out.

REFERENCES

Adamo, P. (1982) Epidemiologia e Ricerca Operativa. Indagine Preliminare, Empirico-Descrittiva, sullo Stato della Psichiatria in Calabria. In: De Salvia and D. Crepet, (ed) Psichiatria Senza Manicomio. Feltrinelli, Rome, pp.59-74.

Attenasio, L.et al (1982) Arezzo: Attuazione della Riforma Sanitaria ed Attualità della Lotta Antiistituzionale. De Salvia, ibid, pp.78-92.

Balduzzi, E. C. (1981) La Loi Psychiatrique du 13.5.1978: Introduction au Probleme. Information Psychiatrique, 57, 5, pp. 567-580.

Basaglia, F. (1980) Problems of Law and Psychiatry: The Italian Experience. International Journal of Law and Psychiatry, 3, 3, pp.17-37.

Bercil-Taini, A. ot al (1982) Università e Nuova Psichiatria Salute e Territorio, Regione di Toscana, Firenze, pp.57-61.

Bondioli, C. (1982) Manicomio, Servizi, Terapia. Sapere, LXXXV, pp. 50-54.

Bottacioli, G. (1982) La Rete dei Servizi Psichiatrici in Umbria. In: De Salvia, op.cit., pp.109-120.

Bussolari, A. et al (1982) Riflessioni sulla Possibilità di Ricomposizione Tecnico-Sociale dell' Intervento Psichiatrico in un Servizio di Territorio della Provincia di Bologna. In: De Salvia, op.cit. pp.121-134.

Casagrande, D. et al (1982) Demanicomializzazione e Neomanicomializzazione nella Realtà di Venezia. In: De Salvia, op.cit., pp.156-172.

Canosa, R. (1984) Nonostante Il Manicomio: La Pratica di un Servizio Psichiatrico nella Periferia di Bari. Psicologia, Lavoro, Società, Rome.

Cerletti, V. (1961) 'Italy'. In: L. Bellak, (ed). Contemporary European Psychiatry, Grove Press, New York.

CNR-Progetto finalizzato medicina preventiva (1981) La Riforma Psichiatria, Il Pensiero Scientifico, Rome.

Cravedi, B. (1982) Analisi Comparativa della Proposte Relative alla Psichiatria, Salute e Territorio, Regione Toscana, Firenze, pp.4-42.

De Plato, G. and Minguzzi, G.F. (1981) A short history of psychiatric renewal in Italy. Psychiatry and Social Science, 1, pp.71-77.

De Salvia, D. et al (1982) La Psichiatria Cambiata. In: De Salvia, op.cit., pp.173-195.

Di Noya, G. (1984) La Valutazione dei Servizi Comunitari di Riabilitazione. L'Esperienza della Provincia di Bari. Paper given at the conference 'La Riabilitazione Psichiatrica: Tra Riforma e Contoriforma', Modena.

Gallio, G. (1981). De-Instituzionalaz e Cultura della Miseria. Paper available from the directorate of psychiatric services, Trieste.

Gallio, G. et al (1982) Note per la Lettura del Modello Organizzativo dei Servizi Psichiatrici a Trieste. In: De Salvia, op.cit., pp.239-265.

Gramsci, A. (1971) Selections from the Prison Notebooks (by Hoare, Q). Lawrence and Wishart, London.

I Tetti Rossi: Dal Manicomio alla Società, Mazzotta, Arezzo, 1978.

Lanteri, A. et al (1982) La Pratica Territoriale. Storia e Risultati dell' Équipe di Salute Mentale di Settimo Torinese. In: De Salvia, op.cit, pp.279-299.

Mauri, D. (1983) (ed) La Libertà E Terapeutica? Fetrinelli, Rome.

Missiroli, A. (1984) Statistica dei Servizi Psichiatrici. USL 10, Ferrara, unpublished.

Mistura, S. (1982) L'esperienza Psichiatrica a Fiorenzuola d'Arda. In: De Salvia, op.cit, pp.309-327.

Montezemolo, A. et al (1983). Mental Health Services in the Community - The Italian Experience, Conference 'Contemporary Issues in Mental Health', London, April 21, 1983.

Mosher, L. (1982) Italy's Revolutionary Mental Health Law: An Assessment, American Journal of Psychiatry, 139, 2, pp.199-203.

Petruzzellis, V. et al (1982) I Nuovi Servizi Psichiatrici Tra Controllo Manicomiale e Nuova Cronicità nel Territorio. Il Caso di Palermo. In: De Salvia, op.cit, pp.346-358.

Piro, S. (1982) Leggi sulla Psichiatria e Meridione d'Italia. In: De Salvia, op.cit,pp.360-370.

Ramon, S. (1983) Psichiatria Democratica: A Case Study of an Italian Community Mental Health Service. International Journal of Health Services, 13, 2 pp.307-324.

Righetti, A. et al (1982) Il Servizio di Diagnosi e Cura nel Circuito Psichiatrico. In: De Salvia, op.cit,pp.37-387.

Ruccia, M. et al (1982) I Servizi Psichiatrici in Basilicata: Bilancio a Quattro Anni dalla Legge 180. In: De Salvia, op.cit, pp.388-401.

Schittar, L. et al (1982) Gli Psicofarmaci Chi Li
    Dà Chi Li Prende. I Quaderni, a cura del
    centro ricerche e documentazione del Centro
    Igiene Mentale di Pordenone.
Simons, T. (1980) Psychiatrie im Übergang: von der
    Verwaltung der sozialen Ausgrenzung zum
    sozialen Dienst. In: Simons, T. (ed). Absage
    an die Anstalt: Programm und Realität der
    demokratischen Psychiatrie in Italien. Campus.
    Frankfurt, pp.83-149.
Telleschi, R. (1982) L'approccio con i Nuovi
    Utenti di un Servizio Psichiatrico
    Territoriale a Milano. Caratteristiche della
    Richiesta e della Tisposta. De Salvia, op.cit,
    pp.402-416.
Vislie, L. (1981) Integration of Handicapped
    Children in Italy: A view from the outside.
    OECD, Paris.
Zanetti, M. (1974) La Realtà manicomiale ed i
    servizi di salute mentale nella prospettiva
    della riforma santaria. Convegno dell' UPI,
    Trieste, pp.25-75.

Chapter Nine

MENTAL HEALTH CARE IN LUXEMBOURG

Danielle Hansen-Koenig and Jean-Jacques Meisch

Conscious that the standards of care posed an
increasing problem, it was at the beginning of the
Seventies that the public authorities in the Grand
Duchy initiated a reform of mental health services.
The situation facing policy-makers at that time was
not encouraging: apart from psychiatrists in office
practice who worked with less serious clinical
caseloads, psychiatric care was largely centred on a
single hospital with 1100 beds providing 3.7 beds per
thousand population. Here 95 per cent of inpatients
were compulsorily detained, 60 per cent of them being
long-stay patients who were likely to be hospitalised
until they died. Medical and paramedical staff were
few in number and resources for occupational and
industrial therapy extremely scarce. Other services,
such as psychiatric units in general hospitals, day
hospitals and specialist psychogeriatric provisions
were, at best, in embryonic state. Consequently, the
more affluent patient tended to go to hospitals in
neighbouring countries enjoying a higher reputation
than the Luxembourg services.
    Policies since the Seventies have been directed
towards the establishment of a comprehensive,
community psychiatric service with the emphasis on
prevention and continuity of care.

THE ORGANISATION OF MENTAL HEALTH SERVICES

The Ministry of Public Health is responsible for
policy and the planning of health services. The
principal instrument for hospital planning is the
health map ('carte sanitaire') which is a similar
process to that employed in France. Because doctors
and the majority of nurses are trained abroad, the

Ministry's functions in medical and nursing education are largely confined to supervising the state diploma granting Luxembourg citizens with foreign qualifications the right to practice. In addition, the Ministry supervises nursing schools in the Grand Duchy, which offer general and psychiatric nursing as basic qualifications. The Ministry of Labour and Social Security is the relevant authority regulating the social insurance system. Since 1978 sickness insurance has been provided by seven funds for wage and salary earners and coverage extends to 90 per cent of the population. Those people who are not insured are eligible for means-tested social assistance (aide sociale) to cover medical expenses. The government pays 50 per cent of the administrative costs of the funds and also subsidises the cost of long and expensive treatments, for which there has been an additional mandatory insurance scheme since 1974.

Hospitals operate on a daily fee basis, whilst doctors in office practice receive a fee for each item of service performed, the fee catalogue being a product of direct negotiations between medical professional bodies and sickness insurance funds. Patients have direct access to medical specialists. As in France and Belgium there is a 'ticket modérateur' system: the lower-paid receive 100 per cent reimbursement of the costs of treatment, but others are liable for a personal contribution (ticket modérateur) of 25 per cent of treatment costs. Many people take out additional private insurance through one of the mutual assurance societies to offset the ticket modérateur.

PRESENT SERVICE PROVISION

The neuropsychiatric hospital continues to function, but capacity has declined to 800 beds (2.2 per thousand population) and there are now other inpatient facilities. At present, certified admissions comprise 50 per cent of the total. The average length of stay has been reduced and the emphasis is now on rehabilitation and re-integration. Since 1974 there has been a considerable increase in the number of mental health personnel. Currently a total of seven psychiatrists and one general practitioner work in multi-disciplinary teams in inpatient services and at mental health centres. In addition, there are now 24 psychiatrists in office practice (6.5 office psychiatrists per 100,000 population).

A range of day care, sheltered workshops and residential provisions have been created, largely through initiatives in the private and charitable sector. These agencies are non profit-making organisations and receive subsidies from public funds or operate under contract to the social insurance schemes. There has also been a significant improvement in specialist inpatient services, most notably in psychogeriatric assessment and treatment provisions. A new forensic unit has been established and services for alcoholic and drug dependent patients extended. These latter services function as therapeutic communities and great importance is attached to social and occupational rehabilitation and after care.

Legislation

The 1880 Act, which is modelled on Belgian legislation, regulates compulsory admissions and provides for the inspection of establishments licensed to receive certified patients. The law requires that a medical certificate be completed by an independent doctor who must give an account of the current mental state of the patient and provide grounds for admission. Patients have the right of appeal to a tribunal which may commission an independent medical report. Until 1982 all certified patients lost their civil rights and control over their property; now these restrictions may only be applied by authorisation of a tutelary judge acting on medical advice.

The legislation is in the process of being revised and a bill, currently before parliament, seeks to introduce a number of new measures, whilst maintaining the legal safeguards of the 1880 Act. The bill proposes that there should be a period of clinical observation prior to certification with subsequent periodic reviews by an independent committee of experts. There is to be increased use of trial leave and forms of trial discharge which may be appropriate in individual cases. The bill will submit to much stricter rules the use of clinical trials and all treatments whose safety and efficacy have not been adequately established. Finally, the bill stresses that, wherever possible, care should be provided in the patient's own milieu; where admission is necessary, all efforts should be made to maintain the patient's links with the family and wider social group.

Conclusion

The past fifteen years have seen the beginnings of a transformation of mental health care in the Grand Duchy, from a custodial neuropsychiatric and hospital-based service to one which is increasingly community based. More effort needs to be expended in extending domiciliary, outpatient and day care provisions, as well as improving the training of staff in psychiatric units in general hospitals. However, the outstanding problem to be resolved is finding an appropriate means of coordinating the various public, private and voluntary agencies active in this expanded services network.

This chapter has been translated and edited from the original French by Steen Mangen.

Chapter Ten

MENTAL HEALTH CARE IN THE NETHERLANDS

Tom van der Grinten

Dutch mental health services originate in private charity and the assistance municipalities gave to indigent lunatics. It was not until the middle of the last century that specific institutions for the mentally ill were created (1). During this period the understanding and treatment of madness increasingly became a medical preserve, a process consolidated by the Insanity Act of 1841 (Krankzinnigenwet) which, among other things, instituted an inspectorate of asylums. Like the French law of 1838, the Act charged the provincial governments with the task of ensuring that an adequate number of asylums were built, though central government did not vote funds for this purpose. Thus, provincial governments were left merely to exhort and persuade the churches and other charitable bodies to found these new institutions on their behalf. Though the Act did represent some measure of advance in public policy, it could not provide a solution for the growing overcrowding of the asylums.

It was not until 1884, when a new Insanity Act was passed, that some amelioration of the situation was possible. Provincial governments became more explicitly responsible for guaranteeing adequate provision of asylums and the municipal authorities were charged with meeting the costs of caring for the inmates. The Act stimulated the creation of many new institutions, although only in Noord-Holland were they founded and administered by the province. In the remaining ten provinces the authorities continued to delegate this task to the churches and other charities. Through this Act a general inspectorate of asylums was established for the whole country, the oldest inspectorate in the field of health in the Netherlands. However, the most important provisions of both the 1841 and the 1884 Insanity Acts were not concerned with the relatively few stipulations on the planning and financing of the asylums, but with procedures governing compulsory admission and legal guarantees protecting against unlawful detention.

The 1884 Insanity Act and its amendments remains the basic legislation regulating compulsory admissions, even though it has always been the object of controversy. Indeed, soon after its implementation there were criticisms that its effects were too conservative, being primarily concerned with the police function: i.e. the maintenance of public order. Its adversaries argued that the law did not provide a means of ensuring adequate care and protection of patients. In addition, there was no legislative support for local schemes in the late nineteenth-century of placing patients with families (boarding-out). An important amendment in 1904 made voluntary admissions possible to licensed institutions and provided for the creation of open wards. However, it soon became evident that the legal position of the growing number of voluntary patients was in essence no better than those compulsorily detained; indeed, voluntary patients were not protected by the provisions of the insanity acts. This situation was only comprehensively reviewed by government in the 1960s, despite the fact that, since the 1920s, there had been a dramatic shift in the nature of admissions, so that, by 1983, voluntary admissions comprised 85% of the total.

The years up to the Second World War were a period of new hospital construction. Existing institutions diversified both in functions and specialisms and there was a large increase in staff and in-patient turnover. In the years following World War Two Maxwell Jones' model of the therapeutic community enjoyed a certain currency. Although there was scepticism later about its general applicability and therapeutic communities have suffered from cuts in government budget, they remain in operation in ten hospitals or psychiatric units.

Mental health services outside hospitals developed incrementally, in the train of the establishment of the national network of asylums. Initially, services were a direct sequel of institutional work and were restricted to a few localities, where they were run by charities and the churches. Gradually, the increasing numbers of in-patient admissions, the rise in costs of care, and the introduction of therapeutic methods such as industrial and occupational therapy which were also applicable outside the institutions, resulted in a demand for extra-mural care. The beginnings of a real growth in community-based provisions can be traced back to the 1920s, when the first psychiatric follow-up services were created. The earliest clinics, founded in 1926, were established by the asylums and were inspired by contemporary experiments in community care in the German towns of Erlangen and Gelsenkirchen(2)

These extra-mural services were gradually assimilated in the new 'social psychiatric services' offering a range of preventive and follow-up care. The new services were established from the early 1930s onwards and were independent of the mental hospitals. The reason for the bifurcation of administrative responsibility for inpatient and 'community' services lies in the failure of many hospitals to undertake catchment area functions, despite the intentions of the Insanity Act. The majority of mental hospitals, managed by the churches and charities, reserved the right to admit patients from the whole country and therefore did not have to confront the problems of after care.

The foundation of the Dutch social psychiatric services (SPD) is above all associated with the name of Dr. A. Querido. At the request of the city of Amsterdam he designed a system of pre- and post-institutional psychiatric care, which has been applied since 1934 in a municipal Social Psychiatric Service. The interest shown by the city authority was not in the first place occasioned by legal obligations or by humanitarian or therapeutic considerations, but economic necessity. In the years of recession in the early 1930s the city was faced with financing a relatively large number of admissions from depleted municipal funds. Extra-mural services were identified as one means of reducing this financial burden, at the same time as offering services more appropriate to the needs of the patient. With the twin goals of increasing discharges from local mental hospitals and preventing new and re-admissions, where possible, Querido created a domiciliary-based service available twenty-four hours a day. Contacts with general practitioners, schools and the police were developed and a 'liaison' service offered. All in-patient

210

admissions were regulated by the Social Psychiatric Service. Before the Second World War other large cities followed the example of Amsterdam by setting up social psychiatric services with a staff of social psychiatrists and nurses who had received a social psychiatric training.

The real expansion in social psychiatric services came after the Second World War and owed much to the initiative of private organisations and charities. The private services did attempt to emulate the Amsterdam model, but in practice they failed to offer a comprehensive service. Round-the-clock availability and the regulation of in-patient admissions, for example, scarcely developed at all and, increasingly, the focus of their work became counselling and psychotherapy for those with less severe disorders.

The late 1920s and early 1930s were also a period of expansion in the clientele of psychiatry. The first child guidance clinics (MOB), for example, were established at this time by private bodies and their work was much influenced by their American counterparts. From the start there was an emphasis on multi-disciplinary teamwork which was alien to contemporary Dutch psychiatry and, consequently, the clinics did not receive immediate acceptance within the profession or from the public authorities. The churches were also active in creating new services. They were concerned about the threat to the family posed by the economic depression and the new sexual ethics advocated by the neo-malthusians. Their solution was to set up marital and family guidance centres (LVG) fashioned after the German 'Eheberatungsstelle'. The religious origin of these centres was initially reflected in the composition of the staff, which, in addition to social workers and sessional work by doctors and psychiatrists, included clergymen. In the Thirties, too, there were the beginnings of specialist services for alcoholics. Later to be known as 'consultation bureaux for alcohol and drugs' (CAD), major expansion came after the War, again due to private endeavours. Finally, the first institute for medical psychology (now called institutes for multidisciplinary psychotherapy (IMP)) was opened in 1940. Initially, the staff were exclusively medically-qualified and they concentrated their work on those suffering the ill effects of war. After demobilisation of the Netherlands, later in the same year, the institute devoted itself to the treatment of patients with neurotic disorders. Over the years these institutes have widened their activities and the change of name reflects their emphasis on a multi-disciplinary approach to psychotherapy.

DEVELOPMENTS SINCE 1960

As time went on, community-based services achieved a considerable degree of informal collaboration and, since the early 1960s, organisational integration has become an explicit policy of government. I have emphasised that these services are largely administered by the churches and other charities; however, the government has gradually assumed responsibility for almost all financing and has increasingly regulated their activities with regard to training programmes, minimum standards of care, and their organisation and administration. Apart from their origins which are independent of the mental hospitals, their common characteristic is an approach which relies heavily on multi-disciplinary team-work. This emphasis continued in the 1960s and the services acquired increasing public and political support, whilst mental hospitals were being criticised on humanitarian, therapeutic and economic grounds. The high regard paid to psychotherapy and government subsidies for non-residential psychotherapeutic services have provided a catalyst for their further growth.

The force of criticism of the mental hospital in the 1960s encouraged innovation and the wider acceptance of new therapeutic approaches already adopted in some institutions. The number of in-patient facilities offering care for specific groups grew considerably: alcohol and drug-dependent units; institutions for the criminal offender; and psychogeriatric units. Many of the psychiatric units in general hospitals were also built in this period. Most of the larger general hospitals now have units and they account for a considerable proportion of psychiatric admissions. The units have tended to operate on classical neuropsychiatric lines and many psychiatrists in independent office practice have their consultation rooms within them (3). Until comparatively recently there was no national policy regulating the development of these diverse forms of inpatient provision, and the assessment of the need for these services was left to the charitable organisations administering them.

212

Psychiatric hospitals and units in general hospitals were relatively slow to establish their own outpatient services. By the end of the 1960s, for example, only five hospitals operated outpatient clinics. Their establishment was rapid in the 1970s and all hospitals and units currently have clinics which offer follow-up treatment, as well as care for patients who have never been admitted. To a considerable extent the work of these clinics overlaps with that of the social psychiatric services; this has led to some degree of competition in practice, a characteristic also of the relationship between office psychiatrists and other forms of outpatient care. Social psychiatric services are now being by-passed by some general practitioners who make direct referrals to hospital services. Similarly, some hospitals no longer refer discharged patients to those services, but refer them to their own outpatient clinics. The social psychiatric services also face competition from independent 'crisis centres' in several large cities which are open twenty-four hours a day, a provision that is not available in all of the social psychiatric services.

Day care and non-inpatient residential services have also been comparatively recent developments. They offer a range of supportive and rehabilitative services financed through social insurance and welfare schemes. As yet, sheltered accommodation occupies a modest place in Dutch mental health care. It is estimated that, in 1980, there were about 4,200 places in day care and residential services for the mentally ill.

THE ORGANISATION, FINANCING AND ADMINISTRATION OF DUTCH HEALTH SERVICES

Dutch social, health and educational services owe their origin to private and charitable bodies rather than to the initiatives of public authorities. The key organisations have been the Protestant and Catholic churches, although later other charitable bodies become involved. Thus, the characteristic of many Dutch services is their denominational adherence: there are Protestant facilities, Catholic facilities and non-denominational facilities. The role of central and local authorities has been governed by the

213

'subsidiary principle': i.e. the responsibility for service provision is delegated to the churches and charities; public authorities have direct responsibility for a restricted range of activities, notably in the field of public health, and exercise a default authority if these organisations fail to meet their obligations. Therefore, though the financing of mental health care depends on public funds, the public authorities' direct involvement in the actual operation of services is minimal: until recently six cities operated their own social psychiatric services and there are three municipal, two provincial and two national psychiatric institutions. To a very large degree, the voluntary bodies are free to formulate their own policies, even though they are heavily dependent on public funds. Various attempts have been made to increase substantially government control, none with any great degree of success, and the system has become the accepted basis for the organisation of health and social services in the Netherlands(4).

Public subsidies to bodies administering extra-mural mental health services increased throughout the first half of the century. National government gradually took over from municipal and provincial authorities the responsibility for these subsidies, covering almost a hundred per cent of the operating costs. However, recently the method of reimbursing these services has been brought into line with other forms of health care and costs are underwritten by the sickness insurance schemes. Currently, only five per cent of total expenditure on health care is met by government subsidies; approximately 25 per cent is met by voluntary private insurance schemes and the remainder by the compulsory schemes.

The compulsory scheme is regulated by the Sickness Fund Act of 1964 and is organised in regional funds, each of which is administered by a non-profit making body. The scheme covers nearly all individual sickness risks of employees below a certain income level which is regularly reviewed. Under this system general practitioners and specialists in 'office' practice are reimbursed for each 'item-of-service' they provide; hospitals and related institutions receive a daily fee. All fees are negotiated by the sickness funds, the doctors' organisations and representative bodies of the hospitals; government plays no direct part in the process. Until recently the level of the annual insurance premium was determined by government on the basis of expected total costs, but nowadays government has become more concerned with cost containment, an issue discussed later.

Since 1968 there has been an additional insurance covering everyone against a limited number of risks: in particular, for long-term inpatient care in general or psychiatric hospitals or in nursing homes.

The administrative and organisational pluralism that is the essential feature of Dutch (mental) health services has led in the past to a duplication of effort and a lack of cohesion in the service network. Thus, in a time of rapid increases in health budgets, the government has sought to intervene in favour of creating a unified framework for the whole field of health care, with adequate instruments for strategic planning. One of its most important acts has been the introduction of global budgeting, primarily for the purpose of cost containment. These experiments have now been in operation for several years. If one judges on the criterion of cost containment, results so far have not been impressive, especially as it has not proved possible to integrate the sickness insurance schemes into the system. On the organisational front, the Health Care Facilities Act was passed in 1982 and provides for organisational streamlining and planning of the whole field of health care, including mental health services. The Act is the most important consequence of the plans for health service organisation promoted by central government since 1974. The details, as they relate to mental health care, are discussed in a later section.

DUTCH MENTAL HEALTH POLICY: TOWARDS AN INTEGRATED SERVICE NETWORK

The plethora of legal and financial regulations, and the 'complex' of care providers and health services bodies, did little to assist in the creation of a coordinated and comprehensive mental health care system. This confusing care network was difficult to negotiate for both patients, staff and administrative authorities alike. The outcome was an inefficient and patchy total service where duplication of effort in certain services coexisted with inadequate or totally absent coverage in

others. It led to an undesirable competitive basis
to community care, affording insufficient scope for
collaboration among service providers.

The need for a greater level of integration
has long been recognised and early initiatives were
made by the service organisations themselves.
Attention was focussed almost exclusively on
ambulatory services which were the least clearly-
structured and most loosely-regulated provisions.
The Roman Catholic organisations, clearly inspired
by the American community mental health centres,
put forward their ideas for a coordinated operation
of outpatient and community services, with the aim
of obtaining organisational integration and
uniformity in methods of financing, if possible by
assimilation in the sickness insurance system.
Initially the role played by government in these
endeavours was small. Of their own accord, in
1972, all the voluntary bodies providing outpatient
and community services amalgamated in the
Netherlands Society for Ambulatory Mental Health
Care (NVAGG), thus creating an administrative
framework in which it was hoped re-organisation
could be more effectively directed.

In practice it soon became evident that each
service organisation had only limited abilities to
steer the re-organisation process. There were no
formal means of exerting control, and the restructuring of services was only able to proceed as
and when the majority of member services permitted
it. Though in a few areas the various services had
voluntarily amalgamated as early as the 1960s, in
the majority organisational integration continued
to be at best partial, with few formalised
agreements between member services. Internal and
external conflicts were rife. External conflicts
centred on the existence of private psychiatrists
and psychiatric hospitals who feared a restriction
in their sphere of influence if independent
outpatient services grew. Internally, there were
conflicts because bodies providing the services for
alcoholics and drug addicts wished to retain an
independent identity in order to improve patient
access to treatment. Accordingly, these services
withdrew from the integration process at an early
stage. The institutes of multi-disciplinary
psychotherapy (IMP) feared that integration would
lead to a dilution of specialist psychotherapeutic
services and that psychotherapy would become a
free-for-all. Here, too, financial considerations
played a certain role: psychotherapists in the IMPs

216

commanded a much higher salary than colleagues in other services and this they were anxious to safeguard (5).

As a consequence of internal dissent the plans of the NVAGG for amalgamation of services were in jeopardy and the national ministry of health, which had been concerned with the issue of incorporating these services into sickness insurance coverage, was progressively drawn into the problem. As mentioned earlier, formal integration - still, however, without the participation of bureaux for alcoholics and addicts - was only achieved in 1982.

The bodies providing extra-mural services, in fact, had been pressing government since the 1960s for recognition under the sickness insurance schemes. For practical reasons government chose the General Insurance for Exceptional Medical Expenses, established in 1968, as the appropriate scheme for extending liability, in preference to the pre-existing sickness insurance schemes, since these being employment-based did not cover the entire population. The social psychiatric services (SPS) were the first to be incorporated into the insurance scheme. But problems arose because of a lack of conformity to the sickness insurance principle of covering 'individual, sickness, risks'. The work of the SPS did not comply with any of these principles, since they were largely engaged in group therapy, had a broad concept of 'illness' which included psychosocial problems, and were actively engaged in prevention and in counselling and consultancy work.

If this lack of conformity to insurance principles was true of the SPS, it applied even more in the case of other ambulatory services. The problems of integrating these services into insurance coverage dragged on for ten years and were only resolved in 1982 when, inter alia, the liability of sickness insurance was extended to include preventive, consultancy, and counselling work, as well as the narrower concept of 'treatment'. Accordingly, Dutch 'sickness' insurance has moved some way along the path towards a 'health' insurance system. Part of the price that the ambulatory services have had to pay to achieve recognition for insurance reimbursement is the surrendering of direct access by patients; these provisions are now regarded as specialist facilities for which patients need GP referral. This condition was imposed in order to conform to the policy introduced from 1974 onwards of

217

'echelonisation' of services, details of which are given below.

1982: THE ESTABLISHMENT OF THE 'REGIONAL INSTITUTES FOR AMBULATORY MENTAL HEALTH CARE' (RIAGGS)

The central health ministry's concern to introduce uniformity in financing and organising outpatient services found expression in the establishment of the RIAGGs, by which the 1974 ministerial policies of 'echelonisation' and 'regionalisation' of health services were enacted. The aims were to create one coordinated ambulatory service within a sectorised mental health care system, which would serve as a locus of specialist treatment for primary care referrals and reduce the existing hospital domination of psychiatric care.

One of the basic foundations of the reform introduced by the 1982 Health Care Facilities Act is the extension of 'echelonisation': i.e. services are organised in tiers according to the level of specialisation. The first echelon includes primary care services directly accessible to the patient. The second are specialised outpatient facilities available only on referral by a first echelon agent; and the third consists of specialised hospital services, including inpatient treatment. The other guiding principle is the 'regionalisation' of services, by which the whole country has been divided into health care regions (or sectors). The sector is now the basic unit for planning and organising health services, a task which continues to be undertaken by the public authorities at the national, provincial and municipal level, although it is envisaged that here the role of the provincial and local authorities will be increased.

In each sector the RIAGG is a second-tier (echelon) service providing counselling, psychotherapy, crisis intervention and physical treatments. It is available on a round-the-clock daily basis for acute cases. The RIAGGs also provide consultation for agents in other services and are involved in preventive work. At present each of the institutes has forty to sixty members of staff drawn from the old component services, which were formally abolished in January 1983 (with the exception of the consultation bureaux for alcoholism and drugs which remain outside the

RIAGGs). Great emphasis is laid on multi-disciplinary teamwork and on peer supervision (6).

A particularly thorny problem, alluded to earlier, has been the status of psychotherapy and the role of former institute of multidisciplinary psychotherapy (IMP) staff within the new service. In a compromise solution the health ministry has sanctioned the creation of so-called 'organisational psychotherapy units' which operate inside the RIAGGs and draw their staff from the former IMPs, but the salaries of these staff have been gradually scaled down to a level analogous to those of their new colleagues.

At the moment, reform and experimentation in service structures is progressing at a fast pace. Currently, several models are being tried: some RIAGGs have a central office with specialist teams receiving referrals from an intake team; others have separate teams for specialist areas such as adolescents and psychogeriatrics; some sectors have a central team supported by a series of sub-sector teams responsible for specific geographical areas.

As a deliberate incentive towards speedy organisational integration, the separate reimbursement by insurance funds of services provided by the previously independent components of the RIAGG was discontinued in January 1983. Now it is the RIAGG as a whole that is reimbursed via a system of budget financing; this means that the RIAGG is reimbursed the costs of an agreed range of facilities and staffing complement. By identifying the whole RIAGG as the unit for reimbursement the health ministry has been able to impose certain pre-conditions relating to organisational functioning and therapeutic objectives.

Though a radical departure, the Act was essentially a compromise and the status of the charitable and private bodies providing services has been largely left intact. However, on the positive side, all organisations providing (mental) health services have been drawn into the planning process at national, provincial and municipal level. It is true that in some quarters there are fears that the reform may progressively fall victim to lengthy and bureaucratic procedures with, ultimately, only modest impact on the integration of the service network. Although there is still no communis opinio on the most appropriate organisational model, or on the precise division of policy-making power between the central ministry, the provinces and the municipalities, it is fair to say that the transfer of planning authority incurred by the Act is the most fundamental and positive change that has occurred in post-war health services policy in the Netherlands.

RE-ORGANISATION OF INPATIENT AND RESIDENTIAL SERVICES

Current policies are based on a planning ratio for acute and medium-term beds of 1.1 per thousand population. Since 1981 the government has sanctioned a programme of renovation of old buildings and partial re-building in existing psychiatric hospitals. There is also a limited building programme of new hospitals in sectors with inadequate inpatient facilities. The overall aims are to obtain a balanced distribution of beds, improve the quality of the provisions and reduce the size of hospitals to a maximum of 500 beds. Within the 'regionalisation' policy each psychiatric hospital has defined catchment area responsibilities for a sector or part of a sector. Unfortunately, the boundaries of hospital catchment areas are not yet coterminous with those of the RIAGGs. In addition, there are specialist psychiatric institutions for the treatment of specific patient groups such as addicts, adolescents, severely disturbed or violent patients and forensic patients which operate on a supra-sectoral basis.

In 1980 there were just over 23,000 beds in psychiatric hospitals and a further 2000 beds in DGH units. University clinics, which are not part of the regionalisation policy, contribute a further 580 beds. In recent years, the number of admissions has been increasing and is in excess of the number of discharges. In common with many other Western countries the average duration of an inpatient spell has been declining rapidly. On the other hand two-thirds of all beds are occupied by those who have been in hospital for over a year, and the 'new long stay' are taking the place of other chronic patients who are being transferred to psychogeriatric nursing homes or other residential accommodation.

There is, as yet, no closely integrated policy for the various services providing inpatient or residential care. However, the government has expressed its firm commitment to a rapid expansion

220

of the residential sector, especially sheltered accommodation, which it intends to finance through the provisions of the Exceptional Medical Expenses Act. Funds previously earmarked for the psychiatric hospital building programme are also to be made available to the voluntary bodies who are to manage residential facilities. The system of financing hospitals has proven a intractable obstacle in transferring resources to residential services: hospitals are reimbursed on a daily fee basis according to the number of beds occupied. Furthermore, the fee is set irrespective of the amount of resources individual patients consume. Consequently, chronic patients, who receive relatively 'low intensity' treatment 'subsidise' acute psychiatric care. Accordingly, if large numbers of chronic patients were to be transferred to sheltered accommodation, hospitals would be faced with the need to treat on a reduced budget the remaining patients who required more intense clinical interventions.

In general, the voluntary bodies administering psychiatric hospitals have criticised the policy of developing alternative services, especially since the government intends to prohibit hospitals from having direct managerial control of sheltered accommodation. The major move away from the hospitals, therefore, has involved elderly patients requiring high inputs of medical and nursing care; in 1980 there were already over 18,000 beds in psychogeriatric nursing homes and they accounted for the great part of the increase in expenditure on mental health services.

Expenditure on the mental health services in recent years has been increasing more rapidly than for health services as a whole, although in 1980 mental health accounted for only 13 per cent of the total health budget. However, even though expenditure on ambulatory services has been the most rapidly expanding area of mental health care in the last ten years, the hospital domination of the budget has remained paramount. Thus, in 1980, the psychiatric inpatient sector employed 90 per cent of all mental health staff and spent 83 per cent of the budget. Day care and sheltered residential services consumed a mere 3.5 per cent of the budget, and ambulatory services which catered for 185,000 patients and office psychiatrist practices (100,000 patients) together accounted for 13.5 per cent of total mental health expenditure (7).

A solution to the problem of transferring financial allocations away from the hospitals has yet to be found. And an additional constraint in the more recent past is the government's policy, as part of its austerity programme, to prohibit further expansion of the social insurance system. These new restrictions will bear most heavily on sheltered accommodation whereas, fortunately, ambulatory services were amalgamated in the RIAGGs and obtained reimbursement status from sickness insurance just in time.

In the past, policy for each area of mental health care has been formulated independently. The result is a disjointed system in which competition and imbalances in funding are regrettable features. The first cautious steps towards the creation of a fully - integrated service are currently being taken, with the aim of establishing a national network of Regional Institutes of Mental Health Care (RIGGs), which will incorporate all psychiatric services, save the university clinics. Unlike the RIAGGs, which provide a unified service, the RIGGs are primarily envisaged as coordinating bodies comprising the various autonomous organisations administering provisions. The hope is that the policy of 'echelonisation' and 'regionalisation' of mental health care can be taken further and that, within this collaborative system, there can be a more appropriate distribution of resources.

THE LAWS GOVERNING PSYCHIATRIC ADMISSIONS:

As well as a concern for adequate financing and organisation of psychiatric care, the mental health professions and other interest parties have been pre-occupied in the 1970s and early 1980s with the question of the legal status of the psychiatric patient. As mentioned earlier, the basic legislation regulating compulsory admissions is the 1884 Lunacy Act. Amendments in 1904 permitted voluntary admissions and, in 1972, the law was again changed to give more guarantees on compulsory detention. Two procedures for compulsory admission exist at the moment: where there is a threat of danger to self or others an 'urgent admission' for an initial period of up to three weeks can be sanctioned by the local mayor and requires judicial authorisation as soon as possible after the detention; the other procedure requires judicial authorisation before admission and concerns persons in such a state of mental distress that treatment is deemed 'necessary and desirable'. The patient may demand that the judge interview him and he may also produce witnesses to support his appeal against admission. In these cases the judge may ask for a second opinion from an independent psychiatrist. The period of initial authorisation is six months. In practice, the 'urgent admission' procedure, followed later by judicial authorisation, is the more common. Compulsory admissions currently account for 15 per cent of all admissions.

Concern about the lack of legal safeguards has been expressed at frequent intervals in the present century. The influence of the anti-psychiatrists and the growth of the 'psychiatric patient movement' in the 1960s, in part, prompted the government to give parliamentary time to this issue. A bill was introduced in 1971 but provoked much opposition, with claims that legal safeguards were still too few, its concept of dangerosity nebulous and the position of voluntary patients unclear. Consequently, the bill failed and the government appointed a commission in 1975 to investigate the whole matter. Its conclusions were published in 1979 and its most important recommendations relate to the establishment of a legal code of rights for both compulsory and voluntary patients, with an explicit right to refuse treatment, except in defined situations of danger. In the same year a revised version of the 1971 bill was proposed, in which some of the commission's recommendations have been incorporated. The bill was subsequently amended in 1981 and, at the time of writing, has almost completed all parliamentary stages, although its enactment is not certain. The bill proposes that the presence of mental disorder shall no longer be a sufficient condition for compulsory admission, but that the disorder must represent a clear danger to self or others. All patients, compulsorily or voluntarily admitted, are to retain their civil rights. There are proposals for stricter procedures for compulsory admission and for shortening the initial periods of detention without judicial review. There will also be improved access of the patient to appeal procedures.

One reform that has already occurred, and with some success, is the experimental scheme of Ombudsmen for psychiatric patients which has been funded by the government since 1980. These functionaries work independently of the hospital and act as mediators for patients and also investigate complaints about compulsory admissions, aspects of treatment, prescription of medication, ill-treatment and interception of mail.

CONCLUSION

The major problem in Dutch mental health care has been the lack of a comprehensive organisational framework, with the resultant failure to coordinate new initiatives. Integration has progressively been a prime concern of the individual services and, later, of government. However, little attention has been paid to the development of an operational model of an integrated mental health care system. In fact, I would argue that Dutch mental health policy has not so much been directed towards innovation as towards re-organisation of services.

The essential question is whether a holistic approach to mental health services is at all viable. To what extent will it, in practice, be possible to reconcile policies of new hospital building and modernisation programmes on the one hand with the expansion of community-based services on the other? What are the real chances for the development of sheltered accommodation services now that reimbursement through sickness insurance is not an option open to them?

Another unresolved issue concerns the appropriate relations between specialist mental health care, primary care and social work. In fact, several interesting experiments are in progress at the moment. The City of Amsterdam, for example, is re-organising its community psychiatric services on a neighbourhood or 'patch' system, in which the basis of the service will be primary care, social psychiatry and crisis intervention. It is, as yet, early days to assess how successful these innovations will be.

Policy development is also taking place at the national level and a major document on the future mental health care system based on the RIGGs is expected shortly. Meanwhile, the full implementation of the 1982 Health Care Facilities Act is progressing sector by sector. Now, however, implementation is to be extended to include the broad range of psychiatric facilities, at least at the planning level, and not merely the ambulatory services. A national consultative body composed of representatives of the various mental health services has also been set up. Finally, the outcome of attempts to amend the laws governing compulsory admissions and the legal status of psychiatric patients is expected very shortly.

Unfortunately no conclusion can yet be drawn on whether the reforms that have been taking place in the last few years have resulted in actual improvements in the quality of mental health care offered in the Netherlands. Only the coming years will tell how well the system works and whether this Dutch variant of psychiatric reform is really worthwhile.

NOTES

(1)   The chapter is concerned with services for the mentally ill. Though some psychiatric facilities also cater for the mentally handicapped, the Netherlands has a long history of providing separate services for these patients.

(2)   Until the Second World War German psychiatry enjoyed considerable influence in the Netherlands.

(3)   Independent office psychiatrists are the only major private practitioners in Dutch mental health care; in 1980, 200 psychiatrists were in office practice. There are also a small number of psychologists in office practice.

(4)   The most important health policy functions retained by the central government include: the supervision of the social insurance system (in the present context, most critically the provisions of the 1964 Sickness Fund Act and the 1968 Exceptional Medical Expenses Act); regulating the planning and building of hospitals and other inpatient facilities (Hospital Facilities Acts 1971 and 1979); regulating the planning of all health services (Health Care Facilities Act, 1982); and

establishing the procedures for determining tariffs in health care (Hospital Tariffs Act 1965 and Health Care Tariffs Act 1982). In addition there are national regulations governing training in the health care professions.

(5)   The financing of non-residential psychotherapy was made possible by the introduction of a government subsidy in the mid-1960s. The Sickness Fund Act authorises reimbursement by sickness insurance of a limited number of psychotherapy sessions.

There is, at present, no officially recognised training in psychotherapy and the title of 'psychotherapist' is not legally protected. Psychotherapists employed in the Institutes for Multidisciplinary Psychotherapy are required to have undergone a training meeting the requirements of membership of the Netherlands Society for Psychotherapy, which is the sole means of gaining recognition for reimbursement as a psychotherapist by the sickness insurance funds. However, psychotherapists with other training are employed in a variety of other settings. At the time of writing, discussions on the regulation of training and legal protection of the title of psychotherapist are at an advanced stage.

(6)   Although the RIAGGs were created in the same year as the Health Care Facilities Act was passed, their organisation is not, as yet, regulated by the Act. Thus, there are at present 60 RIAGG regions varying from 150,000 to 300,000 inhabitants, but boundaries are not coterminous with those of the sectors created by the 1982 Act.

(7)   A further 40,000 patients were receiving psychiatric treatment in hospital outpatient departments in 1980.

BIBLIOGRAPHY

Only English language texts are listed. Interested persons who are able to read Dutch are invited to apply to the author for suggestions on further reading.

Dekker, C.V.C.(1979) 'Mental Health Legislation in the Netherlands: Civil and Administrative Law',International Journal of Law and Psychiatry, 2, 469-484.

Dewez, J.Th.M. and R. Giel. (1972) 'About the regional responsibility of the mental hospitals in the Netherlands' Psychiatrica, Neurologica, Neurochirurgia, 76, 31-38.

Giel, R. (1977) 'Hospital psychiatry in the Netherlands: Buildings or People', Social Psychiatry, 12, 89-93.

Giel, R. and G.H.M.M. ten Horn (1982) 'Patterns of mental health care in a Dutch register area', Social Psychiatry, 117, 117-123.

Hepburn, Andrew W. and Anton F.de Man. (1980) 'Patient rights and the Dutch Clientenbond', Canada's Mental Health, 28, 16-18.

Krul-Steketee, J. and M. Zeegers. (1981) 'Recent Developments in the Field of Forensic Psychiatry in the Netherlands', International Journal of Law and Psychiatry, 4, 445-447.

Londen, J. van. (1976) 'Relationship of intramural and extramural services', International Journal of Mental Health, 5, 64-70.

Querido, A.(1969) 'The shaping of Community Mental Health Care', British Journal of Psychiatry, 114, 293-302. Also published in: International Journal of Psychiatry, 1969. 7, 300-311.

Romme, M.A.J.(1980) 'Working with governments on the provision of therapeutic communities; a Dutch perspective'. In: Jansen, E. (ed), The Therapeutic Community; Outside the Hospital, Croom Helm, London, 355-359.

Straathof, L.J.A. (1975) 'General Policies in the development of Mental Health Services in the Netherlands', International Journal of Mental Health, 5, 59-63.

Trimbos, C.J.B.J. (1972) 'In search of new models in psychiatry', Psychiatrica, Neurologica, Neurochirurgia, 75, 251-259.

Trimbos, C.J.B.J.(1980) 'Developments in intra-mural and extra-mural alternatives to the mental hospital', World Hospitals, 16, 22-25.

Editor's suggestion for further reading:
Mental Health Care in the Dutch Welfare State. Proceedings of a conference at the University of Utrecht, 7-10th April 1983. Obtainable from the Instituut voor Ontwikkelingspsychologie, Bijlhouwerstraat 6, Utrecht.

Chapter Eleven

UNITED KINGDOM: SOCIALISED SYSTEM – BETTER SERVICES?

Steen Mangen and Bridget Rao

It was not until 1911 that legislation for national social insurance came into force in Britain and from then, until 1948, health insurance was administered by friendly societies. The milestone in the history of British health services is undoubtedly the creation of the National Health Service (NHS), a decision taken during the War on the basis of the recommendations of the Beveridge Report. Introduced in 1948 the NHS is a socialised system of health care delivery. Its initial and prevailing goals are equality of access to treatment through a redistribution of resources and a decentralisation of policy-making. The insurance principle of coverage against individual risk gave way to a service which, in large measure, is free at the point of consumption. Membership of individual insurance schemes was replaced by a system which is largely dependent on funding through general taxation (1). Private services and private insurance have had a minimal part to play, although their role has increased since the Seventies (2). Hospitals, most of which had been managed by the municipalities and in the case of mental hospitals by the county authorities, were transferred to the new NHS regional hospital boards. Local authorities were given discretionary powers to provide preventive and after-care services, further stipulations being contained in the 1948 National Assistance Act which, at last, heralded the end of the Poor Law.

Mental hospitals were incorporated into the same administrative structure responsible for the general hospitals. Most commentators of the time agreed that psychiatry was being offered an unprecedented opportunity of close liaison with the rest of medicine and that, together with local authority departments, a comprehensive approach to mental health care had come of age.

This chapter reviews developments in the intervening period - now almost forty years - and assesses the extent to which the hopes of the early post-war reformers have been fulfilled. After a description of the organisation and financing of (mental) health and social services, the chapter is divided into sections reviewing events in what for our purposes seem to be three convenient periods: the history of psychiatric care until the passing of the 1959 Mental Health Act in England and Wales, which was then the most important review of policy this century; events in the Sixties and Seventies until the publication of the government white paper 'Better Services for the Mentally Ill', a document which still forms the basis of policy and planning; and, finally, developments from 1975 until the present day.

Although the chapter's title refers to the 'United Kingdom', most of what is recorded here concerns England or, at most, England and Wales (3). As we will describe, responsibilities for the health and social services are exercised by ministries for each of the four countries of the United Kingdom. Space prevents us from considering each country in turn and we therefore hope that readers will forgive our anglo-saxon bias, which we have attempted to restrain by conciliatory references to the situations in the other home countries when policies depart radically from those in England.

ORGANISATION AND FINANCING OF (MENTAL) HEALTH SERVICES

In England the Secretary of State for Social Services is the senior minister in the Department of Health and Social Security (DHSS). The Department exercises overall responsibility for the NHS in England and, despite considerable delegation of powers, retains a central planning function by determining national policies and allocating capital and revenue funds to the regional health authorities. The supervision of legislation governing the social services is also a DHSS function as is the direct administration of the social security system, a duty that extends to the whole of Great Britain, local social security offices being agencies of the DHSS.

Apart from a small number of centrally administered services, the management of the national health service in England has been delegated to fourteen regional health authorities which, in turn, delegate responsibilities for local service management to 192 districts. The intermediate area health authorities were abolished in 1982 in an effort to reduce administrative costs. The majority of districts serve a population of between 250,000-330,000 although some have populations as low as 120,000 and others have well over 500,000. In many cases health district boundaries are not coterminous with those of local authorities.

The Welsh Office under its own Secretary of State exercises authority in respect of the NHS and the personal social services in Wales. The Welsh Secretary is consulted in cases where legislation covers England and Wales. Since the reform of the NHS in 1974 direct responsibility for the planning and administration of Welsh health services has been delegated to nine health districts.

In Scotland the relevant ministry is the Scottish Home and Health Department. The Scottish Secretary has delegated many of his functions to fifteen health boards which, in turn, are divided into twenty-nine health districts as the lowest-tier authorities. The organisation of the NHS in Scotland is about to be reformed to streamline administration.

The Secretary of State for Northern Ireland is responsible for health and social services in the Province, his duties being exercised through the Department of Health and Social Services in Belfast. The NHS in Northern Ireland is currently in the process of reorganisation. The four area boards are to remain but the seventeen health and social services districts (lowest-tier authorities) are being replaced by units of management. It should be noted that currently only in Northern Ireland is the local administration of health and social services undertaken by the same authority.

Other ministries with functions in health affairs include the Department of Education and Science which is ultimately responsible for educational facilities providing training, although each of the health professions has its own national governing council. The Home Secretary is empowered to detain patients on Home Office orders, either in

230

psychiatric hospitals or special hospitals. The Department of Employment through its Manpower Services Commission (MSC) manages the employment rehabilitation centres and is responsible for disablement resettlement services. The MSC also allocates subsidies to sheltered workshops managed by local authorities or voluntary agencies.

The Organisation of Health Services in England

Since its inception one of the prime goals in the organisation of the NHS has been the delegation of power to regional and lower-tier authorities. The reorganisation of the NHS in 1974, which also incurred the transfer of community health services from local authority to health service control, was intended to create a unified system through a more appropriate and streamlimed division of NHS responsibilities at central, regional, area and district level. Nevertheless, one effect of the reform has been merely to re-align internal divisions in the administration of health and welfare so that primary care services, specialist medical services and the social services remain the responsibility of three separate authorities, a point described in more detail later.

Planning and Administration

An important consequence of the reform is the improvement in the central ministry's ability to formulate an overall strategy for the health services. Since the present economic recession began health services planning has been an increasingly urgent concern of government. Within the tight constraints on public expenditure growth rates imposed on health and social services authorities, the DHSS has identified client groups - the elderly, the mentally ill, the mentally retarded and provisions for children - that should be accorded budgetary priority. A 'community care' approach is also being fostered, with the DHSS exhorting authorities to attach greater emphasis to residential, day care and domiciliary provisions for these groups rather than to rely on inpatient services. To encourage moves in this direction NHS funds have been earmarked for allocation to local authority projects establishing these priority services. In a later section we provide a critique of these policies.

The introduction of the present planning system in 1976 has also provided the opportunity for the DHSS to adopt a stronger dirigist role in planning. Data on service performance indicators (admissions, discharges, lengths-of-stay etc) are forwarded by health regions and districts to the DHSS which, in turn, issues feedback information in the form of comparative performance indices and planning guidelines to assist health authorities in the preparation and monitoring of their plans. Both the regional and district health authorities are required to submit to the DHSS their operational and strategic plans which must broadly reflect national policy priorities for the health services as well as specifying short-term and long-term goals relevant to local needs.

The central supervision of the planning process has been recently reinforced by the introduction of a series of annual reviews undertaken by the Secretary of State with the chairperson and leading officers of each region. The overriding purpose of these meetings, at least from the ministerial viewpoint, is to review the feasibility of the current plans being formulated by the health regions in the light of continuing and increasing budgetary constraints.

The DHSS has periodically issued planning norms which, although intended as guidelines, have tended to be interpreted as fixed targets in regional and local planning documents. However, in recent years the Department has been encouraging health authorities to move away from the idea of planning norms and to consider a range of options which would lead to differential needs for a variety of services, especially those in the inpatient sector. Admittedly this leaves open the question of recommended minimum provisions, but it does represent considerable progress in planning terms. To assist local NHS planning the DHSS has circulated an analysis of differential psychiatric bed needs (Robinson, 1981) (4). More recently a DHSS Operational Research Report (1983) has suggested that the current acute/medium term bed guideline of 0.5/1000 may prove an over-estimate, given the drive towards day care and outpatient services.

The regional health authority is primarily concerned with long-term strategies and with the supervision of the local health plans of the districts. For this purpose a series of annual reviews with district officers is now being instituted on the lines of those between the DHSS and the regions as described above.

The regions receive their budgetary allocations from the DHSS and then allocate funds to their component districts. Both the regions and the districts have tended to enjoy a large degree of autonomy in deciding how their budgets should be spent but, as discussed in the next section, heavy budgetary constraints imposed over recent years by the DHSS have increasingly limited their choice of options.

Each of the district health authorities receives a revenue budget allocation to distribute among the individual services for which it is directly responsible. Primary care services are not administered by the districts but by separate family practitioner committees (FPCs) which receive funds direct from the DHSS. FPC budgets are not subject to the cash limit measures described in this chapter. Within budgetary and regional strategic planning limitations the district authorities have the powers to develop their own local policies.

For the purposes of administration particular kinds of services or groups of establishments form one management unit. Individual psychiatric hospitals, for example, are no longer single administrative entities. A reform of these management structures is at present in progress and some details are given in the final section. Since 1976 there has been a statutory duty for health districts and local authorities to establish joint consultative committees to promote administrative coordination of service areas where responsibility is shared. These committees may set up joint care planning teams to improve local level planning for priority client groups.

Financing the NHS and the Social Services

The rationing of resources has always been a dominant factor in the operation of the NHS. Since 1975 an even tighter grip has been maintained on health services expenditure through the application of the Treasury PESC controls (5). Budgetary increases are now closely linked to a permitted proportional allocation of GNP. As a result of the public expenditure crisis of 1975/6 central control of the capital and revenue spending programmes of health authorities has been strictly enforced. From 1977 cash limits have been applied in the health regions' annual budgets and deficits arising in the course of the year can no longer be made good from central funds. As a very large proportion of NHS expenditure is budget limited the potential for effective central control is considerable. Only the primary care sector has escaped these cash limits; funds here are voted separately by parliament and, to a large degree, the budget is open-ended, total expenditure being a function of such factors as the number of prescriptions issued and the rate of performance of certain medical acts which attract item-of-service reimbursement.

The NHS inherited a health care system characterised by profound inequalities in service provision and, surprisingly, for practically the first twenty years of its existence little was done to remedy the situation: resources continued to be allocated largely on the basis of the existing distribution of services. It was not until 1970 that some success in resource reallocation was achieved through the utilisation of population-weighted indices. However, it was with the publication of the formula proposed by the Resource Allocation Working Party (RAWP, 1976) that the process began in earnest (6).

The RAWP method involves an analysis of regional indicators of health resource allocations and service activities. It excludes statistical indicators from the primary care and private sectors, although in the case of the latter there is some possibility that relevant indicators may be incorporated at a future date. One of the most frequent criticisms of RAWP is its reliance on mortality data as a surrogate for morbidity data. This is particularly unsatisfactory in specialities like psychiatry where there is little correlation between morbidity and mortality rates. Implementation of the RAWP method has been gradual but there is evidence that it has already helped reduce inequalities among the regions, so that the gap between the poorest and richest region has been narrowed. Substantial inequalities do remain, however, with the four south-eastern regions continuing to receive favourable allocations when compared with other parts of England (Harrison and Gretton, 1984).

Inequalities do not merely exist between regions; they can be even more acute within individual regions. It is for this reason that regions are being encouraged to apply RAWP criteria

234

in their allocations of funds to the district authorities. Inequalities among the medical specialities have been pronounced and the DHSS consultative document on priority groups, discussed earlier, suggests means to improve the 'cinderella' services.

Inequalities also exist in closely allied services outside the NHS. This is the case in the social services, the majority of which are administered by local authorities: the counties or, in the major conurbations, the metropolitan boroughs. Other social services are managed by bodies in the voluntary sector. The wide range of social services provisions include social work support, home helps, day centres and a variety of residential accommodation. Unlike standard NHS services, certain social services, such as homes and hostels, are means-tested provisions. Thus, for example, psychiatric patients moving from inpatient wards to hostels may find themselves having to pay towards the cost of their accommodation if their financial resources are above a certain limit.

Local authorities are empowered to formulate their own policies and although, since 1972, they have been required to submit strategic plans for the social services to the DHSS, most of the influence of central government on the positive development of policy takes the form of exhortation through the circulation of consultative documents. Policy, of course, is also directed by budgetary considerations and here central government's role has become increasingly prominent since the introduction of a range of measures to curb local government expenditure. Approximately half of the public funds local authorities spend on the social services are obtained from central government rate support grants; the other half are raised from the rates which are a local taxation on residential and commercial property (7). Monies from the two sources enter a common pool and local authorities then allocate a budget to individual services; this means that central government does not have direct powers to ensure that resources go into the priority areas in the health and social services that it has identified.

With its streamlined organisation and planning process and with central government financing instead of a large number of individual sickness insurance funds, the British National health service is frequently held up as a system offering

value for money, despite the much publicised
waiting lists and sometimes squalid conditions.
Certainly, at approximately 6 per cent of GNP,
public expenditure on the health services in
Britain is the lowest of any Community country.
Combining total public expenditure on the health
and personal social services: in 1982, 84 per cent
was obtained from the central government funds -
principally the consolidated fund - and 16 per cent
came from local authority rates (DHSS, 1982). The
effect of this financial system on present mental
health services is discussed in a later sections.

PSYCHIATRIC SERVICES BEFORE 1959

England's present mental hospitals largely owe
their origins to the provisions of the 1845
Lunatics Act which enjoined each county to erect
asylums for the containment of their mad, earlier
permissive legislation having met with a desultory
response (8). In the following years Connolly
became a celebrated figure for his publication of
the principles of non-restraint. However,
pressures of numbers soon reduced those asylums
attempting to practice humane care to custodial
institutions. Very early on the overcrowding of
asylums became a national problem which further
building did little to alleviate.

From the middle of the nineteenth century
until 1930 - with a break in the First World War
years - there was an enormous rise in the asylum
population (Scull, 1983). Enlightened reformers
despaired that the asylums could be anything other
than houses of containment. Local projects such as
boarding-out schemes were launched in an effort at
finding alternatives to incarceration. Voluntary
associations such as the Mental After Care
Association (1879) were formed to provide after
care for discharged patients. However, these
developments remained small-scale and had little
national impact.

Major legislation was passed in 1890. The new
Lunacy Act was the embodiment of legalism,
carefully prescribing the requirements for
certification which was to be authorised by the
local magistracy. Jones (1972) has argued that the
Act was outmoded medically even before it had
received the royal assent and, moreover, that it
hindered progress for decades. The Act did

236

authorise voluntary admission of 'private' although not of 'pauper' patients, but the gain, at least initially, was more apparent than real, since conditions in the asylums were sufficient to deter all but the desperate from seeking admission of their own volition.

On the eve of the First World War the first signs of some amelioration of asylum practice were beginning to emerge. In 1914 a central board of control was appointed with medical and legal members whose task was to exercise supervisory control of establishments for the mentally ill and mentally retarded. The War itself provided a significant opportunity for psychiatry to prove itself: ten per cent of army officers were invalided out with shellshock and the military hospitals were swamped with victims of all ranks. The condition was accepted as a functional nervous disorder and psychiatrists were recruited to treat it.

The Twenties were a period of increasing interest among psychiatrists in the classification of neurosis and the new ideas emanating from Vienna began to find their way across the Channel. The movement for mental hygiene took root in Britain at this time and child guidance and family guidance clinics were opened in several of the larger cities. Outpatient clinics were founded too and even within the asylums there was a wind of change: patients were permitted to wear their own clothes and industrial and occupational therapy was introduced. In 1924 the Maudsley Hospital, which had pioneered clinical work with the victims of shellshock, became Britain's first psychiatric teaching hospital.

The 1929 Local Government Act created the public assistance boards with, inter alia, duties to provide extra-mural services for the mentally ill. This and the 1930 Mental Treatment Act represented the first major formal revision of mental health policy in the present century. The 1930 Act made legal provision for voluntary admission of all categories of patients; it encouraged the creation of observation wards; local authorities were authorised to establish outpatient clinics and to provide after care facilities; the board of control was reorganised; and the use of Victorian terminology was discontinued, 'asylums' giving way to 'mental hospitals'. The juridical basis of certification of the 1890 Act was, however, retained.

237

In the 1930s several of the mental health occupations took their first serious steps towards professionalisation. Training courses in psychiatry were organised for nurses and general practitioners. Several universities offered training in psychiatric social work; indeed, the first course began at the London School of Economics as early as 1929. In 1936 a professional association of occupational therapists was formed and the first training course organised in 1938 (Jones, 1960).

By the end of the 1930s 40 per cent of patients were voluntarily admitted. Then came the Second World War which disrupted the normal routine of the mental hospitals with staff being conscripted into the armed forces and establishments requisitioned. Yet, again, war provided psychiatry with new opportunities. Psychiatrists were recruited to screen military personnel and new techniques of group therapy were exploited to treat the casualties of war, a development that presaged the establishment of therapeutic communities in the early post-war years. The creation of the National Health Service in 1948 brought the mental health services into the mainstream of health service administration. Instigated in the same period and inspired by the work of Maxwell Jones were the now celebrated services offering social therapies. These and the open-door policies introduced in progressive hospitals like Dingleton in south-west Scotland and Mapperley in Nottingham led to a decline in inpatient numbers locally several years before the introduction of the phenothiazines. Finally, the late 1940s saw the opening of the first formal day hospital.

1954 was the year with the peak post-war inpatient rate (3.44/1000). Thereafter, inpatient rates declined steadily with the introduction of the neuroleptic drugs. All in all, the mid-1950s were a period of great optimism in psychiatry: a variety of new forms of care had been tested in the decade since the end of the War and psychotropic medication was then having unprecedented success. It was in this atmosphere that a royal commission was appointed to make recommendations for a reform of mental health legislation. When it reported, in 1957, it proposed sweeping changes, most of which received official endorsement and uncharacteristically government acted quickly: a new mental health act was passed in 1959.

238

The 1959 Mental Health Act put an end to authorisation of certification by the magistracy and abolished the board of control. Instead mental health review tribunals were appointed to protect the patient's interest. The Act represents the apotheosis of psychiatry: the pre-occupation of the 1890 Act with legal safeguards was replaced by concern for the clinical state of the patient. The psychiatrist, not the justice of the peace, was recognised as the most appropriate agent to pass judgment, although the local authority mental welfare officer was entrusted with the task of ensuring that certification was justified. The Act's emphasis is unambiguously on the promotion of clinical competence; it looked forward to the closer integration of psychiatry with the rest of medicine and it advocated the primacy of informal patient status. Only those needing round-the-clock care were to be hospitalised; compulsory admission was to be a last resort.

The 1959 Act is generally regarded as the first official statement propounding the principles of community care. Yet the Act made no financial provisions for this new policy; neither did it become a statutory duty. Indeed, apart from the appointment of mental welfare officers, the local authority services the Act cites as essential to help reduce inpatient numbers were to remain discretionary provisions.

The Minister of Health's speech to the conference of the National Association of Mental Health in 1961 was to exploit the prevailing optimism still further. He declared that the 150,000 beds in psychiatric hospitals should be cut by half by 1975. Ultimately, the psychiatric hospital would be redundant, its place being taken by psychiatric units in general hospitals. This was a major shift in policy, for the 1959 Act had said nothing about the mass closure of psychiatric hospitals. In the following year the Hospital Plan was published and projected that the national average bed ratio would decline from 3.3/1000 in 1961 to 1.8/1000 in 1975. These estimates were based on the celebrated gaffe of Tooth and Brooke, who predicted future bed needs on the basis of a crude extrapolation of trends between 1954-1959 without any allowance being made for demographic changes or the impact of alternative services on bed usage (9).

239

Between 1961 and 1971 mental health policy remained unchanged, although the Hospital Plan was slightly amended in the 1966 Hospital Building Programme. By the mid-1960s the naive optimism in the future of the mental health services was beginning to be shaken. Sociologists - and psychiatrists - had described the pathological consequences of 'institutionalism' (Goffman, 1961; Wing & Brown, 1970). Anti-psychiatry had become a hip movement: Laing (1965; 1967) and Cooper (1972) were its gurus. Public scandals about appalling conditions and brutality inside some psychiatric hospitals followed hot on its trail.

By the early Seventies, perhaps for the first time, there were growing signs of widespread disillusion with the ideals of the welfare state. It was a time of reorganisation: reform of social services in 1971 led to the creation of generic social services departments; in 1973 the national health service was reorganised; and in the following year came the reform of local government.

The 1971 White Paper 'Hospital Services for Mentally Ill' predicted a further decline in recommended ratios for acute/medium term beds to 0.5/1000 population. It confirmed the government's commitment to community care and, once again, there were predictions of the closure of the psychiatric hospitals in the long-term. Preference was reaffirmed for psychiatric units in general hospitals, each with a multi-disciplinary team providing an integrated hospital and community service for an average population of 60,000. As an interim measure, psychiatric hospitals were to undergo internal sectorisation so that each unit could fulfil catchment area obligations for this population. An additional long-term aim was that chronic patients should be treated in general hospital psychiatric units or else be transferred to small 'community hospitals'.

The principal planning document of the Seventies is the 1975 White Paper 'Better Services for the Mentally Ill' which remains the basic reference for present-day policy. In a sense it was incumbent on government to undertake a major review of mental health policy at this stage because the planning period envisaged in the 1962 Hospital Plan was expiring. Although inpatient numbers had declined in the intervening period, the predicted ratio (1.8/1000) was still a few years off from being achieved and nothing much had come of hospital closures. In sharp contrast to its predecessor, the tone of the 1975 plan was modest: planning horizons were pushed into the next century and even then, as the health minister herself acknowledged, there could be no guarantee that planning targets would be achieved. For a government shaken by the oil crisis there could be no question of allocating the huge increase in capital expenditure that would be required for the large-scale establishment of new provisions in the short-term. Accordingly, it was stressed that reforms would have to be achieved mainly through a redistribution of existing allocations.

The long-term aim of 'Better Services' is the creation of a comprehensive and locally-based service. Within each district, with an average population of 250,000, there was to be an integrated network of services: primary care services, to which 'Better Services' attached great importance; specialist psychiatric services ideally based at a psychiatric unit in a local general hospital, or in psychiatric hospitals which were to be internally sectorised; and local authority and voluntary social services. Priorities were to be given to community services which reduced demand on the inpatient sector: day hospitals and day centres; hospital-hostels for the 'new long stay'; and other forms of sheltered residences. Staff ratios were to be improved and the old hospitals were to be modernised, their gradual substitution having replaced medium-term mass closure. A range of planning ratios were provided as guidelines and, despite the lapse of ten years, they remain active targets in many areas (10) (DHSS, 1975).

AFTER 'BETTER SERVICES'

Hard on the heels of the 1975 'Better Services' White Paper came the government white paper on public expenditure forecasting the bleak times ahead until 1980. Capital expenditure was to be cut back in order to allow some small growth in current expenditure on certain public services. Although the increased allocation to the personal social services was slightly more favourable than the projected rise in the NHS budget, both service areas faced annual increases in expenditure averaging less than three per cent, barely sufficient to maintain services at their existing level. (In the event a slightly higher rate of

241

growth was permitted in the last financial year of the programme). Clearly, it was the end of the period of high spending of the early Seventies when, for example, local authority social services budgets had benefitted from annual increases in the order of twenty per cent. It was with these dismal prospects in view that the government issued the 'Priorities' consultative paper in 1976 recommending on what services the small budgetary increases should be spent.

According to 'Priorities' additional allocations to acute hospital services were to be held in check in favour of increased expenditure on NHS and local authority services for the elderly, the mentally ill, the mentally retarded, and children. Yet, curiously, the projections for expenditure on services for the mentally ill belie any original intention to attach priority. The annual recommended percentage increase to be allocated to these services, at 1.8 per cent, was below the projected average. Indeed, the paper predicted a standstill in the share of current expenditure on health and personal social services for the mentally ill which, up to 1980, was to be eight per cent of the total. Combining current and capital expenditure the relevant projected increase was a mere 0.4 per cent, to stand at 8.2 per cent of the total in 1980. Within these allocations there was a preference for day care and residential provision which were seen as promoting the development of 'community care' through an emphasis on low cost solutions. Overall, the paper's clear message was a reiteration of 'Better Services': it again stressed the long-term approach to policy implementation (DHSS, 1976).

1976 was to prove something of a year for resource reallocation in health and welfare services. The report of the Resources Allocation Working Party, discussed earlier, was published and government announced a novel scheme whereby NHS 'earmarked' resources could be allocated to local authority social services to subsidise the provision of community services for priority groups, including the mentally ill. This 'joint finance' scheme was part of a general policy aimed at encouraging joint planning between health and social services authorities for provisions where, to a significant degree, their duties coincided and where the division of responsibility had led to patchy service development. As we have described it was introduced at a time of near stagnation in

242

health and social services budgets. Thus, this
infusion of new money was regarded as a modest but
timely means of inducing local social services
authorities to provide the much needed alternative
residential and day care facilities without
infringing on normal NHS budgetary allocations.
Whilst it would have been naive to entertain high
hopes of a major effect on community services in
the short-term, the scheme was better than simply
allowing existing funding arrangements to take
their course.

The principal undertakings of local
authorities wishing to avail themselves of the
scheme are that they are willing to develop the
kind of provisions envisaged in 'Better Services'
and are prepared to accept full financial liability
for these services at the end of the period of
subsidisation. In its early years the period of
one hundred per cent subsidisation of capital and
revenue costs was limited to three years, with a
lower rate of subsidies continuing for a further
two years. The brief time scale of these subsidies
proved a disincentive to many local authorities
which were unwilling to accept full liability for
new services a mere five years after their
creation. The scheme was therefore amended in 1977
to permit extensions of subsidisation of up to
seven years. Further amendments were introduced in
1983 extending the period of subsidy,
exceptionally, to up to thirteen years, with one
hundred per cent subsidisation for the first ten
years.

Whilst the scheme now appears to be more
generous, stricter stipulations for accepting funds
have been introduced. In the past local
authorities tended to use joint finance more to
create additional day care, domiciliary and social
work services than alternative residential
accommodation for discharged patients. To some
extent this may reflect a difference in the meaning
attached to 'community care' on the part of health
authorities and social services authorities. Since
1983 the improvements in subsidies have been tied
more closely to measures leading to the movement of
patients out of hospital and into alternative
provisions. In addition to 'earmarked' subsidies,
district health authorities are empowered to make
lump sum payments or grants without pre-specified
time limits out of normal budgetary allocations
they receive from regional health authorities.
These awards are forthcoming only in respect of

identified patients being transferred from hospital to community services.

As well as social services departments, education authorities, municipal housing authorities, and voluntary housing associations are now eligible under the scheme. Uptake of available funds is currently running at over 95 per cent. None the less, the scheme has been - and is likely to continue to be - relatively small-scale. In its first five years of operation it is estimated to have added a half per cent annual growth rate to the total social services budget. Approximately thirty per cent of the 'earmarked' funds were allocated to services for the long-term psychiatric patient.

How far the scheme will continue to attract local authorities now facing unparalleled budgetary constraints remains to be seen. The majority of subsidies are still allocated in the seven year programme and it is too early to say how strict an interpretation will be given to the 'exceptional' circumstances allowing subsidisation to continue for up to thirteen years. Local authorities, then, are being asked to accept additional liabilities for services at a time when budgets for other public services they provide are being strictly limited. There is concern that, in the future, these authorities will increasingly expect health authorities to make supplementary lump-sum or other grants before they will participate in the scheme (Wistow, 1984).

In the late Seventies the regional health authority strategic plans began to appear. In general, in the first generation of plans goals for psychiatric services were too vague to be operationalised and critically failed to take account of the resource constraints announced in the 1976 white paper. Although priority was given to the cinderella services the plans varied in the degree to which they were closely based on the policies of the 'Priorities' consultative paper. All the plans contain a prediction that progress towards establishing the required services would be slow and the majority did not envisage that psychiatric hospitals within their region would be closed.

The 1979 election returned a government deeply committed to an expansion of the economy through the fostering of private enterprise and the restriction of the growth of public expenditure. A year later, in 1980, central government 'block grants' to local authorities were introduced as a measure to increase central control over local government budgets. In 1981 the government issued the consultative document 'Care in the Community' in which it exhorted health and social services authorities to redouble their efforts to develop alternative services to the psychiatric hospital. This requirement had become all the more pressing, since it was acknowledged that several large mental hospitals had reached the end of their life as viable buildings; the modernisation and maintenance expenditure they required simply could not be justified in this era of financial crisis. Once again, twenty-one years after the Hospital Plan, a government made an explicit statement on the future of the psychiatric hospitals: up to thirty psychiatric hospitals - about one third of the stock - should be closed over the following ten years. Alternative services were therefore urgently required. But local authorities were facing cuts in the real level of central government rate support grants and NHS budgets were at a standstill. The government acknowledged that the required alternative services were discretionary duties of local authorities who, under prevailing economic conditions, were hardly being presented with an incentive to take action. As a small palliative to the budgetary crisis of both the district health authorities and local authorities an increase in the joint finance scheme was announced in 1983 and, as described above, the subsidisation period was prolonged in certain circumstances.

However, since this announcement further cuts in the real level of public expenditure have gone on unabated. In 1983 stricter cash limits were imposed on the NHS budget which, for the first time in thirty years, entail a reduction in manpower. Regional health authority budgets were pruned once again even though guidelines suggested that expenditure over the following ten years would grow at a maximum annual rate of 0.5 per cent. Five health regions were allocated amounts insufficient to maintain existing services, even in the short-term. Moreover, four of these five health regions have an outstanding task of de-institutionalising psychiatric patients which is of enormous proportions, since of the fourteen English regions they have the highest percentages of 'old long stay' patients.

245

It is doubtful that local authorities will be willing or able to shoulder much more of the burden of providing alternative services to cope with the flow of literally thousands of patients who will be discharged as the run down of the hospitals gains pace. As part of the government's explicit policy of reducing public expenditure there have been increasingly tighter restrictions on central government subsidies for local authority services, with further reductions in the pipeline. The alternatives for local authorities of raising extra money from increases in the rates (local taxation on property) or from their own reserves have also been limited. Local authorities now face financial penalties in the form of a further reduction in central government subsidies if the increase in the rates they approve is above the government's guidelines. In the case of certain local authorities regarded as having 'overspent' central government has imposed the level of rate poundage that may be levied.

In the meantime regional strategic plans have been revised to reflect the increased emphasis now laid on the hospital closures programme. At the time of writing a contentious issue concerns how much of the money saved by closing hospitals will eventually filter through to the new services and to the patients who have been transferred. There are some fears that, with the present curbs in NHS and social services expenditure, the programme will be used as a means of reducing investment in the psychiatric services. Certainly, the budgetary allocations for the transfer programme to be initiated in several hospitals on the edge of London are hardly reassuring.

Currently, one solution to the short-fall in funds in the period before total closure of the hospital is a bridging loan or mortgage scheme under which central government funds are allocated to meet the costs of patients' transfer and are then repaid once the hospital is closed, a process extending over several years. Other proposals involve the allocation of a 'dowry' to long stay patients being discharged from hospital to a variety of sheltered and informal residential accommodation in order to help them build a new life in the community.

On the basis of epidemiological and survey research, it is estimated that 95 per cent of patients presenting with psychiatric or psychosomatic symptoms are treated by general practitioners (Shepherd, Cooper, Brown and Kalton, 1966). Only a minority are ever referred to psychiatrists (the NHS does not give patients direct access to medical specialists) (Goldberg and Huxley, 1980). General practitioners are not employees of the NHS but work under contract to the Family Practitioner Committees. Their income is derived from a capitation fee including local supplements, payments related to their seniority and item-of-service reimbursement for certain medical procedures. At the present time about 20 per cent of general practitioners have their surgeries in health centres where they are supported by multi-disciplinary clinical teams.

The overwhelming majority of psychiatrists are employees of the NHS, although they may contract out for a number of sessions in order to treat private patients. Psychiatrists in academic posts cannot be personally reimbursed for any private treatment they provide. The number of private psychiatric practices is exceedingly small and they are mostly located in the fashionable postal districts of London. However, the past few years have seen some increase in private facilities, especially in south-eastern England.

The professional qualification of psychiatrists is membership of the Royal College of Psychiatrists which is obtained by examination. The College's licence extends to the whole of the United Kingdom and, through the Irish section, to the Republic of Ireland. In 1981 there were over 4700 doctors in English mental illness hospitals (10.3/100,000); and there were 2.63 consultant psychiatrists (senior practitioners heading clinical teams) per 100,000 population, this ratio being in line with that recommended by the Royal College of Psychiatrists (DHSS, 1984a).

In Britain psychiatric nursing is offered as a basic qualification. Student nurses may follow a two-year training leading to the qualification of state enrolled nurse (SEN(M)) or a full three-year training for registration (Registered Mental Nurse - RMN). New curricula devised by the national boards in each constituent country of the UK are

247

now being implemented. There are also university courses leading to degrees in nursing. Since the publication of 'Better Services' the government has attached priority to increasing the number of qualified psychiatric nurses. Currently, the ratio of nurses in mental illness hospitals and units in England is 118/100,000, i.e. above the ratio of 100/100,000 recommended in 'Better Services'; 52 per cent of these nurses hold a qualification in psychiatric nursing (DHSS, 1984a).

Of nurses who are qualified approximately 95 per cent are employed in inpatient work. However, in the past fifteen years there has been a considerable increase in the number of community psychiatric nursing services. The latest estimate indicate there are just over four CPNs per 100,000 population, but only about fifteen per cent have undertaken a specialist training in community psychiatric nursing. CPNs work in a variety of settings, with the emphasis on domiciliary visiting. Studies suggest that outcomes of CPN interventions with certain patient groups are comparable to those of outpatient psychiatrists (Mangen, Paykel, Griffith, Burchell and Mancini, 1983). A smaller-scale development has been the creation of posts of nurse behaviour therapists with similar claims of effectiveness (Ginsberg and Marks, 1977).

There are almost eight hundred clinical psychologists employed in psychiatric hospitals and units (1.7/100,000). In Britain clinical psychology is a postgraduate qualification regulated by the British Psychological Society. Courses are organised by universities and regional health authorities (11). Since 1971 social workers have been employed in unified social services departments of local authorities and most have a generic training, although there are a small number of specialist courses in psychiatric social work. In order to fulfil duties under the 1983 Mental Health Act social workers are required to undertake a brief additional training to acquire 'approved' status. Of the 2400 occupational therapists and assistants (5.1/100,000), 38 per cent have formal qualifications. The relevant ratio for industrial trainers is 1.2, 51 per cent of whom hold appropriate qualifications (DHSS, 1984a – the data in this paragraph refer to hospital and units with more than 200 beds).

The majority of inpatient care is still provided by approximately one hundred <u>psychiatric hospitals</u> (12). Bed capacity has fallen considerably, although not as sharply as earlier plans predicted. In the United Kingdom as a whole the average number of beds occupied daily declined by 27 per cent in the decade 1971-1981 (CSO, 1984). In England on the 31.12.1981 the total number of available staffed beds was just over 85,000 (1.8/1000) of which approximately 73,000 beds were occupied (1.6/1000) (DHSS 1984a: data refer to hospitals and units with more than 200 beds). The latest estimate suggests that at the end of 1983 approximately 69,000 beds were occupied (1.5/1000). The average length-of-stay has been reduced, only 4 per cent of current admissions remaining in hospital for more than one year. Although statistics are subject to considerable regional variation, first admission rates declined by some 25 per cent in the Seventies, but there was almost a ten per cent increase in the re-admission rate. At the present time there are 2.4 re-admissions for every first admission (DHSS, 1984a). One factor which will determine the pace of further decline in inpatient numbers is the margin between decreases in the number of 'old long stay' patients and the accumulation of the 'new long stay'. When, and if, a balance will be reached cannot be predicted accurately.

In the course of the last twenty years hospitals have been modernised and progress has been made on providing patients with more space and improved facilities. An official survey has indicated that 54 per cent of resident inpatients have some form of day-time occupation. In six of the fourteen health regions certain psychiatric hospitals failed to meet all of the 1972 DHSS recommendations on staffing levels, living space requirements for each patient and the allocation of individual cupboards for patients' personal belongings (DHSS, 1984a: data refer to hospitals and units with more than 200 beds).

By 1980 there were almost 160 <u>psychiatric units</u> in general hospitals, but many were too small to fulfil catchment area responsibilities. These units now account for ten per cent of all psychiatric beds and, in 1981, they received forty per cent of psychiatric admissions compared with 15 per cent in 1970 (DHSS, 1984b). One follow-up study suggests that long-term outcomes in a group of patients treated in psychiatric units were superior to those in a matched group of psychiatric hospital patients (Goldberg and Jones, 1980). However, other researchers have expressed doubts about the functions of these units, arguing that they provide an inappropriate environment for mental health care and, in the absence of firm evaluative data, are an act of faith on the government's part (Baruch and Treacher, 1978).

There are few office psychiatric practices. Specialist outpatient services are based at NHS hospitals. In 1981 there were almost 21 million psychiatric outpatient consultations at United Kingdom hospitals, a nine per cent increase over the figure for 1976 (CSO, 1984).

Day care provisions offering a range of social and occupational rehabilitation facilities are still considerably below the guidelines established in 'Better Services' and the indications are that, at the current rate of progress, it will take the best part of half a century to achieve the recommended ratios. Seventy-five per cent of all day care places are provided by NHS services and twenty per cent are provided by local authorities. The remainder are in the voluntary sector. It is estimated that by 1981 there were over 15,000 places in day hospitals (33 places per 100,000). Thirty-two per cent of day patients were of pensionable age and nineteen per cent were using day hospital facilities whilst being inpatients. A further 3,800 patients were day visitors to inpatient wards (DHSS, 1984a).

In contrast local authorities provided only 8200 places in day centres in 1982 (DHSS, 1983a) and, although there was more than a fifty per cent increase in places between 1976-1982, the ratio of provisions (including places for the elderly mentally infirm) was 17/100,000, i.e. less than one third of that recommended in 'Better Services'. In 1979 one quarter of English social services authorities still had no day centre provisions and only 30 per cent of day centre staff held any form of qualification (Vaughan, 1983). Moreover, the results of a survey of forty day care establishments suggest that staff-patient ratios of day centres are only half those of day hospitals (Edwards and Carter, 1980).

Unfortunately, data on the number of former psychiatric patients in sheltered workplaces subsidised by the Manpower Services Commission are not routinely collected. In order to be eligible for sheltered employment candidates must prove they have at least a thirty per cent work capacity in relation to tasks performed by a non-disabled person in any given job. It is not accurately known how many of the 14,500 places in sheltered workshops are occupied by ex-patients, but it is thought that approximately twelve per cent of persons working in sheltered industrial groups in normal workplaces are former psychiatric patients (Manpower Services Commission, personal communication).

In England and Wales there was a 47 per cent increase between 1976-1982 in the number of places in homes and hostels for the mentally ill. In total there were 6900 places, two-thirds of which were provided by local authorities, the remainder being in the voluntary or private sector (CSO, 1984). In 1983, the estimated number of local authority supported residents (financial or social work support) suggested that the ratio of assisted places in England was a mere 9.2/100,000. In addition, it was estimated that some five hundred former patients were being supported in lodgings in private households. These latest statistics suggest that there has been some reduction in the number of local authority supported residents in voluntary and private homes and hostels. The largest increase in the number of places in the last ten years has been in unstaffed premises and it is estimated that almost forty per cent of places are now in these establishments (DHSS, 1983b).

In the late 1970s less than half of English local authorities provided hostels. Their patients were therefore dependent on voluntary hostels or boarding houses that had formerly catered for the holiday-maker or casual guest but were now increasingly turning towards a clientele from the psychiatric hospitals. There is good reason to believe that the number of local authority hostel places will not increase dramatically in forthcoming years. Current curbs on public expenditure have hit social service budgets hard: official statistics indicate that in real terms local authority expenditure on the personal social services has been declining since 1979. Discretionary provisions such as residential accommodation for the mentally ill are among the first to be sacrificed. Although the 1983

Residential Homes Act introduces stricter registration and inspection procedures to be carried out by local authorities in licensing voluntary and private establishments, it is unlikely to have great effect since these authorities are increasingly dependent on placements in independent facilities.

Yet, despite these constraints, current national policy seeks to accelerate the trend towards transferring long-term hospital patients to a variety of residential accommodation outside. Standards vary, although the results of a survey in three areas of London suggest that the majority of hostels investigated offer reasonable accommodation and a de-institutionalised environment. The researchers were more critical of long-stay hostels which in their view were no better than the worst of the old back wards (Ryan, 1979). More startling observations are currently being made of conditions in some boarding houses. In the worst cases patients have been transferred to seaside resorts where they have no personal connections and are sharing inadequate accommodation from which they are locked out during the day.

Mental Health Services: An Audit

In the 1970s there was considerable growth in the proportion of the NHS budget devoted to mental health services, so that at the end of the decade 23 per cent of total current expenditure was allocated to psychiatric care. (In the inpatient sector occupied psychiatric beds comprised 27 per cent of total occupied beds at this time.) However, in 1981 a psychiatric bed still cost on average only 40 per cent of an acute medical bed in a non-teaching hospital. Over 90 per cent of the NHS psychiatric budget continues to be allocated to mental illness inpatients, with less than nine per cent being consumed by outpatient and day care services (data exclude joint finance funds and expenditure on welfare benefits).

The proportion of the social services budget local authorities allocate to provisions for the mentally ill is even more meagre. It is true that between 1975-1980 their current expenditure on residential services for the mentally ill rose by fifty per cent and expenditure on day care by sixty per cent, partly as a result of the joint finance scheme discussed in an earlier section. However, in the financial year ending 31st March 1981, only

252

just over one per cent of total current expenditure of local authorities on the social services was allocated to these provisions (DHSS, 1982).

If the health and social services budgets are combined and spending on inpatient services excluded, the rate of current expenditure on 'community' mental health services is miserly. One extrapolation of recent official statistics puts the figure as low as 1.3 per cent of the combined total budget (excluding primary care and welfare benefits) (Richmond Fellowship, 1983).

PSYCHIATRIC LEGISLATION

Until 1983, the 1959 Mental Health (England & Wales) Act governed compulsory admissions to psychiatric hospitals. The Act broke with the tradition of juridical control. Ordinarily certification required a request for admission by a near relative or a designated mental welfare officer who was a local authority social worker. This was supported by two medical signatures, one obtained from the patient's general practitioner, the other from a psychiatrist. Patients could be compulsorily admitted for up to 72 hours (emergency section) or up to 28 days for 'observation', or for up to twelve months for 'treatment'. Four categories of mental disorder were recognised for the purpose of certification: mental illness; subnormality; severe subnormality; and the controversial inclusion of psychopathy. Although the emphasis of the Act was on voluntary admission, informal patients could be subjected to similar restrictions as those formally detained (e.g. loss of certain civil rights, restricted access to mail) and, initially, were required to give three days notice of their wish to discharge themselves, with the possibility that certification might be initiated to prevent their departure.

The Act instituted a new appeals procedure through the creation of mental health review tribunals in each region, composed of medical, legal and lay members. However, in practice less than five per cent of formally admitted patients made use of the tribunals. Those compulsorily admitted under the common sections of the Act - the 28-day observation order and the 72-hour emergency order - had no right to apply. Even of those patients eligible, only twelve per cent on average appealed to the tribunals.

253

Psychiatric legislation elsewhere in Britain contains notable departures from the 1959 Act. Both the 1960 Scottish Act and the 1961 Northern Ireland Act exclude the category of psychopathy. In Scotland the procedures for request for non-emergency admission and the requirements for independent medical certificates are similar to those in England and Wales, but the role of the magistracy has been retained, this form of certitication requiring the ultimate authorisation of the sheriff. Emergency seven-day admissions, however, do not require initial authorisation of the sheriff and ninety per cent of compulsory admissions are made under this procedure. Many of these orders are renewed without being converted into the 28-day orders requiring the sheriff's authorisation. The Scottish Act established a mental welfare commission which is chaired by a judge and is independent of the health service. It has the general task of protecting the interests of psychiatric patients.

In England in 1981 nine per cent of patients were compulsorily admitted (DHSS, 1984b). The percentage was similar in Scotland. As in Scotland the emergency procedure was the most frequently used section, despite the original intention of the legislation.

The 1983 Mental Health Act excludes the subnormality categories and psychopathy is included only if there are reasonable prospects for treatment. In general, the legislation increases patients' rights: there is improved access to the mental health review tribunals; more frequent reviews of detention orders; and an emphasis on consent to treatment. There is also a more salient role for non-medical members of the psychiatric team. In part, these changes reflect contemporary concerns for the protection of civil rights, but, in comparison with the 1959 legislation, they also represent a more measured assessment of the effectiveness of psychiatry.

Procedures for certification are similar to those in the 1959 Act, with the exception that the social worker making the application for admission must be 'approved' for the purpose, having at least two years post-qualification experience and having completed a brief designated training. Each local authority social services department is required to have a minimum number of approved social workers. The three-day and twenty-eight day orders remain, although they now refer to 'assessment' instead of 'observation'. A six-month admission order for treatment replaces the one-year certification. Patients now have the right to appeal to the mental health review tribunal within fourteen days of admission and patients detained on home office orders have also been granted access to the tribunal. Interim hospital orders and hospital remand orders give improved opportunities of psychiatric assessment and treatment for those appearing before the courts.

Important innovations relate to the patient's consent to treatment. Three categories of treatment are specified. The first are hazardous or irreversible treatments and those whose effectiveness has not been fully established. Psychosurgery is so far the only treatment in this category. Here the patient's consent and a second medical opinion are required. The case must then be referred to a multi-disciplinary panel which must include a psychiatric nurse; the members of the psychiatric team must also be consulted before authorisation can be given. In the second category is electro-convulsive therapy. This may be given without the patient's informed consent providing an independent doctor agrees, after having consulted non-medical members of the psychiatric team. In the third category are all other forms of care, which may be given without consent or a second medical opinion. As regards commonly prescribed psychotropic medication, drugs may be administered without the patient's consent for up to three months. Thereafter, a second medical opinion is required from a doctor authorised by the new Mental Health Act Commission.

This new Commission has the important task of overseeing the protection of the rights of detained patients and will review the use of powers under the Act. The Commission is also formulating a code of practice, part of which concerns the identification of treatments 'of special concern' (Bluglass, 1983).

PROSPECTS

Strict budgetary constraints facing both health authorities and social services authorities preclude any real growth in most services in the planable future. In fact, as we have reported, there will be a reduction in current expenditure in certain areas. Capital expenditure has been cut to a minimum, especially in the social services. As for planning, in the present circumstances authorities can hardly look beyond each cash limited annual allocation. Strategic plans formulated in earlier years, such as those for the social services when public expenditure was rising at a rate in double figures, are now redundant.

The current and projected near-stagnation in budgets scarcely improves the prospects of effective coordination of mental health services. Indeed, since public services are increasingly having to rely on provisions in the voluntary and private sector the task of coordination takes on even wider dimensions. One attempt at improving the integration of services at the local level, the joint consultative committees, on the whole have not worked well. Membership of these committees has now been extended to local housing and education authorities and to voluntary housing associations. How effective they will be in a future marked only by further financial constraints is open to doubt.

A government-commissioned report on the organisation and management problems of mental illness hospitals was published in 1978. It recommended the establishment of a psychiatric services management team in each health district with a broad membership from all local services. The team would be responsible for all local provisions for the mentally ill and would report directly to the health district management team. Some health districts have already formed teams of the kind envisaged in the report, but the recommendations have not been formally adopted on a national level (Nodder, 1978). Further recommenda- tions on the organisational integration of psychiatric services have been made in unofficial reports: by the NHS trades union, the Confederation of Health Service Employees (COHSE, 1983); by the national presure group MIND (the National Association of Mental Health) (MIND, 1983); and by the voluntary organisation, the Richmond Fellowship (1983). In the meantime a managerial solution has been adopted by government, through the appointment of general managers at each level of the NHS hierarchy. This policy is now in the process of being implemented and it is primarily a bid to improve efficiency within the NHS by replacing the consensus decision-making of the management team by an official at each level who will have ultimate responsibility for administration.

Other urgent problems in British mental health policy are shared by Community neighbours. The growing numbers of the elderly, especially those over 85 years old, are expected to put an increasing strain on psychogeriatric services. The government recently announced a small project in which demonstration districts will be established in each health region, preferably in areas participating in the joint finance scheme. The project seeks to expand and evaluate local services for the elderly mentally infirm.

Psychiatric disability has also become an important issue and, largely as a result of a report by the Royal College of Psychiatrists, the DHSS has sponsored several 'demonstration centres' to monitor the experiences of provisions attempting to offer rehabilitative services to long stay patients.

Rehabilitation has become all the more pressing a concern since the acceleration of hospital closures was announced. Although it is generally accepted that closures can only proceed after adequate alternative services have been created, some early indications are far from reassuring, with some reports of ex-patients being transferred en bloc to boarding houses in towns with insufficient or non-existent day care provisions. What is urgently required, before the programme accelerates further, is evaluative research of the individual needs of patients to be transferred and the degree to which existing forms of provision can meet them. A beginning has already been made in research programmes such as the DHSS-financed Worcester Development Project which commenced in the late 1960s and has been monitoring new services established in the wake of the planned closure of a local psychiatric hospital. This and evaluative research of services in Camberwell, South London, are able to draw on case register data (Wing, 1982). An extension of this kind of research to other service settings is necessary before a cumulative assessment of alternative provisions can be made on a national level.

The past twenty years have seen a general expansion of multi-disciplinary mental health teams. Several professions have created new specialities and their members have moved into new therapeutic settings. Mental health services have developed, too, especially within the NHS, with the growth of the number of inpatient units at general hospitals and an increase in the number and variety of day care settings. Nevertheless, the psychiatric hospitals continue to have command over the overwhelming majority of resources allocated to mental health care. Equally apparent in the same period has been the growth of consumer interest in all aspects of health care, with community health councils having been established in all health districts to represent lay interests. Pressure groups for the mentally ill have also become increasingly influential and several also provide local voluntary services.

Yet, despite the positive developments that have occurred, it is the feeling of uncertainty about the future that dominates. Health and social services planners are confronted with the task of attempting to implement strategies for services which straddle the boundary of responsibilities of separate authorities; where, outside the NHS, duties to provide the kind of services discussed in this chapter are discretionary and are among the first victims of public expenditure cuts. It is now ten years since the publication of 'Better Services' and planning horizons are as distant as ever.

NOTES

1. In the financial year 1980/1981 89 per cent of the costs of the NHS were derived from general taxation (consolidated fund), 2½ per cent came from charges to patients and most of the remainder was obtained from national insurance contributions.

2. In the 1970s there was some increase in the size of the private sector and in the activities of private insurance schemes whose members enjoy tax concessions on their subscriptions. The majority of those with private insurance are subscribers to one of three provident assurance societies. By 1982 8 per cent of the population were members of a private scheme, half of whom had coverage arranged collectively by their employer. Private underwriters have only recently begun to enter the mental health field in earnest, and they generally provide acute services

only, although there has been something of a thriving business in the provision of private long-stay nursing homes, especially for the elderly infirm.

3. The United Kingdom (UK) comprises England, Scotland, Wales and Northern Ireland. Certain UK legislation also applies to the Channel Islands and Isle of Man, but they retain control of health and social security affairs; and although they are not members of the European Community they have associate status. Great Britain is formed by England, Scotland and Wales and excludes Northern Ireland which, until its prorogation in 1972, had its own provincial parliament. In general usage 'Britain' connotes the 'United Kingdom'.

4. Robinson provides 'low' and 'high' forecasts for 1991 for three categories of bed needs. Services for children and adolescents and the elderly mentally infirm are excluded.

Rates per thousand population	Low	High
Short stay (up to one year)	.46	.52
New Long Stay (in hospital since December 1970)	.53	.62
Old Long Stay (in hospital before December 1970)	.12	.19
Total	1.11	1.33

5. Criteria laid down by the Public Expenditure Steering Committee (PESC).

6. RAWP applies in England only. The other home countries have introduced resource allocation methods of their own. In fact, Scotland and Northern Ireland have always had higher per capita rates of health expenditure than England and Wales. Maynard and Ludbrook (1980) have demonstrated that, if RAWP criteria were applied in all four home countries, the two northern countries would each stand to lose about 14 per cent of their present health budget to the benefit of England and Wales.

7. 85 per cent of expenditure on local authority social services is obtained from local rates or central government support grants; 15 per cent is obtained from charges made to service users (DHSS, 1982).

8. The 1840s saw the beginning of separate services for the mentally retarded, with the first school opened in 1846 and the first asylum in 1847. It was not until the Mental Deficiency Act of 1913 that services independent of the mental hospitals developed on a national scale.

9. The 1966 Scottish Hospital Plan did not contain projections of a substantial decline in inpatient capacity. Scottish - and, indeed, Ulster - inpatient bed ratios have always been higher than those in England and Wales.

10. 'Better Services' planning guidelines per 100,000 population:

Psychiatric beds in general hospitals	50
Day hospital places	25
Hospital-hostels for the 'new long stay'	17
Acute and rehabilitation hostels	4- 6
Long stay accommodation (excluding the elderly)	15-24
Day centre places	60

Day hospital places and inpatient beds exclude services for long stay patients, the elderly mentally infirm and children and adolescents. As regards day care provision 'Better Services' wished to see a reversal of existing trends, so that the larger number of places would be in local authority or voluntary day centres rather than in NHS day hospitals.

11. The term 'psychotherapist' is not a protected title. Proposals for state registration of psychotherapists were made in 1978 and 1981. However, no agreement has been reached among the relevant professions and it is unlikely that action will be taken in the foreseeable future.

12. In addition there are four special hospitals for the psychiatric offender and violent patients. These hospitals are the direct responsibility of the Secretary of State for Social Services and they house about 2000 patients, two-thirds of whom are detained under Home Office restriction orders (Dell,

260

1980). There is also one special hospital in
Scotland.
Since 1974 there has been an official policy
to establish 'medium secure units' in
psychiatric hospitals in all English regions,
providing in total approximately one thousand
places. The first permanent unit opened in
1980 with the aim of offering 'medium secure'
accommodation and forensic psychiatric
services for up to two years for behaviourally
disturbed patients.

REFERENCES

Baruch G & Treacher A (1978) Psychiatry Observed.
    Routledge & Kegan Paul, London.
Bean P (1980) Compulsory Admissions to Mental
    Hospitals. Wiley, Chichester.
Bluglass R (1983) A Guide to the Mental Health
    Act, 1983. Croom Helm, London.
CSO (1984) Social Trends No: 14, 1984. Central
    Statistical Office, HMSO, London.
COHSE (1983) The Future of the Psychiatric
    Services. Confederation of Health Service
    Employees, Banstead, Surrey.
Cooper D (1972) The Death of the Family. Penguin,
    Harmondsworth.
Dell S (1980) The Transfer of Special Hospital
    Patients to NHS Hospitals. Special Hospitals
    Research Report No. 16, London.
DHSS (1975) Better Services for the Mentally Ill.
    Department of Health and Social Security (Cmnd
    6233), HMSO, London.
DHSS (1976) Priorities for Health and Personal
    Social Services in England: A Consultative
    Document. DHSS, HMSO, London.
DHSS (1981) Care in the Community: A Consultative
    Document on Moving Resource for Care in
    England. DHSS, HMSO, London.
DHSS (1982) Health and Personal Social Services
    Statistics for England. DHSS, HMSO, London.
DHSS (1983a) Health Care and Its Costs. DHSS,
    HMSO, London.
DHSS (1983b) Homes and Hostels for the Mentally
    Ill and Mentally Handicapped at 31st March
    1983. DHSS Local Authority Statistics
    (England) A/F83/11, London.

DHSS (1984a) Facilities and Services in Mental Illness and Mental Handicap Hospitals in England, 1980-1981. DHSS, HMSO, London.

DHSS (1984b) Inpatient Statistics from the Mental Health Enquiry, 1981. DHSS, HMSO, London.

Edwards C & Carter J (1980) The Data of Day Care. National Institute of Social Work, London.

Ginsberg G & Marks I M (1977) Costs and Benefits of Behavioural Psychotherapy: A Pilot Study of Neurotics Treated by Nurse-Therapists. Psychological Medicine, 7, 701-707.

Goffman E (1961) Asylums: Essays on the Social Situation of Mental Patients and Other Inmates. Penguin, Harmondsworth (Editions in several European languages).

Goldberg D & Huxley P (1980) Mental Illness in the Community: The Pathway to Psychiatric Care. Tavistock Press, London.

Goldberg D & Jones R (1980) The Costs and Benefits of Psychiatric Care. In L N Robins, P J Clayton & J K Wing (eds). The Social Consequences of Psychiatric Illness. Brunner/Mazel, New York, Chapter 5.

Harrison A & Gretton J (1984) (eds) Health Care UK 1984: an Economic, Social and Policy Audit. Chartered Institute of Public Finance and Accountancy, London.

Jones K (1960) Mental Health and Social Policy. Routledge & Kegan Paul, London.

Jones K (1972) A History of the Mental Health Services. Routledge & Kegan Paul, London.

Laing R D (1965) The Divided Self. Penguin, Harmondsworth (Editions in several European languages).

Laing R D (1967) The Politics of Experience and the Bird of Paradise. Penguin, Harmondsworth (Editions in several European languages).

Mangen S P, Paykel E S, Griffith J H, Burchell A & Mancini P (1983) Cost-Effectiveness of Community Psychiatric Nurse or Outpatient Psychiatrist Care of Neurotic Patients. Psychological Medicine, 13, 407-416.

Maynard A & Ludbrook A (1980) Applying Resource Allocation Formulae to the Constituent Parts of the UK. Lancet, 1, 85-87.

Mind (1983) Common Concern: A Manifesto for a new Mental Health Service. Mind Publications, London.

Nodder (1978) Report of a Working Group on the Organisation and Management Problems of Mental Illness Hospitals (Nodder Report). DHSS, HMSO, London.

RAWP (1976) Report of the Resource Allocation Working Party. DHSS, HMSO, London.

Richmond Fellowship (1983) Mental Health and the Community: Report of the Richmond Fellowship Enquiry. Richmond Fellowship Press, London.

Robinson G (1981) The Provision of Inpatient Facilities for the Mentally Ill: A Paper to assist NHS Planners. ORS, DHSS, London, unpublished.

Ryan P (1979) Residential Care for the Mentally Disabled. In J K Wing & R Olsen (eds). Community Care for the Mentally Disabled. Oxford University Press, Oxford, Chapter 4.

Scull A (1983) The Asylum as Community or the Community as Asylum: Paradoxes and Contradictions of Mental Health Care. In P Bean (ed). Mental Illness: Change and Trends. Wiley, Chichester.

Shepherd M, Cooper B, Brown A C & Kalton G W (1966) Psychiatric Illness in General Practice. Oxford University Press, London.

Vaughan P J (1983) The Disordered Development of Day Care in Psychiatry. Health Trends, 15, 91-94.

Wing J K & Brown G W (1970) Institutionalism and Schizophrenia. Cambridge University Press, London (Editions in several European languages).

Wing J K (1982) (ed) Long-Term Community Care: Experience in a London Borough. Psychological Medicine Monograph Supplement No. 2.

Wistow G (1984) Joint Finance and Community Care. In A Harrison & J Gretton (eds) Health Care UK: An Economic, Social and Policy Audit. Chartered Institute of Public Finance and Accountancy, London, 69-74.

Chapter Twelve

TOWARDS A EUROPEAN MANDATE

Steen Mangen

To varying degrees three key European organisations
are involved in mental health, either in promotion
and research, or in the provision of a limited
range of services. In this final chapter I have
attempted to describe and assess the role of each
of these bodies: the World Health Organisation, an
organ of the United Nations; the Council of Europe;
and the European Community itself (1).

WORLD HEALTH ORGANISATION

The European Region of the World Health
Organisation (WHO) extends to the whole of the
geographical continent. The WHO publishes reviews
of health policy and health services in each of its
member states as well as the proceedings of
international seminars it arranges for invited
experts. The principal aim is to promote
international collaborative research. The WHO also
launches regional and worldwide public health
campaigns. A current campaign 'Health for All by
the year 2000' was adopted in 1977 and an official
document was issued in 1982. Within this worldwide
campaign there are specific targets for the
European Region: in particular, the promotion of
healthier life styles to reduce epidemiological
risk factors; a reduction of inequalities in
service provisions; and an improvement in the
access of underprivileged groups to health care.
The role of the WHO in the campaign is exhortative
and its success depends on the sustained
cooperation of the member states who agreed the
principles of the programme.

Two research projects currently being promoted by the WHO European Office will, it is hoped, produce valuable comparative empirical data on mental health services. The first is, in part, the outcome of a survey of European mental health services undertaken in the mid-1970s in which it was found that in many countries important statistics vital for effective planning were either not available, or of dubious quality, or else available in a form that did not permit comparison (May, 1976). Work on the new project got underway before the publication of this survey and it was decided that small areas would be selected as subjects for intensive study and data gathering. From its original six centres the project has been extended to twenty-one centres in rural and urban areas of varying size throughout Europe, although the majority are located in Western Europe. Services in each centre will be described and analysed and, in particular, there will be an attempt at evaluation of new forms of care. There will also be an assessment of unmet needs and outstanding planning problems. The final report of the project is expected to be published in 1985.

Another WHO report being published in the same year concerns the outcome of a project aiming to standardise official data collection which was initiated at a meeting of national mental health advisers in 1979. The report will present a country-by-country profile of mental health resources.

COUNCIL OF EUROPE

This twenty-one member organisation includes all EC states and exists to facilitate economic and social progress. The Council has a series of specialist committees dealing with various aspects of health, welfare and social security affairs. A European Social Charter of rights in these areas has been prepared, to which all EC member states except the Benelux countries are signatories. Current activities are directed towards the harmonisation of social security regulations and legislation on pharmaceutical products and foodstuffs.

In the field of mental health the Council shares a similar brief with the WHO. It promotes campaigns and collaborative research on such subjects as the prevention of mental illness, alcoholism and drug dependence and issues recommendations on topics such as the training of psychiatric personnel and the establishment of medical data banks. A charter of psychiatric patients' rights is also under consideration. Ten Council of Europe countries are at present collaborating on a research project on the rehabilitation of the disabled, and recently six countries set up a research group to prepare a report on 'new trends in the organisation of mental health services at the primary level' which will be presented to the conference of European ministers of health in 1985.

These roles of the Council of Europe, like those of the WHO, are advisory and exhortative. However, two of its organs have formal powers in the field of human rights, which in a small number of notable cases in recent years have been exercised in favour of appellants who were compulsorily detained in psychiatric hospitals. The European Commission is empowered to examine complaints of violations of the European Convention for the Protection of Human Rights and Fundamental Freedoms. Actions may be brought by contracting parties to the Convention, or by individuals or non-governmental organisations. The first task of the Commission is to establish that the appeal can be allowed and, after having assessed the full facts of the case, it attempts to reach a friendly settlement between the parties. If this is not possible the case, may be referred to the Committee of Ministers or the European Court in order to obtain a final judgement as to whether a violation has occurred. The decision of the Court, in which judges from all member states sit, is final.

Actions have been brought under several sections of the European Convention and friendly settlements or judgements of the Court have occasioned some European countries to amend long-standing practices and, in certain cases, relevant legislation. All the cases have been presented after court appeals in the respective countries failed. From information available it would seem that, so far, there have only been a small number of cases, involving psychiatric patients in the United Kingdom, Belgium, the Netherlands and Ireland. In fact most of the appellants have been UK citizens, who have been assisted by the voluntary organisation 'Mind', and have complained about the lack of independent reviews while they were being detained on Home Office orders in special hospitals. As a result of pronouncements in their favour an amendment to the review procedure was made in England and Wales and was enschrined in the 1983 Mental Health Act which gives patients subject to Home Office detention orders the right to appeal to mental health review tribunals after the lapse of a certain period. In another British case concerning the use of solitary confinement a friendly settlement was reached. As a result, stricter guidelines were drawn up by the British Department of Health and Social Security and the plaintiff was offered a small ex gratia payment by the government (information supplied by the Legal Department of Mind).

THE COMMISSION OF THE EUROPEAN COMMUNITY (2)

Despite its long-term aim of achieving social, economic and political integration, there is no reference to the integration of health policies in the 1957 Treaty of Rome, on which the European Economic Community is founded. Article 117 which refers to the harmonisation of social security systems and Article 57 on the mutual recognition of professional qualifications have some bearing on health policy, but no attempt is currently being made to seek an integration of the diverse health care systems of Community countries. Nor is such harmonisation likely in the future, since it is improbable that national governments will be willing to surrender responsibilities in areas of social policy such as health care which consume significant proportions of their GNP.

Some indication of the relatively marginal status of general health affairs may be obtained from the fact that the first meeting in council of ministers of health of EC countries did not occur until 1978. Within the Commission itself no one directorate has sole responsibility for health affairs and the possibility of creating a special directorate must be ruled out on the grounds of cost, particularly in the present state of the Community's budget. On a broader level James (1982) has criticised the lack of real coordination of social policy and its relegation to issues largely relating to employment. His argument that, within the directorates, units responsible for specific areas of social affairs merely exist to maintain a 'presence' and undertake 'passive surveillance' applies a fortiori to mental health.

The Commission's interests in (mental) health affairs have focused on occupational health and safety at work (e.g. studies of alcoholism and employment) and the rehabilitation programme for disabled people subsidised by the European Social Fund. It is likely that any further action in favour of the mentally ill will continue to be part of this programme which, although sponsoring relatively small-scale services, is significant in being the only permanent programme funded by a super-national body that assists in the financing of mental health provisions in European countries. This programme is discussed later. Other developments in favour of disabled people include the formation of an all-party group by members of the European Parliament. Furthermore, appeals against discrimination in employment on the grounds of physical or mental disability may be taken to the European Court of Justice which pronounces on violations of the Treaty of Rome. However, the number of cases brought by disabled people has been small.

One area of health affairs in which the EC has made considerable progress is the harmonisation of professional qualifications. In 1977 the Commission prescribed minimum criteria for mutual recognition of the qualifications of general practitioners and medical specialists, including psychiatrists. A further directive was issued in 1981 which has laid down more specific qualitative criteria for the training of all doctors. Harmonisation of qualifications for general nurses was achieved in 1979. A working party was appointed in 1984 to prepare a report initiating the process of mutual recognition in countries with basic and specialist qualifications in psychiatric nursing. In general, the scale of movement of health personnel between Community countries has so far been modest.

The EC also fosters health care research, although direct funding is limited to activities necessary for the coordination of international projects. In 1982 a medical and public health research programme was proposed with investigations of disability, alcoholism and drug abuse. Mental illness and psychiatric services evaluation were not included at this stage; indeed, the most important official scientific action in this broad field has been a seminar on evaluation of mental health care which took place in 1980. The seminar recommended that a centrally available information

268

source should be compiled and a European study
centre for mental health established. No official
response to these suggestions has yet been
forthcoming.

THE EUROPEAN SOCIAL FUND

Direct EC action in the provision of services for
psychiatric patients is limited European to Social
Fund (ESF) subsidisation of projects directed
towards the rehabilitation of disabled people. The
ESF is primarily intended to help fund 'pilot' or
'demonstration' projects designed to retrain
workers for employment on the open market or, in
the case of the physically disabled, to adapt
physical conditions in normal workplaces to meet
their needs. ESF subsidies are restricted to the
operating costs of pilot services. For each
project the proportion of funding cannot exceed
that by the authorities in the country in which it
is located, except in the 'priority regions'
(Greenland (formerly), Northern Ireland,
Mezzogiorno, Greece and the French Overseas
Departments).
     Because projects are intended as pilot or
demonstration services they are generally small-
scale and the ESF subsidies short-term. It is not
possible to assess accurately the amount of
expenditure specifically allocated to the mentally
ill, since many of the projects are intended to
serve a multiple clientele. However, an
examination of the recent annual reports of the
Fund's activities suggests that the greater
proportion of the budget is awarded to schemes for
the physically handicapped, followed by those for
the mentally retarded.
     ESF activities in favour of disabled people
have been growing since the early Seventies,
although their share of the total budget has
remained small. In 1974 the ESF helped finance a
network of innovative rehabilitation centres with
the aim of evaluating and publicising their
experiences. Since 1976 limited funds have been
made available for experimental housing projects
for the disabled, with subsidies for both capital
and operating costs. Each of the five-yearly
reviews of the Fund since 1972 has increased the
priority given to the needs of the disabled.
However, the ongoing crisis in the Community's

budget since the late 1970s has meant that all EC Funds have had to concentrate their efforts on particular areas. Since 1980 the majority of the ESF budget has been allocated to projects in districts nominated by the Regional Fund as assisted areas. Only a small amount of the budget has been allocated to projects outside these areas and they have been awarded on average only half of the grant requested. Further restrictions were enforced in 1984, when it was announced that in future three-quarters of the budget was to be allocated to retraining and rehabilitation projects for the younger age-groups.

According to the latest report, in 1982, the Fund aided thirty-seven demonstration projects for the disabled throughout the Community and gave other direct assistance in the form of subsidies for retraining programmes and adaptations of normal workplaces.

The policy of increased priority accorded disabled people is reflected in the increase in their ESF allocation, which in the early 1980s achieved annual growth rates varying between twenty and thirty per cent. However, the share of the budget taken up by these allocations has remained relatively stable at around eight per cent of the total. Allocations amounted to 125 million ECU (approximately £71 million) in 1982. In the same year the ESF as a whole received only 5.8 per cent of the total Community budget.

In response to a council resolution adopted in 1981, the International Year of the Disabled, a special allocation within the ESF has been awarded for measures seeking to promote the social and economic integration of disabled people. This five-year programme - the 'Accord' project - was announced in 1983 by the newly-created EC 'Bureau for Action in Favour of the Disabled. Accord has been established in sixteen areas in all EC countries, representing a variety of urban and rural environments with populations varying from 150,000 to 300,000 (3). Fifty per cent of the funding is derived from the ESF with the remainder being obtained from the home authorities. ESF finance is intended to cover the cost of the small project teams as well as the evaluative exercise and the publicising and exchange of information.

Accord is intended as an integrated project, although each of the sixteen districts will vary to some degree in the priorities they adopt. The main emphasis will be on promotional projects and information exchange that will help in the coordination of current services and will highlight gaps in provisions. The first theme to be developed will be the employment of the disabled and the Commission has been concerned that each of the projects should have a training element. Some of the districts are creating experimental training centres to equip their clients with skills necessary for open employment. There are also to be trial schemes for sheltered industrial groups in normal workplaces and the establishment of cooperatives. Other activities to be sponsored are the development of local information exchange networks for employment, housing, health and education affairs. Advisory services and self-help groups will also be promoted. A report on the experiences of the Accord project is expected in 1986.

CONCLUSION

The activities of European organisations in the field of mental health are limited and in the short-run are unlikely to be expanded. In general, the organisations cited are active in promoting preventive campaigns and in assisting mental health research. The Council of Europe has an important function in the safeguarding of civil rights. In the case of psychiatric patients its powers have been invoked on a limited number of occasions but its interventions have led to important changes in practices in several member countries. The European Community is the only organisation with a permanent programme to provide financial assistance for services, but these are limited to relatively small-scale pilot projects for the disabled and - critically in the case of many of the mentally ill - subsidies are restricted to actions directed towards returning clients to the open labour market rather than their long-term placement in sheltered employment.

(1)   The United Nations Educational, Scientific and
Cultural Organisation (UNESCO) and the Organisation
of Economic Cooperation and Development (OECD) have
fields of interest which touch on mental health and
mental retardation.   The Centre for Educational
Research and Information, for example, subsidised a
schools integration project in Italy in which
physically handicapped, mentally disturbed, and
mentally retarded children are being integrated
into the normal schools system.
     Voluntary agencies and informal groups are
also   involved   in   efforts   at   cooperation   and
dissemination of information about new developments
in mental health care.   The International Hospital
Federation instigated the project 'Good Practices
in Mental Health' in 1977 as a result of an
international study of health care in large cities
in which mental illness arose as one of the most
prevalent problems for which existing services were
inadequate.   The project, which has now been funded
for a two-year period by the British Department of
Health and Social Security, aims at describing and
publicising local-level services which are judged
to be effective and imaginative.   This London-based
project   is   collecting   information   from   other
European countries and is collaborating with a
project   in   Bonn,   financed   by   the   European
Community's Social Fund: 'The International Centre
for   the   Social   Integration   of   the   Disabled'
(Internationales Zentrum sozialer Integration der
Behinderter).   Information   from   the   'Good
Practices' project is also being incorporated in
the data archive on the elderly housed at Leuven
University.
     As well as the many international professional
congresses on mental health that are held regularly
in   Europe,   mention   should   be   made   of   an
alternative: the 'Reseau International', founded in
1974 at a symposium in Brussels.   The Reseau is
intended as an international colloquium for those
within   and   outside   mental   health   who   take   a
critical view of psychiatry at both the theoretical
and empirical level and wish to work   towards   a
'de-psychiatrisation' of mental illness.   Since its
foundation the Reseau has met on six occasions and
has addressed topics ranging from the relationship
between politics and mental health to psychiatry in
Latin America.

(2) Strictly speaking the title should read 'Commission of the European Communities'. There are three Communities: the European Economic Community, the European Coal and Steel Community and the European Atomic Energy Community (Euratom).

(3) The sixteen districts are Genk-Hasselt, Liege, Berlin (Spandau), Gelsenkirchen, Achaia, Dijon, Montpelier, the Irish midland counties, Piacenza, North Basilicata, Luxembourg, Dordrecht, North Limburg, West Berkshire, London (Lambeth) and Aarhus.

REFERENCES

James, E. (1982) The role of the European Community in Social Policy. In C. Jones & J. Stevenson (eds). Yearbook of Social Policy in Britain, 1980-1981. Routledge & Kegan Paul, London.
May, A.R. (1976) Mental Health Services in Europe: A Review of Data Collected in Response to a Questionnaire. World Health Organisation, Geneva.

CONTRIBUTORS

FRANZ BARO
Professor of Psychiatry, Katholieke Universiteit, Leuven, Belgium

FRANÇOISE CASTEL
Until her death, Chef de Secteur, Corbeil-Essonnes, France

TOM van der GRINTEN
Director, Nederlands centrum geestelijke Volksgezondheid, Utrecht, Netherlands

DANIELLE HANSEN-KOENIG
Assistant Director of Health, Grand Duchy of Luxembourg

STEEN MANGEN
Formerly Department of Psychiatry, University of Kiel, West Germany. Currently member of scientific staff, Medical Research Council Social Psychiatry Unit, London

ALAN MAYNARD
Professor of Economics and Director, Centre for Health Economics, University of York, UK

JEAN-JACQUES MEISCH
Director of the State Neuropsychiatric Hospital, Luxembourg

ANDRÉ PRIMS
Professor, Faculty of Social Medicine, Katholieke Universiteit, Leuven, Belgium

SHULAMIT RAMON
Lecturer in Social Work, London School of Economics
and Political Science

BRIDGET RAO
Research Psychologist, St. George's Hospital
Medical School, London

PIERRE de SCHOUWER
Secretary-General, Ministry of Health, Brussels

ERIK STRÖMGREN
Formerly Professor of Psychiatry and Director,
Institute of Psychiatric Demography, University of
Aarhus, Denmark

DERMOT WALSH
Psychiatrist, Medico-Social Research Board, Dublin
and Editor, Irish Journal of Psychiatry